# THE SECRET SOCIETIES BIBLE

JACQUES DE MOLAY, chef des Templiers.

# THE SECRET SOCIETIES BIBLE

## THE DEFINITIVE GUIDE TO MYSTERIOUS ORGANIZATIONS

JOEL LEVY

# FIREFLY BOOKS

# A FIREFLY BOOK

Published by Firefly Books Ltd. 2010

First printing

**Publisher Cataloging-in-Publication Data (U.S.)**
Levy, Joel.
   The secret societies bible : the definitive guide to mysterious organizations / Joel Levy.
[400] p. :  photos. (chiefly col.) ;  cm.
Includes bibliographical references and index.
Summary: comprehensive guide to secret societies, from the Freemasons and the Knights Templar to the Rosicrucians and Chinese Triads, including their history, beliefs and secret rituals.
ISBN-13: 978-1-55407-734-2   (pbk.)
ISBN-10: 1-55407-734-6   (pbk.)
1. Secret societies.  I.  Title.
366 dc22    HS125.L489  2010

**Library and Archives Canada Cataloguing in Publication**
A CIP record of this book is available from Library and Archives Canada

Published in the United States by
Firefly Books (U.S.) Inc.
P.O. Box 1338, Ellicott Station
Buffalo, New York 14205

Published in Canada by
Firefly Books Ltd.
66 Leek Crescent
Richmond Hill, Ontario L4B 1H1

Printed in China

# CONTENTS

 **PART 1**
**A WORLD OF SECRETS** 6
CHAPTER 1   THE CHARACTERISTICS OF SECRET SOCIETIES 8
CHAPTER 2   THE ROOTS OF SECRET SOCIETIES 22

 **PART 2**
**RELIGIOUS, MYSTICAL AND OCCULT SOCIETIES** 62
CHAPTER 3   TEMPLARS AND NEO-TEMPLARS 64
CHAPTER 4   ROSICRUCIANISM 90
CHAPTER 5   FREEMASONRY 124
CHAPTER 6   OCCULT SECRET SOCIETIES 174
CHAPTER 7   OPUS DEI 210
CHAPTER 8   THE PRIORY OF SION AND THE MYSTERY OF RENNES 220

 **PART 3**
**POLITICAL AND CRIMINAL SOCIETIES** 234
CHAPTER 9   THE ASSASSINS 236
CHAPTER 10  ILLUMINISM 264
CHAPTER 11  ELITES OF THE NEW WORLD ORDER 288
CHAPTER 12  ITALIAN MASONRY'S PROPAGANDA DUE 316
CHAPTER 13  THE DARK BROTHERHOODS AND THE MAFIA 332
CHAPTER 14  THE TRIADS AND THE TONG 354

GLOSSARY 362
BIBLIOGRAPHY 376
INDEX AND ACKNOWLEDGEMENTS 385

# PART I
# A WORLD OF SECRETS

A secret society is a group of people gathered together in a self-governing institution with a definite structure or system, such as a hierarchy, set of rules, agenda or maybe even just a name, which keeps its membership, organization, proceedings and actions more or less secret. Membership is not open to all and usually depends on some specific process of initiation. Thanks to popular books and films, secret societies are a hot topic, yet the level of ignorance and misunderstanding surrounding them is probably greater than ever. People find themselves interested in secret societies, but know little about them, leading to a host of questions. What are secret societies all about? What is the point of them? Should secret societies be viewed with suspicion? Why do they feature strange rituals, theatrical ceremonies and exotic language? Above all, people want to know what is the big secret?

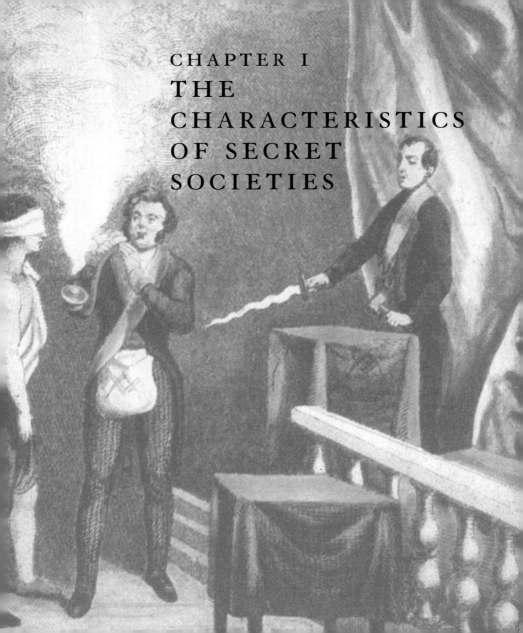

# CHAPTER I
# THE
# CHARACTERISTICS
# OF SECRET
# SOCIETIES

# SECRET SOCIETIES — THE BASICS

Most readers will be familiar with some of the terminology of secret societies, but it is worth going over the basics. A secret society may be large or small, with membership running into the millions or just a handful, but even large societies tend to be organized into small local groups. These may be called chapters, colleges, cadres, units, commanderies or cells, but the most common term, following the Freemasons, is lodges.

The Freemasons provide many of the terms and references for the topic of secret societies as a whole, because Freemasonry is the most popular and successful secret society in the Western world, and one of the oldest, and many other secret societies, including the modern-day Rosicrucians and Templars are or were originally offshoots of the Freemasons (see, for example, pages 92–123 and 66–69). 'Freemasonry' is often shortened to 'Masonry', which gives the adjective 'Masonic'.

Most secret societies require members to go through a process of initiation before they are allowed to join, and therefore members are often referred to as initiates. After initiation there may be several levels or ranks within a secret society; these are often called degrees or orders, and further processes of initiation may be required to progress through them. Some secret societies may be run without any presiding authority, but most have a leader or head, often called a Master or Grand Master, although other titles include Prior, Commander, Navigator or Chief.

Initiation, special occasions or simply normal meetings may involve rituals or ceremonies, and these can involve regalia (special clothing or whole costumes, along with other special items), recitations, incantations and elaborate symbolism. Symbolism is at the heart of many of the processes of a secret society, and may take the form of images, symbolic words or sayings, or ritual actions. Initiates of secret societies are often given signs so that they can recognize each other and confirm that they have been initiated. These can take the form of handshakes, grips, passwords or markings (such as symbols scratched on a door).

Secret societies may differ widely in their goals and concerns, but many of the best-known ones in the West are concerned with personal development, spiritual self-exploration and the study of topics that come under the heading of the mystical, esoteric or occult.

*A new member being sworn into the Tigers Eyes Society in 1922. The society's aim was to combat the Ku Klux Klan. The secret society was known as the invisible jungle and the knights wore black gowns and masks that hid their faces and bodies.*

# SECRECY

Secrecy creates mystery, allure, romance and excitement, but it also generates suspicion, frustration, hostility and fear. Some commentators argue that secrecy is inherently wrong or even evil. A good example of this belief is contained in the 1991 classic of paranoia *Behold a Pale Horse*, by arch-conspiracy theorist Bill Cooper: 'THE VERY FACT THAT SOMETHING IS SECRET MEANS THERE IS SOMETHING TO HIDE.' The use of capitals is as per the original text. Some secret societies claim that they are merely private, as opposed to secret. The Freemasons famously claim to be 'a society with secrets', rather than 'a secret society'. But the fact remains that their teachings are available only to the initiated, and that they swear blood-curdling oaths not to reveal them (see pages 153–154). So the question remains, why is this secrecy necessary? Secrecy is important for a number of reasons, including safety, freedom and cohesion.

## FEAR OF FREEDOM
Although today secret societies in the West are generally free from fear of persecution, this has only been the case until relatively recently, and is not the case in many parts of the world. For most of history, simply being a member of many secret societies was illegal and/or dangerous. In Soviet Russia and Nazi Germany, for instance, Freemasons were hunted, imprisoned and often murdered. In 19th-century America, Masons were attacked by angry mobs (see Anti-Masonry, pages 169–173). Masonry is still illegal in China and in other authoritarian states. It is also illegal throughout most of the Islamic world, where it is deemed unlawful under sharia law.

The modern Freemasons and many of the other important secret societies to which they are linked can trace their formation back to the 17th–early 19th centuries. In Europe this was a time of revolution, religious division and war, in which people could be persecuted and even killed for their beliefs or suspected beliefs, especially if these were of a revolutionary or unorthodox flavour. Yet unorthodox and potentially revolutionary philosophies were central

to the Freemasons as well as other secret societies, such as the Rosicrucians.

An important concept in the world of secret societies is heterodoxy. Heterodoxy is the opposite of orthodoxy, and refers to beliefs that are different from the mainstream, one of the most important examples being the heterodox Christian belief, Gnosticism (see pages 46–51). In Late Antiquity and the Middle Ages, heterodoxy was classed as heresy, and the orthodox religious and secular authorities hunted down and

*'The Torture of John Cousos in Lisbon, 1744',* from The Freemason *by Eugen Lennhoff (1922). Membership of a secret society could be perilous.*

suppressed it ruthlessly. Heretics might be tortured or burned at the stake. Later, in the 18th and 19th centuries, there was widespread fear among the Establishment (the mainstream powers of Church and state) about political heterodoxy, which was regarded as one step from revolutionary politics. Revolution was a genuine threat to

THE CHARACTERISTICS OF SECRET SOCIETIES

the ruling classes, especially given that in England and France monarchs had been beheaded, and in America an entirely new system of government had been introduced. To the established powers, the philosophy of the Rosicrucians and Freemasons, which included freethinking, belief in moral and social reform, and explicitly stated programmes of social and political change, were extremely heterodox and therefore threatening.

Whenever and wherever societies have expressed heterodox views or beliefs, they have been perceived as a threat and therefore have been threatened themselves, making secrecy advisable if not essential. Even where the safety of initiates was not threatened, secret societies have felt the need to keep their inner workings private so that their freedoms would not be curtailed.

## FRATERNITY, TRANSFORMATION AND CONSPIRACY

Secrecy also serves other roles. Having a secret in common can bind society members together, increasing group

*Poster for the French League ('for purging, mutual aid and European collaboration'), a movement founded in 1941 to oppose Jews, Freemasons and the dastardly English.*

cohesion and building fraternal feeling. If membership of the society confers benefits or privileges, such as the facilities that many fraternal societies in the USA provided in the 1950s, secret signs may be required to prevent the uninitiated from taking advantage. For societies concerned with the exploration of mysteries and the pursuit of personal development, secrecy may be a necessary first step. John Michael Greer, a scholar of secret societies, practising magician and high-level Mason, argues that keeping a secret is a transformative act, which focuses the mind of the initiate and 'awakens [him] to a new awareness of himself and his world'.

Finally, it is important to acknowledge that sometimes societies maintain secrecy for precisely the reasons that conspiracy theorists fear: because they are plotting, scheming or conspiring. There have been some secret societies that have engaged in conspiracies to perform criminal acts (for instance, the Mafia or Propaganda Due, and the Triads), political killings (for example, the Assassins) or even whole-scale revolution (such as the Carbonari, or Charcoal Burners, a Masonic secret society founded in Napoleonic Italy c. 1800 that spread around much of the Mediterranean and launched uprisings from France to Greece).

# INITIATION

Most secret societies are to some degree selective and/or exclusive, and nearly all of them require members to undergo a process of initiation, which forms part of the barriers of secrecy they erect. Critics of secret societies sometimes complain that this requirement for initiation is suspicious and unnecessary. In particular, the theatrical/ceremonial element often involved in initiation is criticized as being either silly and demeaning, or blasphemous and even Satanic. Why do secret societies practise initiatory rites? Why require a process of initiation at all?

## FUNCTIONS OF INITIATION

Secret societies typically claim that initiation is important for the benefit and protection of the initiate. The nature of the heterodox knowledge that many secret societies teach is often challenging and difficult, and the theory is that initiatory rites/tests weed out those who cannot or do not deserve to benefit from the teachings, while at the same time preparing the mind of the successful initiate for proper understanding and

assimilation of the teachings. Typically secret societies reveal new levels of knowledge as members progress through the degrees or orders, and secret societies claim that this is a stepwise process, where each step can only be taken by building on the steps already taken.

However, all the secrets cannot be revealed at once because the uninitiated will either fail to understand them or, worse, misunderstand them. Initiation tests and stepwise progression through the degrees also serve to prevent the misuse or abuse of knowledge by those unworthy or unprepared to wield it. Initiates may even harm themselves, physically, psychologically or spiritually, by trying to 'go it alone' or 'run before they can walk'.

Secret teachings are often referred to as 'esoteric', meaning inner or reserved only for the initiated, in contrast to 'exoteric' teachings, which are 'for public consumption' – easily accessible and in plain view. This is an important distinction that goes to the heart of the need for secrecy.

## EXPERIENCE VERSUS INSTRUCTION

Ritual, ceremony, regalia and all the other elements of secret society practice also exist for a reason, and are particularly important aspects of initiation. These elements combine to produce direct visceral experiences, which are very different from instruction. In other words, initiates

*At an initiation ceremony, a new member of the Oddfellows sect is presented with the badge of the sect. The badge has three intertwined links, which together represent friendship, truth and love.*

cannot simply be told the secrets of the society; they have to experience them for themselves (see pages 33–40 on initiation and the Eleusinian Mysteries).

# CATEGORIZATION OF SECRET SOCIETIES

Throughout the book you will see that the entries on each secret society begin with a quick rundown of basic facts: what categories the society falls into, its dates, the other societies to which it is most closely related and a brief statement of its main aims and purposes. The first of these is intended to provide a broad definition only – categorization of secret societies is difficult and contentious, as most of them occupy more than one category simultaneously. The basic categories used in the book are:

• **Fraternal** Many secret societies – notably the Masons – admit only men, but 'fraternal' is used here in the wider sense of encouraging interpersonal bonding between members of the group for the purposes of mutual support, protection and understanding, whatever their gender. The Masons traditionally put much emphasis on the moral virtue of 'fellow feeling' as an end in itself, but fraternal societies often expressed this in practical terms as well – for instance, taking collections to support sick members or the widows and orphans of members who died. The Oddfellows are a quasi-Masonic secret society that was once widespread in the Anglo-Saxon world; they combined trade union-like functions with insurance services for their members. The Masons themselves claimed descent from the medieval guilds, which had similar functions.

• **Religious** Some secret societies explore or emphasize mainstream religion along more or less orthodox lines. Many neo-Templar groups (see pages 84–89), for instance, are explicitly Christian, while the Assassins were an Islamic sect (see pages 238–263).

• **Mystical** Many secret societies concern themselves with religious philosophies, but in a very heterodox fashion, focusing on direct personal experience of the divine/spiritual or complex metaphysics. These can be categorized as 'mystical' to distinguish them from societies with more mainstream religious concerns.

• **Esoteric** Esoteric societies are based around a loosely defined set of teachings

that include the teachings of Pythagoras, Plato and later philosophers who developed their work (see pages 42–43), Hermetic lore, alchemy, Kabbalah, gematria, symbolic architecture and mathematics, Tarot and related topics. Generally they can be said to reveal 'inner' or 'hidden' teachings of philosophy, mathematics, history and science that are not taught by conventional schools of thought. 'Esoteric' here is closely related to both 'mystical' and 'occult'.

*A 19th-century depiction of a candidate for apprenticeship to the Freemasons undergoing the dramatic initiation ceremony, which combines exhortations to fraternal feeling with heavy doses of mystical and esoteric symbolism.*

- **Occult** Occult simply means 'hidden', but in this context it refers to the use of esoteric and mystical teachings to pursue 'operative' ends: the application of mystical and esoteric theory. Occultism includes all of the same topics as esotericism, together with psychic and paranormal powers, magic and supernatural powers, and spiritualism and contact with the dead. As a category, occult is closely related to 'esoteric' and 'magical'.

- **Magical** Magic can mean the application of supernatural power, as in witchcraft or Satanism; or it can mean 'natural magic', which is the application of knowledge of the secret laws of nature to manipulate and control nature as a form of paranormal technology; or it can mean the art and science of changing consciousness through the application of the will. Magical secret societies are those that use occult techniques to pursue magic, particularly the latter definition. All 'magical' societies also fall into the category of 'occult'.

*Portrayal of a Knight Templar after a 14th-century manuscript original. The Templars were a religious and paramilitary order who may also have developed esoteric teachings, and who were accused of occultism and magic.*

- **Paramilitary** Secret societies that use violence, force or strength of arms to achieve their ends, or specifically include warriors in their membership, are categorized as 'paramilitary'. This includes both medieval orders such as the Knights Templar, which was created to be a society of warrior monks, and groups with paramilitary activities or arms like the Assassins or the early Triads.

- **Criminal** Secret societies concerned with illegal activities either for personal profit or for the benefit of the group are categorized as 'criminal'.

- **Political** This category includes secret societies set up to pursue a specific political agenda, where that agenda is the sole reason for the existence of the society, but also societies with a political dimension alongside their other pursuits, where a mystical or criminal agenda also serves to advance an ideology or political goal. For instance, the pre-Nazi neo-Templar society *Ordo Novi Templi* (Order of the New Temple, or ONT) was concerned with a mystical interpretation of history and occult means of bringing that history to life, but it also served to develop and promote a fascist ideology with definite political ends – that is, the creation and support of the Nazi regime.

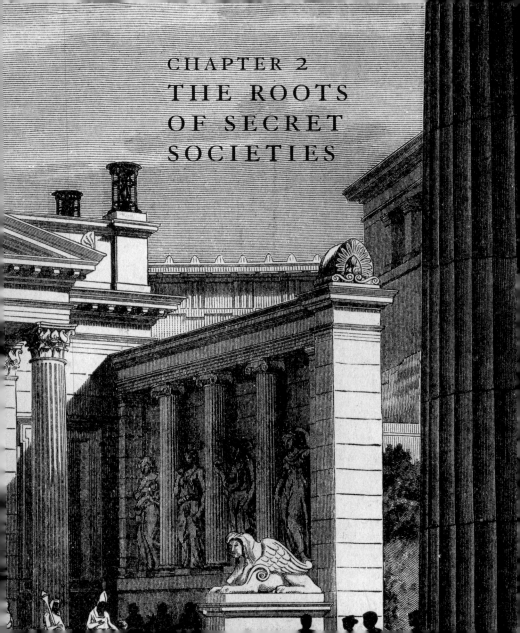

# CHAPTER 2
# THE ROOTS
# OF SECRET
# SOCIETIES

# SPIRITUALITY IN THE ANCIENT WORLD

Secret societies are probably almost as old as human culture. Evidence of the development of religion can be traced back at least 50,000 years, with the appearance of carvings and cave paintings, and possibly much further. The oldest vestiges of human ritual burial are from a cave at Qafzeh in Israel, where bones stained with red ochre have been dated to 90,000 years

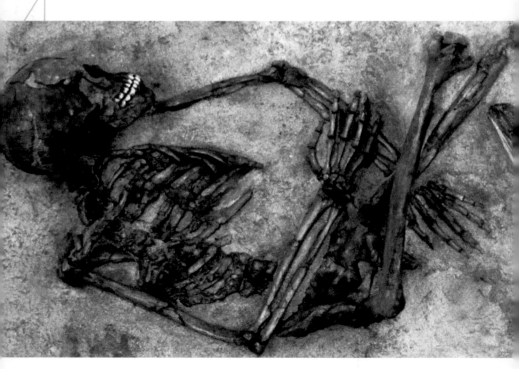

ago. With religion came spirituality, mysticism, knowledge of the world of spirits and otherworldly powers: the kind of knowledge that humans have always, throughout history and around the world, sought to protect and keep secret. As soon as a group of people know something that others do not, and work to maintain that secrecy, a secret society is born. From these primitive roots a long tradition stretches down through time. Where prehistory shades into ancient history it is possible to catch the first recorded glimpses of this tradition, in the form of mystery religions, lost cults and the esoteric knowledge of the ancients.

*Buried 90–100,000 years ago at Qafzeh in Israel, these are some of the oldest human remains in existence and provide evidence of a developed sense of spirituality among even the earliest* Homo sapiens.

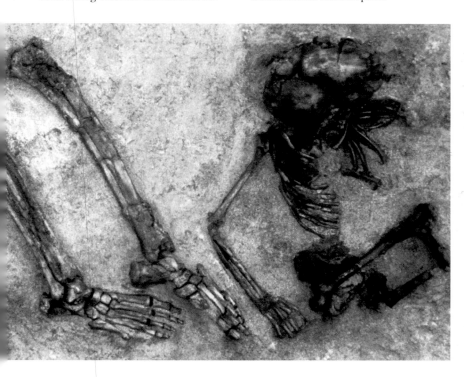

# LOST CULTS OF THE STONE AGE

Evidence from tribal peoples who have practised a Stone Age lifestyle in modern and historic eras, such as the !Kung of the Kalahari, the Australian Aborigines or the Inuit peoples of the Arctic, suggests that shamanistic beliefs and practices are likely to have been common to most human societies. These included the use of psychedelic techniques and potions, journeys to the spirit world and communication with supernatural beings and the dead.

Although all members of a society might have shared some of this knowledge and taken part in some of these practices, much of the shamanistic lore would have been reserved for the shaman himself. This made sense for a number of reasons. The sheer amount of knowledge the shaman needed to learn, including botany, zoology, geography, magic, myths, legends and other oral traditions, made it a specialized job of which only a few individuals were capable. So shamanistic practices inevitably meant that shamanistic knowledge would be restricted to a select few, who passed on by word of mouth (no other means being available) their traditions, which were not accessible to ordinary people. Whether or not they intended it, these early shamans had formed the first secret societies.

In pre-modern societies the shaman was respected, even feared. Knowledge is power, and human nature being what it is, those with power seek to protect and continue their power. Perhaps it was inevitable that the shamans would therefore want to guard their secrets jealously, giving access only to people they felt they could trust: those who had been specially initiated. Initiation also served other purposes (see page 16).

Scholars agree that the earliest recorded secret societies, the mystery religions covered over the next few pages, had ancient roots reaching back into prehistory, reflecting prehistoric cults of fertility, agriculture and the spirits of the dead. These cults are known as chthonic (from the Greek for 'under the earth') to distinguish them from the Olympian religion familiar from Classical Greece (with Zeus and the other gods of Mount Olympus).

*An elder of Botswana's San bushmen weeps in a trance. Shamanic rituals involving trance and mystical experience are common to many tribes who follow pre-Neolithic lifestyles.*

Characteristics of chthonic cults included arcane rituals, the use of caves as sacred spaces and shamanistic practices such as use of psychedelics and ecstatic dances and communing with the otherworld. Most of these became features of later religions, but more specifically they lived on in the mystery religions, and through them were passed down to later secret societies.

# THE MYSTERY RELIGIONS

Religious worship in the ancient world was usually a public act, but alongside the conventional exoteric (outwardly displayed) forms there were important esoteric (inner or hidden) traditions. The best known are the Greek mysteria or mystery religions. These were religious experiences and teachings available only to those who had been initiated. Indeed, this is the root of our modern word 'mystery'. 'To initiate' in Greek was 'myein', and an initiate was known as a 'mystes'. The mysteries appear to be remnants of prehistoric cult practices, and particularly involved fertility rites, reference to underground deities, ecstatic dances and the use of psychedelics and alcohol.

The Eleusinian Mysteries (see pages 30–41) are the best documented and probably the most important, but there were others. The Orphic mysteries concerned hymns and teachings purported to have derived from Orpheus, who travelled to the Underworld and returned, and whose head survived being torn from his body. The Dionysian rites concerned Dionysus, the god of wine, who had been killed and then resurrected. The revelation of secret truths about death, and more importantly life after death, seems to have been at the heart of all the mysteries. According to an ode by the poet Pindar (518–c.438 BCE): 'Happy is he, who having seen these rites, goes below the hollow earth; for he knows the end of life and he knows its god-sent beginning.'

## THE ORACLE AT DELPHI

A related cult in ancient Greece was the Apollonian oracle at Delphi (associated with Apollo, the sun god and also the god of prophecy) – the greatest oracle of the ancient world. Like the mysteries, it may also have had roots stretching back to prehistoric shamanic practice, and it too contributed important elements to the heritage of secret societies. At Delphi enquirers approached the temple through a series of symbolic rituals, but the oracular mystery at the heart of the cult – the high priestess Pythia, who was said to achieve an ecstatic trance state, perhaps through inhalation of

*Gustave Moreau's 1865 painting* Orpheus *shows the severed yet still animated head of the legendary poet recovered by a young maiden, who gazes at it, entranced. Orpheus was credited with the composition of a numer of 'hymns' concerning the secret of life after death, and became the centre of a mystery cult that passed on his 'teachings'.*

psychoactive fumes – was concealed within the adytum, or inner sanctum. There are links here to the Templars, among whose secrets was said to be an oracular head; the Masons, who focus heavily on the symbolism of sacred architectural spaces, specifically the adytum; and the modern Rosicrucian society, Builders of the Adytum (see page 189).

# THE ELEUSINIAN MYSTERIES

| | |
|---|---|
| TYPE | Religious, mystical, esoteric |
| EXISTED | c.700 BCE–393 CE |
| RELATED TO | Other mystery religions, Mithraism, Gnosticism |
| GOALS AND CONCERN | Life after death; spiritual growth |

The mysteries of Demeter, the Greek goddess of crops and agriculture, and her daughter Persephone were celebrated at Eleusis, 12 miles (20 km) from Athens, for at least a thousand years until 393 CE, when the Emperor Theodosius I suppressed all non-Christian religions. Three years later, the cult site with its great temple and sacred complex was sacked by the marauding Visigoths. During its millennium or more of existence, the mystery cult had grown in importance to become one of the defining characteristics of first Athenian and later Greek identity; poets, philosophers and even emperors had joined the ranks of initiates. The mysteries left an indelible legacy that lasts to this day. The development of Christianity was heavily influenced by the mystery cults, while many of the core elements of the modern secret society were predated and prefigured by the Eleusinian Mysteries.

## DEMETER AND PERSEPHONE

The myth of Demeter tells how she was distraught when Persephone was carried off to the Underworld by the god Hades. Seeking her child, she abandoned her heavenly abode and wandered the Earth,

*The Temple of Demeter in Naxos, Greece, as it would have appeared in ancient times. It was a sanctuary of the sacred mysteries of Eleusis.*

plunging the world into an era of infertility in which no green thing would grow and the survival of humanity and all the other animals was threatened.

The Olympian gods were alarmed and Zeus forced Hades to release Persephone so that she could return to her mother, but the cunning god of the Underworld managed to trick her into eating six seeds of a pomegranate. In a motif that recalls faery folklore of much more recent vintage, having eaten otherworldly food, Persephone was thus doomed to spend time in the land of the dead – a month for each seed. For the rest of eternity she would spend half the year above ground, in the realm of light and life, and half of it below ground, in the realm of the dead and the chthonic gods of the pre-Olympian age.

The return of her daughter roused Demeter from her grief and restored fertility to the Earth. However, during the six months of the year Persephone spends in the land of the dead, Demeter is plunged once more into depression, with unfortunate effects for earthly life. For some ancient Greeks, this provided the explanatory myth for the seasons, which in ancient Greece were not the same as the four seasons of north-west Europe and north-east America, but were divided into the cold/wet season and the hot/dry season.

## REVEALING THE MYSTERIES

During her gloomy wanderings, Demeter had stopped at the town of Eleusis, and because of the kindness shown to her by the people there, she had taught them her mysteries. Exactly what were these amazing revelations? One of the most important rules of the Eleusinian Mysteries was that they could only be revealed to the initiated, and amazingly this rule seems to have been obeyed for centuries. Although many ancient writers wrote about the mysteries in a general sense, or gave clues as to their content, there is no surviving account of their exact nature. Enough is known to speculate, however.

For instance, it is known that the mysteries concerned the issue of life after death, and that the whole point of initiation was that it offered a guarantee of something more than the dreary eternity of grey nothingness to which most souls were condemned. In other words, it promised some sort of heaven or paradise: a free pass to the Elysian Fields perhaps. It is likely that a key element of the mysteries was that initiation depended on an actual

*Frederic Leighton's 1891 painting,* The Return of Persephone. *Persephone is depicted here emerging from the Underworld to be greeted by her mother Demeter.*

experience – you could not be told what the mysteries were, you had to experience them for yourself. The impact of the initiation experience was immense, as a passage from *On the Soul*, by the Graeco-Roman writer Plutarch (*c.*46–*c.*120 CE) makes clear:

'The soul [at the point of death] has the same experiences as those who are being initiated into great mysteries... At first one wanders and wearily hurries to and fro, and journeys with suspicion through the dark as one uninitiated. Then come all the terrors before the final initiation: shuddering, trembling, sweating, amazement. Then one is struck with a marvellous light, one is received into pure regions and meadows, with voices and dances and the majesty of holy sounds and shapes. Among these [the initiate] wanders free; [he is] released and, bearing his crown, joins in the divine communion, and consorts with pure and holy men. [Meanwhile] those who [were not] initiated – an unclean horde – are trodden under his feet and huddle together in mud and fog, abiding in their miseries through fear of death and mistrust of the blessings of the afterlife.'

## THE ELEUSINION

The Sanctuary of the Two Goddesses (Demeter and Persephone) at Eleusis was unique in the Classical world. There

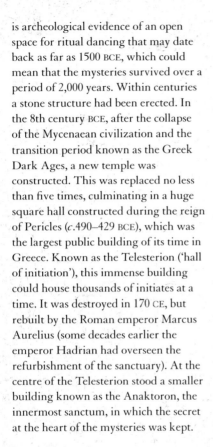

is archeological evidence of an open space for ritual dancing that may date back as far as 1500 BCE, which could mean that the mysteries survived over a period of 2,000 years. Within centuries a stone structure had been erected. In the 8th century BCE, after the collapse of the Mycenaean civilization and the transition period known as the Greek Dark Ages, a new temple was constructed. This was replaced no less than five times, culminating in a huge square hall constructed during the reign of Pericles (c.490–429 BCE), which was the largest public building of its time in Greece. Known as the Telesterion ('hall of initiation'), this immense building could house thousands of initiates at a time. It was destroyed in 170 CE, but rebuilt by the Roman emperor Marcus Aurelius (some decades earlier the emperor Hadrian had overseen the refurbishment of the sanctuary). At the centre of the Telesterion stood a smaller building known as the Anaktoron, the innermost sanctum, in which the secret at the heart of the mysteries was kept.

## THE LESSER AND GREATER MYSTERIES

Initially, the Eleusinian Mysteries were local and tribal, part of what constituted citizenship of the Eleusinian city-state, but when this became part of Athens,

the mysteries became an elective religion open to all as a matter of personal choice. Eventually – and unusually for ancient mystery cults – membership was even open to women and non-citizens.

Initiation involved two stages. Candidates first had to undergo instruction in the Lesser Mysteries, the *Myesis*, which were celebrated annually in February at Agrae near Athens, on the banks of the Ilissos River. Candidates underwent ritual purification by bathing in the waters and then sacrificed a pig, before learning about the story of Demeter and Persephone.

Those who had graduated from the Lesser Mysteries were now eligible to take part in the Greater Mysteries, the *Teletai*, which were celebrated in the month of Boedromion (September–October), the time of sowing, signalling the association between the Eleusinian Mysteries and fertility rites of the chthonic era. On the 14th of Boedromion, baskets of sacred objects from Eleusis were brought to Athens either by priestesses or *epheboi* (young men), depending on the source. On the following dawn, candidates, who had

*Ruins of the Telesterion, Eleusis, where the mysteries were celebrated for over 2,000 years until all 'pagan' religions were suppressed by the Christian emperor Theodosius I in 393 CE.*

THE ROOTS OF SECRET SOCIETIES

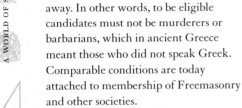

started fasting a few days earlier, gathered to hear a priest open the festival with a declaration warning that those 'who are of not pure hands and speak an incomprehensible tongue' should keep away. In other words, to be eligible candidates must not be murderers or barbarians, which in ancient Greece meant those who did not speak Greek. Comparable conditions are today attached to membership of Freemasonry and other societies.

## PROCESSION TO ELEUSIS

Candidates were then led down to the sea to bathe and purify themselves, and more unfortunate swine were sacrificed. After two days of seclusion, the candidates gathered at the Athenian Eleusinion for a ceremony, and then marched off along the Sacred Way to Eleusis, bearing the baskets of sacred objects, in a great procession rich in symbolism and ritual. Initiates were crowned in myrtle wreaths and waved branches of a sacred plant called *bakchoi*. Plato, a devotee of the Eleusinian Mysteries, quoted what was probably an Orphic verse (supposedly composed by the mythical figure Orpheus, himself at the centre of another set of mysteries) in his Socratic dialogue *Phaedo*: 'There are many who bear the wand, but few who become *Bakchoi*.' Wands would later

become a feature of Masonic ritual and were important tools in the system of magic created by the Hermetic Order of the Golden Dawn (HOGD – see pages 184–187). Participants would raise a rhythmic shout of *lakch' o lakch* – a way of invoking the god Iacchus, believed to be one of the aspects of Bacchus because of the similarity of names.

As they crossed over bridges along the route to Eleusis, the initiates were met by priests. At one bridge the priests gave each of them a sip of a sacred drink known as *kykeon* ('the mixture'), an alcoholic brew made from roasted barley and the herb pennyroyal. It has been speculated that *kykeon* was psychoactive, perhaps because the barley was infected with ergot fungus, which causes ergotism, a form of poisoning involving profound psychedelic effects. At another bridge the priests tied ribbons or threads to the right hand and left foot of each initiate.

This great procession may have been a ritual re-enactment of the main elements of the myth of Demeter and Persephone: the wanderings of Demeter, the marriage of Persephone to Hades and

*Details from the side of an ancient Greek* krater *(wine vessel), from 470* BCE, *showing Demeter with Triptolemus, to whom she taught the secrets of agriculture, a myth that featured strongly in the Eleusinian Mysteries.*

her restoration to the sunlit world, which in the myth was marked by the birth of a divine child (Dionysus or Bacchus), himself symbolized by an ear of wheat.

Elements of this myth, such as death, resurrection and a divine birth, were powerful archetypes that almost certainly fed into the evolution of Christianity in

*Late 4th-century BCE relief showing a sacrificial procession at Eleusis in honour of the goddess Demeter (her deity is demonstrated by her superhuman size, and her identity by the sheaf of wheat she carries).*

## REVELATION

At dusk the procession would arrive at Eleusis and the initiates would crowd into the Telesterion, where the chief priest, or Hierophant (later to become one of the characters in the Tarot), was seated on a throne at the threshold of the Anaktoron. What happened next has remained a secret, which is an amazing feat considering that massive numbers of people took part in the mysteries over the course of a millennium or more, including many who, as with modern-day Masonry, probably did not take it too seriously.

Some clues do exist. The mysteries were reputed to have been divided into *legomena*, *dromena* and *deiknymena*: what was said, what was done and what was revealed. Initiates learned the *synthema*, or password, which was related by the 2nd-century CE Christian writer Clement of Alexandria as: 'I fasted, I drank the *kykeon*, I took out of the chest, having done my task, I put again into the basket, and from the basket into the chest.' In other words, a central element of the ceremony was the transfer and

the early centuries CE, and have their parallels in the ritual dramas that are central to Freemasonry and related secret societies in the modern era.

display of the sacred objects. According to one account, the climax of the revelations involved a bright light issuing forth from the Anaktoron and the holding aloft, in silence, of a single ear of wheat. In practice, the details are not important – what counted was the experience, which was able to free initiates from fear of death and instil faith in a better hereafter.

In some sources those who had celebrated both the Lesser and Greater Mysteries were said to be *teleios*, which can be translated as 'fully initiated' but also means 'perfect'. This term resonates with later movements such as the Cathars, whose priests were known as *Perfecti* (see pages 55–56), and the Illuminati, or Perfectibilists. Among the ranks of the initiated were major figures such as Plato, Cicero and the first Roman emperor Augustus.

## LEGACY OF THE MYSTERIES

There is no direct line of descent from the ancient mysteries to modern Freemasonry or any other secret society, no matter what any fantasy-prone 19th-century Masons might have claimed. But there are many parallels between the movements, which could mean that some sort of tradition endured from ancient times to the modern era, or perhaps that some elements and characteristics are fundamental to secret societies regardless of where or when they arise.

The most obvious parallel is secrecy. According to the *Homeric Hymn to Demeter*, which dates back to the 7th or 6th century BCE, the revelations involved were 'awful mysteries which no one may in any way transgress or pry into or utter, for deep awe of the Gods checks the voice'. This recalls the bloodcurdling oaths that used to be administered to those undergoing initiation into Freemasonry (see pages 153–154). Freemasonry also makes heavy use of passwords, ritual drama and re-enactments of myths and the symbolism of 'sacred' objects as allegories for those myths – all features of the mysteries. The three degrees of Freemasonry (see page 132) recall the three-fold nature of the Eleusinian revelations, or perhaps its division of the initiation process into Lesser and Greater Mysteries.

Like modern secret societies, the ancient mysteries attracted their fair share of influential, highly placed people as initiates. As in Freemasonry, all initiates began their journey as equals; whether the initiate was an emperor or a pauper had no impact on their status within the secret sect, at least in theory. But the involvement of big-name members also feeds into the kind of speculation that swirls around both

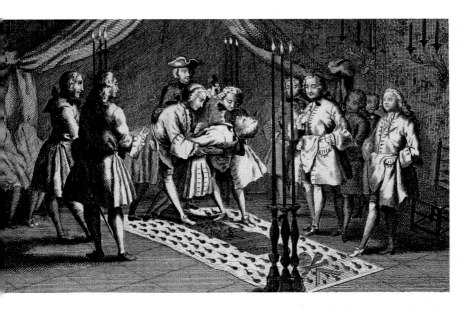

ancient and modern secret societies –
the suspicion that they are pulling the
strings of history, even that there has
been a chain of secret masters of the
world (secret masters featured heavily
in the founding myth of the Hermetic
Order of the Golden Dawn, or HOGD,
for instance – see page 185).

Perhaps the most significant parallel
between mysteries ancient and modern
was their ultimate purpose. Although
both the Eleusinian Mysteries and
Freemasonry have revolved around
colourful rituals and apparently sinister
secrecy, both have also had serious and

*Eighteenth-century Freemasons laying a
newly initiated member on a shroud. Ritual
enactment of dying and rising is believed to
have been common to both Masonry and the
ancient mysteries.*

high-minded goals. The purpose of the
mysticism and the play-acting has
always been self-improvement of a
spiritual sort. Plato himself commented:
'It looks as if those also who established
rites of initiation for us were no fools...
[they were,] in my opinion, no others
than those who have given their lives
to true philosophy.'

# THE PYTHAGOREAN BROTHERHOOD

| | |
|---|---|
| TYPE | Esoteric, mystical, occult, political |
| EXISTED | c.530 BCE–c.450 BCE |
| RELATED TO | Mystery religions, Rosicrucians, Freemasonry |
| GOALS AND CONCERNS | Mathematics; metaphysics; social and political reform |

Pythagoras was a legendary ancient Greek philosopher. Born *c.*570 BCE in Samos, he moved to Magna Graecia (the network of Greek colonies in Southern Italy) where his potent blend of mathematics and mysticism attracted young men from aristocratic backgrounds to form the Pythagorean Brotherhood, a secret society or cult.

According to legend, Pythagoras had acquired his wisdom during his travels in Egypt and the East (similar claims were later made in modern times for Madame Blavatsky and Aleister Crowley – see pages 180–183 and 191–194), but he also borrowed heavily from the ancient mystery religions. He was said to have made important mathematical discoveries (such as the theorem that still bears his name),

identified the ratios that govern music, originated the doctrine of 'transmigration of the soul' – essentially reincarnation – and stressed the importance of sacred geometry (a concept central to Freemasonry). Pythagoras believed that number was the organizing principle of the universe, and that he could hear the music of the spheres. Because of his belief in reincarnation, Pythagoras preached strict vegetarianism, in which beans were also banned.

Candidates for the Pythagorean Brotherhood had to undergo a strict initiation procedure. After a tough interview, they had to swear an oath on a sacred triangle known as the *tetractys*, sign over all their worldly possessions to the group and take a five-year vow of silence. During this period they became *akousmatikoi*, or listeners, allowed to listen to Pythagoras teach only from behind a veil. Eventually they would graduate to become *mathematikoi*, members of the inner circle. Later these two classes diverged, so that those known as *mathematikoi* followed the scientific, philosophical aspects of Pythagorean teachings, while those called *akousmatikoi* followed the mystical oral teachings, or *symbola*, of Pythagoras.

The Pythagorean Brotherhood became powerful and politically influential, but ended up supporting the losing side in a clash between local political parties that descended into violence. Their headquarters in the city of Crotona was burned to the ground and many of the Brotherhood were killed. Pythagoras himself escaped into exile, but died a few years later *c.*495 BCE. His philosophy lived on, however. Plato was an avid admirer, and indeed much of what is attributed to Pythagoras may be Platonic invention. Versions of Pythagorean mysticism became profoundly influential in the Western tradition that led to Hermeticism, alchemy and Rosicrucianism. It has been claimed that the Brotherhood lived on in one form or another to form the roots of many subsequent secret societies, such as the Freemasons.

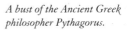

*A bust of the Ancient Greek philosopher Pythagorus.*

# MITHRAISM

| | |
|---|---|
| TYPE | Religious, mystical, fraternal |
| EXISTED | c.100 CE–c.450 CE |
| RELATED TO | Mystery religions, Freemasonry |
| GOALS AND CONCERNS | Life after death; fraternal fun |

Related to the ancient mystery cults of the Greeks, Mithraism was the worship of the god Mithras. Originally a sun god from the Persian pantheon, Mithras became very popular in the Roman Empire, and the Mithraic religion flourished from the 2nd century CE, rivalling Christianity until the latter got the upper hand. Mithraism eventually died out in the 5th century CE. In practice it had many similarities with Christianity – the two religions probably shared the same sources and cross-fertilized each other. Mithras was regarded as a saviour or messiah figure; his holy day was Sunday and one of his main festivals was held on 25 December.

The Mithraic cult had many important parallels with modern secret societies such as the Freemasons. It was open only to men (and was particularly popular with soldiers, minor officials and freedmen), who had to undergo initiation rites. Within the cult, rank in the secular world was of no importance – all initiates started off at the same rank and worked their way up, so that a

*A 2nd–3rd-century CE marble relief of Mithras sacrificing the bull. Such images were a feature of every Mithraeum, their symbolism encoding teachings of the cult. Note the god's Phrygian cap, the Sun and Moon and the animals below the bull (dog, scorpion and snake), thought to symbolize constellations and heavenly bodies.*

legionnaire could be superior to his centurion. There were seven grades of initiation, corresponding to the seven 'planets': Raven, Nymphus, Soldier, Lion, Persian, Heliodromus and Father. The Mithraic equivalent to a Masonic lodge was the 'cave' – an underground (or mock underground) chapel, or Mithraeum, where members would meet for a ritual meal of bread and wine.

Each Mithraeum was equipped with low benches running on either side of an aisle. The men would recline on these benches while they ate. At the head of the aisle was a carved relief or mural displaying the iconic image of Mithras performing his greatest exploit, the slaying of a bull. These icons conformed to a strict symbolic code, with Mithras (wearing his characteristic Phrygian cap) and the bull always shown in the same pose, while animals related to the zodiacal constellations also featured. No texts remain to explain the exact meaning of these symbols, but one explanation is that they are an allegory of the cosmological journey of the soul, which descends to earth at birth but ascends to heaven at death. As with the older forms of mystery religion, Mithraism did not survive antiquity and there is no direct line of descent to secret societies in the modern era, although some have used Mithraic symbolism.

# THE ETERNAL BATTLE

Secret societies like the Freemasons incorporate many religious ideas that come from non- and pre-Christian sources, so to understand the secret knowledge that such societies teach to their initiates, it is necessary to look at the pagan religions that were the original sources of these ideas. One of the most important of these ideas is called dualism. Dualism first became central in the religion known as Zoroastrianism.

## ZOROASTRIANISM

Zoroastrianism was the first monotheistic (believing in one god) religion, based on the teachings of the legendary Zoroaster, or Zarathustra, a Persian priest who probably lived around 1200 CE. Zoroaster preached that there was one supreme god, Ahura Mazda, but that he was opposed by an evil force called Angra Mainyu, which actually controlled the material world. He believed that life was an eternal battle between the forces of light and dark. Each individual had to choose his or her side in this battle. This teaching is a form of dualism: the belief that all of creation is defined by two opposing forces – light and dark, good and evil, spirit and matter. Dualism would become enormously important to the philosophical underpinning of secret societies.

## GNOSTICISM

Gnosticism is not a specific religion but more of a philosophy that can be applied to any religion. As a school of thought it probably began in Alexandria in the 1st century CE and is most commonly associated with Christianity, although there are also influential varieties of Jewish and Islamic Gnosticism. Gnosticism is important in the history of secret societies as the source of a radical form of dualism that would give rise to the Cathars, influence the Knights Templar and inspire the secret heart of Freemasonry and related groups.

*The Persian prophet, Zoroaster or Zarathustra, c.628–551 BCE, who was a reformer, is shown educating his people.*

in corde suo: non est deus .

oruna sunt  abhomunabiles fac

Gnosticism was concocted from a diverse brew of influences, including Zoroastrianism, Pythagoreanism and Platonism, Egyptian religion, Jewish mysticism, Christian theology and even Buddhism. Its name comes from the Greek *gnosis*, meaning 'knowledge', a reference to the essential knowledge at its heart: that the universe has a dual nature, and that we are consigned to the bad part. According to Gnosticism, the realm of light and goodness is the non-material universe, while the physical, material world – the world of reality, of human beings and their physical bodies – is the realm of darkness and evil. Gross matter is viewed as a corruption of the purity of spirit, while God is a sort of non-material divine essence of pure light and spirit. As physical beings, men and women are separated from the heavenly bliss of union with this divine essence, often called the Godhead. Fortunately for mankind, each human has a soul or spirit, often described as a spark of divine essence, and the struggle against evil and for salvation is actually a struggle to liberate this spark of the divine from the

*Illumination from a 14th-century English psalter (book of psalms and other texts) showing the expulsion of Lucifer. Some gnostics, including many Christians, argued that Lucifer was the good guy, battling the evil demiurge to bring purifying light to a corrupt universe.*

gross material world so that it can become reunited with the divine Oneness.

The key point here is that this struggle is individual to each person, and that the route to salvation lies within. *Gnosis* involves direct experience of the divine, through accessing the divine spark within. By stressing a personal route to salvation, Gnosticism inevitably undermines the claims of people or institutions (such as priests or the Church) to act as intermediaries between the common people and God. If salvation comes only from within and is unique to each individual, what need is there for priests, temples or religious dogma of any sort? It is hardly surprising that established religions, and the Catholic Church in particular, have always been hostile to 'heretical' beliefs such as Gnosticism, and to secret societies such as the Freemasons that share some of these beliefs.

As Gnosticism evolved it took many forms, and the basic *gnosis* was interpreted in many ways. According to some interpretations, the physical world was created by an evil spirit, or demiurge, equivalent to Zoroastrianism's Angra Mainyu. This evil demiurge was responsible for the created world that we live in, with all its attendant evil and suffering. Since the Bible, for instance, tells us that the god known as Yahweh

was responsible for Creation, for some Gnostics it followed that Yahweh was actually the evil corruptor, and that his enemy Lucifer, the Bringer of Light, was the force for good. In fact, one of the names attributed to Jesus in early texts was Lucifer, and in some forms of Gnosticism, Jesus and other figures such as Mohammed and Buddha are seen as beings of light, emissaries sent by the Godhead to help mankind achieve *gnosis* and to battle against God. From the point of view of mainstream biblical religions, this is shocking heresy and blasphemy.

Some interpretations of Gnosticism went still further. Since being imprisoned in physical bodies was a tragedy for the divine spark within, it made sense to stop perpetuating this tragedy, so that some Gnostics believed in celibacy and others even sanctioned suicide and murder. Alternatively, some believed that the actions of the body could not affect the pure, incorruptible spirit within, and therefore it was acceptable to behave with total moral and sexual licence. Again, this was not calculated to appeal to the authorities, intent on maintaining order and the status quo. Accordingly, Gnosticism was vigorously persecuted and Gnostic beliefs had to become closely guarded secrets, revealed only to those who

had proved themselves trustworthy and who had been prepared for the shocking revelations by undergoing initiation tests.

The Gnostic version of Christianity was as popular in the early centuries CE as what became the orthodox version, and some traces of it can still be found in the New Testament. In fact, the Bible as it is known today is a canon of scriptures that was whittled down from a larger pool of books or scriptures circulating in the early first millennium. Many of the books were Gnostic in nature, but were suppressed and lost when orthodoxy triumphed, finally fixing the canon at the Synod of Hippo in 393 CE. When a cache of ancient scrolls was found in the Egyptian village of Nag Hammadi in 1945, many of these Gnostic books were rediscovered.

The Gnostic sects that had sprung up were mostly suppressed, and although this drove Gnosticism out of the mainstream, it proved impossible to eradicate altogether. Versions of Gnostic Christianity have continued to be practised up to the present day, while Islamic Sufism and Jewish Kabbalism also kept alive Gnostic traditions. Some of the versions of Gnosticism most significant for the development of secret societies were the Manicheans, the Bogomils and the Cathars.

The Nag Hammadi Gnostic gospels, discovered in Egypt in 1945, provide a fascinating glimpse into the range of heterodox beliefs that characterized early Christianity.

# THE CATHARS

| TYPE | Religious, mystical, political, military |
|---|---|
| EXISTED | c.1100–c.1315 |
| RELATED TO | Gnosticism, Knights Templar |
| GOALS AND CONCERNS | Religious observance; spiritual perfection; religious and political independence |

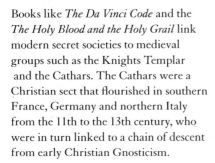

Books like *The Da Vinci Code* and the *The Holy Blood and the Holy Grail* link modern secret societies to medieval groups such as the Knights Templar and the Cathars. The Cathars were a Christian sect that flourished in southern France, Germany and northern Italy from the 11th to the 13th century, who were in turn linked to a chain of descent from early Christian Gnosticism.

## THE MANICHEANS

The early centuries CE were a time of religious ferment across Europe and Asia. Christianity was spreading fast, as were Mithraism and Gnosticism. In Sassanid Persia, a young Zoroastrian named Mani (216–276 CE) was overtaken by visions and became a prophet, preaching a Gnostic gospel of radical

dualism. Supposedly, primal man, a being of pure light and spirit, had shattered into particles and been swallowed by the powers of darkness so that the particles of light were now imprisoned in matter – the human body, specifically the brain. Salvation was the ongoing process of freeing the sparks of light from their physical prisons in order that they could rejoin the divine, and a series of apostles of light, including the biblical prophets Buddha, Zoroaster, Jesus and Mani himself, had been sent to spread the word.

Mani and his followers were actively evangelical and for a while Mani succeeded in gaining the ear of the Sassanid emperor Shapur I, but later he fell foul of political manoeuvring and was flayed alive. His Church lived on,

*Mani, founder of Manicheanism. Born in Persia, Mani's influence was far-reaching; this portrait is from the Indian town of Kotcho, and Manicheanism spread from the Roman Empire to China. Its Gnostic teachings were hugely influential on subsequent Gnostic movements such as the Bogomils and Cathars, but also the early Christian mainstream.*

spreading through Central Asia and reaching China, where it was practised in one form or another up until the modern era. Manicheans were divided into two classes: the Elect (the Righteous) and the Auditors ('hearers'). The strict code of Manichean ethics meant that the Elect were forbidden to gather food for themselves and depended for their sustenance on the Auditors, who were free from these restrictions. The Cathars would later have a very similar system.

Manicheanism became popular in the Roman world and particularly in Alexandria, and the Church Father St Augustine was originally a Manichean before becoming a Christian. The triumph of orthodox Christianity saw it suppressed along with other forms of Gnosticism.

THE ROOTS OF SECRET SOCIETIES

## THE BOGOMILS

In the 10th century, Gnosticism gripped the Balkans with the flourishing of a Christian sect founded by a priest who took the name Bogomil. The Bogomils, or Friends of God, subscribed to the teachings of an earlier sect called the Paulicians, who argued that the physical world and human beings had actually been created by Satan, not God, and that Jesus had not been a physical being, but had simply had the appearance of one. Their dualism was probably passed down from the Manicheans, and they shared a similar hierarchy and moral code. The strictest code – abstinence from sex, marriage, meat and wine, and the giving up of all worldly possessions – was practised only by a select few, known as the *Perfecti*, while the ordinary men and women lived normal lives but could achieve the state of grace of the *Perfecti* by taking the *consolamentum* – a sort of spiritual baptism – on their deathbed.

The Bogomil movement was popular in the Balkans and the Byzantine Empire up until the 14th century, but the conquest of Asia Minor (Turkey) and the Balkans by the Ottomans led to the adoption of Islam

*A Bogomil tomb situated in a graveyard near Stolac, Herzeg. It shows a relief with an archer and dates from the 12th–14th century.*

across the region. In Western Europe the sect was known as the Bulgars because their heartland was Bulgaria; in France Bulgar became *Bougre*. The typical response of orthodox Christianity to heretical groups was to slander them with accusations such as homosexuality and sexual deviance, and hence the term 'bougre' or 'bugger' became associated with certain sexual practices.

## RISE AND FALL OF THE CATHARS

The Bogomils had a direct influence on the best-known Gnostic sect of all, the Cathars, possibly by converting Crusaders passing through their territories, who took their new faith back to Western Europe. Like the Bogomils, the Cathars believed that the material world was corrupt and that salvation lay in freeing the divine spark within to reunite with the Godhead. They shared a similar organization, with a small number of elect known as *Perfecti*, and the mass of laypeople known as *bonshommes*. The word 'Cathar' itself is said to derive from the Latin for 'pure ones'. As with the Bogomils and the Manicheans before them, the Cathar Perfecti rejected sex, marriage and meat; initiates to the rank of Perfecti even had to renounce their marriages. Meanwhile, the bonshommes were less restricted, waiting until near death to take the *consolamentum* and become purified. Also like the Bogomils, the Cathars had an anti-establishment character. The piety and simplicity of the Perfecti stood in stark contrast to the corrupt and worldly clergy of the time, and there was an egalitarian aspect to the sect – men and women were accounted as equals.

Catharism took root in Germany (where it was first recorded, in 1143) and northern Italy, but its heartland was in southern and central France, particularly the Languedoc region. The town of Albi was considered to be the centre of the sect, and they were accordingly known as the Albigensians. At this point in the Middle Ages the Languedoc was very different from the rest of France, with its own language and a culture formed from a blend of influences (including Moorish). The nobles of the region were more or less independent from the French monarch, and their embrace of Catharism, coupled with its growing popularity in other parts of Europe and the fact that it had set up its own hierarchy of priests and bishops, meant that the movement posed a great threat to the Catholic Church and its temporal allies.

After failing to 'correct' the heretical errors of the Cathars, the Church instituted the Inquisition in 1184 to suppress it by force. Initially, progress was slow, but it gained impetus in 1199 when Pope Innocent III declared that local authorities could share in the property of convicted heretics. In 1208 the Pope declared a new crusade against the Albigensian heresy, unleashing a century of conflict and atrocities across the Languedoc region. Catharism was not finally crushed until 1255 (and there was even a brief revival in the early 14th century), but its defeat was sealed when its greatest stronghold, the impenetrable fortress of Montségur, fell in mysterious circumstances in 1244. According to some writers, the Cathars guarded a mysterious secret, perhaps a treasure, and this was spirited out of Montségur the night before it fell. Despite the fact that this appears to be pure invention with no basis in evidence, it has become part of the tapestry of legend that weaves together the Cathars, the Knights Templar, the Rosicrucians and the Freemasons. (See page 72 for more on the legendary secret/treasure guarded by secret societies throughout history.)

*A 20th-century illumination by Daniel Lemozy of Carcassonne from Languedoc showing the capture of Montségur castle, France. Over 200 Cathars were burned alive during a 13th-century crusade that was ordered by Pope Innocent II against Cathar heretics.*

# THE SECRET STREAM

In the West, the rich variety of philosophy, religion and mysticism in the ancient world gave way to a much more uniform, monolithic arrangement in the post-Classical world, as a Christian orthodoxy took shape and the Church established itself, first as the religion of the Roman Empire, and later as the unifying force of the Dark Age era. It was in this era that the mysteries, Mithraism and Gnosticism were all suppressed, and that exoteric forms of religion – those played out in the open, and publicly accessible to all – largely won out over esoteric forms – those hidden forms available to only a few. But, as the great mythologist Joseph Campbell explained in his magnum opus *The Masks of God*, published 1959–1968, 'the mysteries, like a secret stream, went underground'.

## THE WESTERN ESOTERIC TRADITION

The result of being driven underground was what scholars of the occult call the Western esoteric tradition. This is the chain of descent of mystical and magical

*Neoplatonists believed that Hermes Trismegistus was a deity of alchemy and possessed magical as well as oracular powers.*

knowledge from the Classical era down to the modern day, a span of around 1,700 years. During much of this period the Western tradition included knowledge that was considered very dangerous, immoral and often illegal, so that those who followed this tradition had to be extremely careful about broadcasting it. Accordingly, much was kept secret or at least hidden (in other words, 'occult'). Occasionally, however, aspects of the tradition would break out into public view and become popular and even commonplace, such as in the case of Tarot and playing cards (see page 177).

## HERMES TRISMEGISTUS

Ancient Egypt had a tradition of magic and mysticism stretching back to at least 3000 BCE. When Alexander the Great conquered Egypt and a new Hellenic culture took root in and around Alexandria, these ancient traditions were overlain by and melded with Greek traditions such as Pythagoreanism and Platonism. The Egyptian god of wisdom, Thoth the Thrice-Great (or *Trismegistus* in Latin), was identified with the Greek god of writing and communication, Hermes, to create a compound figure: Hermes Trismegistus. Writings about magic and mysticism were frequently attributed to his authorship, while at the same time he

became a legendary, sub-divine figure – a real person who had existed in pre-biblical times and recorded prehistoric wisdom. In early Freemasonry, for instance, Hermes Trismegistus became the legendary founder of architecture and masonry.

In practice, almost all of the works supposedly 'by' Hermes Trismegistus were written in Alexandria in the first three or four centuries CE. This body, or *corpus*, of work became known as the *Corpus Hermeticum*, and dealt with topics such as magic, spells, Gnostic religion, Pythagorean mathematics, Platonic philosophy and alchemy. Islamic scholars preserved some of these works, and they were rediscovered in the West when an Italian scholar translated a manuscript found in Greece in 1453. Scholars of the period believed they had found a direct line to prehistoric wisdom, and Hermetic philosophy, known as Hermeticism, went on to be enormously influential in the development of secret societies.

## KABBALAH

As with Christianity, so Judaism also had exoteric and esoteric elements. The latter are known collectively as Kabbalah (or Qabala or, typically when practised by Christians, Cabala). They feature magical and mystical knowledge, including secret names of God that have supernatural power, and theories about the significance of number. Because Hebrew letters are also used as numbers, words in Hebrew can be read as numbers and collections of numbers. The study of these numbers, their patterns, relationships and significance, is known as gematria.

Important cabalistic texts were written in the Middle Ages and spread to non-Jewish scholars, so that Kabbalah became an important element of the occult tradition in the West, and fed into the philosophical and spiritual basis of secret societies such as the Masons. A well-known element of Kabbalah is the Tree of Life, a diagrammatic representation of the ten aspects of God/creation and the 22 paths that link them.

## MAGIC AND ALCHEMY

As well as metaphysics (philosophical musings on the relationship between mankind and God and the nature of reality), the Western esoteric tradition was concerned with magic – the manipulation of Nature by paranormal or supernatural means. Magic could include telling the future (divination), communing with spirits (including angels, demons and the dead) and casting spells. It was governed by

laws, such as the Doctrine of Correspondences, according to which there are secret correspondences between different aspects of the universe – for instance, the Sun corresponds to the element gold. Another law was 'as above, so below', the doctrine that things on Earth are related to things in Heaven – for example, the zodiacal constellations relate to things and events on Earth. These magical laws were highly influential on the thinking of Rosicrucians, Freemasons, occultists and others involved in secret societies.

A special example of magic was the practice of alchemy, a sort of magical chemistry. Alchemists sought to achieve spiritual and material transformation through manipulation of the elements. Specifically, by heating, distilling and fermenting chemicals, they hoped to find the Philosopher's Stone, which could transmute base metals into gold and bestow immortality. Many of those who played a role in setting up secret societies in the 17th century were also alchemists.

*An alchemist at work, after David Taniers the Younger's 17th-century painting* The Chymist. *Note the alembic, or alchemical still, atop the furnace, composed of the alembic proper and the cucurbit. Such terms recur in the language of mystical and occult societies, symbolizing the transforming power of esoteric instruction.*

# PART 2
# RELIGIOUS, MYSTICAL AND OCCULT SOCIETIES

From the obscure mysteries of the ancient world, a tradition of esoteric knowledge lived on in the West, surviving the end of the Classical world and the coming of the Dark Ages, preserved by Islamic scholars and rediscovered in the Renaissance before spreading to the New World with European colonization. As the Middle Ages gave way to the early modern era, secret societies sprang up that would come to define the concept and form of nearly all secret societies that followed them. Freemasonry was the most important and successful of these societies, but there have been hundreds of others, the most significant and interesting of which are described in this chapter. What connects them all is the Western mystery or esoteric tradition. This includes Hermeticism, alchemy, Kabbalah and Tarot, plus many things now thought of as mainstream knowledge but that have esoteric, symbolic and occult aspects, such as architecture, music and mathematics. As the esoteric tradition developed, it came to encompass science and pseudoscience (including dangerous misinterpretations of Darwinism and evolutionary theory), psychic powers and spiritualism, and new versions of magic.

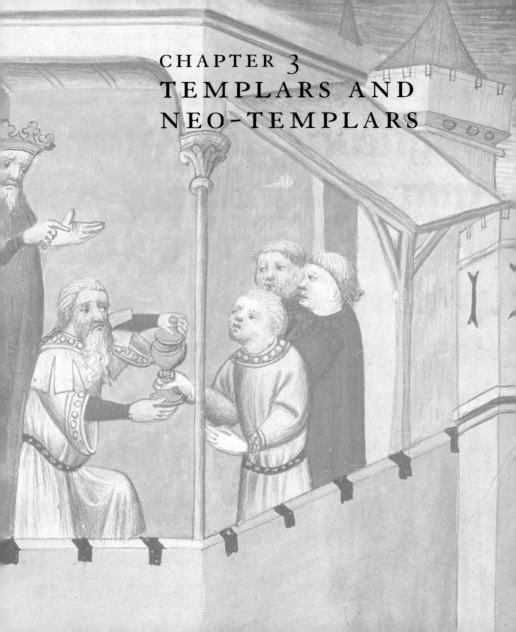

CHAPTER 3
# TEMPLARS AND
# NEO-TEMPLARS

# THE KNIGHTS TEMPLAR

| TYPE | Military, religious, esoteric |
|------|------|
| EXISTED | 1119–1312 |
| RELATED TO | No direct connections to other secret societies |
| GOALS AND CONCERNS | Protect pilgrims to Holy Land; support Crusader kingdoms |

A medieval order of warrior-monks, the Knights Templar were a major force in medieval geopolitics, but were dissolved in the early 14th century. In the 18th century their reputation was revived by Masonic sources and they became an important inspiration for secret societies up to the modern day. Whether there was any genuine link between the original Templars and these latter-day 'neo-Templar' organizations is doubtful, but this has not stopped a huge and evolving body of popular myth attaching to the Templars that relates them to everything from the Holy Grail to the discovery of America.

## POOR FELLOW SOLDIERS

The successes of the First Crusade opened the way for Christian pilgrims to visit the Holy Land and in particular the city of Jerusalem, but the road from the Levantine port of Joppa (now known as Jaffa) to the city was dangerous and beset with bandits. In Jerusalem in 1119, a group of nine knights led by the Frenchman Hugues de Payens formed an order to protect pilgrims travelling along this dangerous road. Basing their rules on those of the Cistercian order, the knights took vows of chastity, poverty and obedience. King Baldwin of Jerusalem assigned them quarters in part of the Temple Mount compound, next to the site where the Temple of Solomon had once stood. Accordingly, they called themselves the Poor Fellow Soldiers of Christ and of the Temple of Solomon, or the Knights Templar.

*This seal of the Knights Templar, which dates from around 1119–1314, portrays two Knights seated on one horse.*

Although at first the Templars were indeed poor – so poor that supposedly two of them had to share a horse, hence their emblem of two knights on one horse – this was to change radically. In 1128 Hugues travelled to Europe to raise funds, and the cause of the Templars was taken up by influential cleric Bernard de Clairvaux, and found favour with the Pope, who exempted them from normal jurisdictions (and therefore from tax). Soon donations (mainly of property) were pouring in. The Templars set up a network of commanderies across Europe to manage their estates and channel the funds to the Holy Land, and this developed into one of the first banking systems in Europe. Kings, nobles,

pilgrims and Crusaders would deposit their wealth in the strongrooms of the commanderies, and the Templars would issue promissory notes, transfer funds across Europe and the Near East and circumvent rules on usury to become moneylenders. Eventually, they were shipping men and goods across the Mediterranean in large quantities, although whether or not they ever had a navy of their own, or simply chartered vessels, is the subject of debate.

Meanwhile, men were flocking to the Templar banner (which took different forms before settling on a red cross on a white field); the order had almost a thousand brother knights by 1170, and far more men in total – perhaps 10,000 – thanks to the other ranks. The Templars became one of the mainstays of the Crusader fighting force in the Holy Land, while in Europe too they were increasingly powerful. In England, for example, the Master of the Temple was the first baron of the realm, and in the early 13th century the then Master William Marshal ruled the country as regent for the young King Henry III.

*A 15th-century version of the fall of Jerusalem to Saladin. The loss of Jerusalem, followed by the expulsion of the Crusaders from the Holy Land in 1291, robbed the Templars of their* raison d'etre, *making their position vulnerable.*

But this rise to power culminated in a terrible fall. In 1187 Jerusalem fell to Saladin, the leader of the Islamic forces, and a century later the last Crusaders were driven out of the Holy Land. The Templars were now bereft of purpose and struggling to stay afloat, presenting an easy target for their enemy, the powerful Philip IV 'the Fair' of France. Philip coveted the Templar lands and resented their influence. Having installed Clement V as pope, he could order him to comply; consequently, he obtained papal authority to suppress the order on charges of heresy. On Friday 13 October 1307, Philip's officials simultaneously arrested every Templar in France, and they were accused of a variety of crimes, including sexual and occult outrages and worshipping an idol they allegedly called Baphomet. Through the use of torture, lurid confessions were obtained, and over the next few years around 60 Templars were executed, including the last Grand Master, Jacques de Molay, who was burned at the stake in 1314. Elsewhere in Europe some arrests were made, but there was much less appetite for condemning the order. Philip forced Pope Clement to dissolve the Templars in 1312. The order had existed for less than 200 years, but its afterlife would be long and strange.

# TREASURE OF THE TEMPLARS

These are the bare facts about the Templars, but they are almost obscured by the multitude of myths that have sprung up about their origins, purpose, treasures and fate. Alternative or speculative histories of the Templars date back to the 18th century, and these in turn provided the spurious basis for the speculations of later writers.

The alternative or pseudo-historians begin their arguments by pointing to the small number of knights who founded the order. How could just nine men usefully guard pilgrims in the Holy Land? Surely they must have had some ulterior motive? Perhaps their true goal was to set up shop in the precincts of the ancient temple so that they could search its ruins for secrets. According to this theory, the original Templars were tipped off by existing guardians of ancient secrets – perhaps by the Assassins or the Bogomils (see page 55) – and set up their order as a cover for

*View of the Temple Mount. According to legend mystical treasures are buried within, secreted in its labyrinth of chambers and tunnels.*

excavations. The Temple Mount is indeed riddled with tunnels and chambers, and the theory is that the Templars discovered something wondrous, something that could explain their meteoric rise to wealth and power.

This logic is shaky, however. The original nine members of the order could easily have performed a useful function within their limited original remit. The road from the coast to Jerusalem was only 40 miles (64 km) long, and the knights may have had retinues of squires and men-at-arms, allowing them to provide a formidable unit more than capable of seeing off bandits. They may have renovated parts of the area where they were quartered, but there is no evidence that they ever undertook excavations or investigations of the Temple. Historian Kevin McClure has traced claims about the excavation myths to a book by Gaetan Delaforge, a member of the Order of the Solar Temple (*Ordre du Temple Solaire*, or OTS), later responsible for the murder or suicide of over 70 people (see page 208). His claims are unsourced and almost certainly pure invention.

## SECRETS OF THE TEMPLE MOUNT

The myth of the Templar treasure is firmly embedded in the public mind. The exact nature of this treasure varies according to the teller. For instance, if the treasure is assumed to have been excavated from the bowels of the Temple Mount, a number of possibilities suggest themselves. According to Jewish folklore, the caverns of the Temple Mount were a possible resting place for the lost Ark of the Covenant. Alternatively, the Templars could have recovered a secret stash of scrolls, perhaps a lost gospel, similar to the ancient documents of the Nag Hammadi find (see page 51). This fits in with claims that the Templars were or became Gnostics; perhaps they found an alternative gospel that gave the Gnostic account of the life and teachings of Jesus?

Another claim is that, either by discovering it in the ruins of the Temple or by inheriting it from its previous guardians, the Templars gained possession of the Holy Grail, and this was the source of their influence, power and riches. Thanks to Dan Brown's novel *The Da Vinci Code*, many people are now familiar with the notion that the Holy Grail was really the Sang Réal or royal bloodline of Christ. According to this myth, Jesus married Mary Magdalene and had children, then his family moved to southern France, where the holy bloodline gave rise to the Merovingian dynasty of kings. The true story of Jesus, recounted in lost versions of the gospels and other Gnostic texts, was suppressed by what became the Roman Catholic Church so that it alone could claim authority to intercede between man and God, maintaining its grip on power. By uncovering the secret at the heart of Christianity, the story goes, the Templars were able to attract powerful adherents and blackmail the papacy into giving it special status. This also ensured that the established powers of Roman Catholic Europe would seek the destruction of the order – hence King Philip and Pope Clement's attack on the Templars.

The link between the Templars and the Holy Grail dates back to the early 13th century, when German poet Wolfram von Eschenbach wrote *Parzival*, one of the early Grail romances. In *Parzival*, Munsalvaesche, the Grail Castle – home to the guardians of the Grail – is guarded by the Templiesin, fictional versions of the Knights Templar. Did von Eschenbach have access to secret knowledge, or was he reflecting the prestige of the powerful Templars?

*Illumination showing the Ark of the Covenant being carried into Jerusalem, accompanied by King David playing a psalterion (a sort of harp).*

A persistent element of the Templar legend is that they had strong links with the Assassins, the medieval Islamic sect whose legendary status matches their own (see pages 238–263). In the world of alternative history, the Assassins practised a Gnostic form of Islam and were inheritors of the Gnostic and esoteric tradition of the Classical period, guarding mystical secrets of their own. Like the Templars, they were a group that mixed religion and combat, blurring the lines between monk and warrior, and, like the Templars, they became a major force in the geopolitics of the medieval Middle East.

There is little doubt that the Templars did cross paths with the Assassins. Although the Crusades seemed mainly to pit Christians against Muslims, in reality they involved local politics, with shifting allegiances that crossed religious lines. The Assassins were often on friendly terms with Christian kingdoms in the Holy Land, and formed alliances when it suited them. It is known, for example, that in 1129 the Assassins joined forces with Crusaders, including the Templars, for an attempted assault on Damascus. It is also likely that after a century and more in the Holy Land, the Templars had grown accustomed to the language and habits of the region. Many of the knights would have spoken Arabic, for instance, and some of these might have taken part in the cultural exchanges that helped in the recovery of knowledge lost in the West but kept alive in the Islamic world, and which eventually helped kick-start the Renaissance.

The accusation levelled at the Templars by their prosecutors in the 14th century, however, was that they had 'gone native' and actively conspired with the forces of Islam to return the Holy Land to Muslim control. More recent conspiracy theorists have imagined the Assassins and Templars swapping Gnostic teachings, occult mysteries and ancient secrets. (The latter, they conjecture, could include the secrets of advanced masonry, handed down from the architects of Solomon's Temple, the pyramid builders of ancient Egypt and perhaps even the Atlanteans before them.) Like many of the other charges levelled at the Templars, the

suggestion of complicity with the forces of Islam can be dismissed as trumped-up and false, the product of a sustained campaign of anti-Templar propaganda cooked up to legitimize King Philip's attempt to seize their wealth. As for the more recent conspiracy theories, there is no direct evidence that secrets were transmitted between the Assassins and Templars, or even that either group was guarding deep secrets. It is, however, possible that sustained contact with other religions and philosophies, including Gnostic flavours of religion, may have influenced the Templar approach to Christianity, but this is pure speculation.

*This illumination c.1410–12, shows Hassan i Sabbah leading the initiations at Alamut and giving drugged wine to his followers.*

# TEMPLARS — SCOTTISH SURVIVORS?

Many Masonic and quasi-Masonic secret societies claim descent from the Templars. These claims are largely based on the idea that the Templars survived the persecution of Philip the Fair, and particularly on the legend that on the night of 12 October 1307, forewarned of the imminent arrests, a cadre of knights spirited away the mysterious treasure of the Templars and carried it off to Scotland, where the order lived on in other guises.

According to this legend, the escaping knights made their way to La Rochelle, base of the Templar fleet, and sailed away to Scotland. Thanks to a dispute with the papacy, Scotland was under excommunication in 1307 and free from papal authority. Given a friendly welcome by the Scots, Templars supposedly fought alongside Robert the Bruce against the English at the battle of Bannockburn in 1314. Prominent among the ranks of Scottish Templars were the Sinclair family, and according to the legend they maintained the secret traditions for more than a century, until William Sinclair purportedly founded

the Freemasons to continue the mysterious work of the Templars. William Sinclair also built the enigmatic Rosslyn Chapel in Lothian, which both encoded the secrets of Masonry and recorded evidence that his ancestor, Templar Henry Sinclair, had used their secret seafaring knowledge to navigate across the Atlantic to America before Columbus. The possible aim of such an epic journey was to hide the Templar treasure there; the mysterious Oak Island Money Pit in Nova Scotia, Canada, is one suggested hiding place.

This convoluted fiction has little basis in fact. Templars did not fight alongside Robert the Bruce against the English, and although one Sinclair may have been a Templar, on the whole the family were not great friends of the order. Rosslyn Chapel has no links with either Templars or Freemasons, and there is no evidence linking William Sinclair to Freemasonry, which did not appear until several centuries after his time. The story of Henry Sinclair's pre-Columbian trans-Atlantic voyage is based on forged letters, and if the

supposed fleet of the Templars ever existed (which it probably did not), it would in all likelihood have consisted of Mediterranean galleys, not ocean-going caravels.

*Rosslyn Chapel in Lothian, Scotland. Conspiracy theorists claim the chapel's half-finished appearance relates to the Temple in Jerusalem in terms of a Masonic role in its construction and its ruined state. Sceptics say that the Sinclairs simply ran out of money.*

# TEMPLARS —
# A SECRET SOCIETY?

If the popular legends about the Templars are based on such shaky foundations, why are they surrounded by so much mystery? Much of it derives, as discussed above, from the slanders spread at the time of their persecution, but even these were based on kernels of truth. The Templars seem to have created an air of mystery by using many of the trappings of a secret society, but even here things are not always what they seem.

## TEMPLAR ORGANIZATION

Secret societies like the Freemasons or the Golden Dawn are marked by their hierarchies, and one of their key characteristics is that initiates all start off equal, whatever their rank in the outside world. The Templars also had hierarchies, but theirs were rather different. The main distinction within the order was between brother knights and serving brothers, but in contrast to the Freemasons, rank within the order

*Woodcut portraying Jacques de Molay, officially the last Grand Master of the Templars, although conspiracy theorists claim he had many successors.*

was very much dependent on rank in the wider world. Only men of noble birth could become brother knights, and only they were able to have a voice in governing the order.

Serving brothers included squires – young men of noble birth in training to become brother knights; sergeants – soldiers not of noble birth, who could therefore not become knights; and all the support staff needed to equip and maintain an army and the huge organization behind it, including craftsmen, cooks and stablemasters. In addition there were chaplains – priests who tended to the spiritual needs of the warrior monks; lay men and women, who were not fully part of the order but supported it; and, in the Holy Land, Turcopoles – mounted archers from the local region. But these various classes and categories had nothing in common with Masonic degrees.

Jacques de Molay is usually described as the Grand Master of the Templars, implying that perhaps within the brother knights there was a Masonic-style hierarchy, but in practice each region had its own Master or Commander. Such ranks were natural in a monastic order.

The Templars were governed by their monastic rule, which was based on the rule of the Cistercian order. It has been claimed that there was also a secret rule running in parallel with the public one, which perhaps set out the guidelines for a secret society within the Templars. However, this rumour may have resulted from a misunderstanding. The rule of the Templars included sensitive information about their military organization and tactics, so they were keen to keep it secret in case their enemies got hold of it. In fact, copies of the rule still exist and can be read today.

## APPLICATION AND INITIATION

One of the key allegations of the case against the Templars was that becoming a Templar involved a bizarre and blasphemous initiation ritual, in which initiates were expected to spit to one side of the cross and kiss another man's anus. Again, the details are probably slanders cooked up by the Templars' prosecutors, but it is possible that prospective knights had to prove they could withstand the potential horrors of being captured and taunted by their Saracen enemies.

It is more likely that the initiation ritual was much more tame. The applicant had to be voted in by other members of the relevant chapter house, and had to affirm that he met the conditions of entry. In other words, he must declare that he was not pledged to another order, was not in debt, was in good health and was a freeman (that is, not a serf). A simple ritual was followed by a lecture on the responsibilities and requirements of the order, in similar fashion to the procedures governing entry into other medieval institutions, such as guildhalls and monasteries. Members were expected to give up all their possessions to the order, and one point of similarity to Freemasonry was the dire threat issued if any money was found on their person when they died – their body would be left for animals to eat.

## THE HEAD OF BAPHOMET

Another lurid allegation was that the Templars worshipped a demon named Baphomet, which they had given idolatrous form in the shape of a head. Under torture, captured knights were likely to admit to almost anything, and records of their testimonies show that

*In 19th-century occultism, Baphomet – a demon alleged by papal inquisitors to have been used by the Templars – became a symbolic hermaphroditic goat-headed figure with alchemical connotations.*

CLIPHAS
LEVI DEL

*Detail from a fresco by Tommaso da Modena c.1352 of Albertus Magnus or Saint Albert the Great.*

they gave varying accounts of this supposed idol. Nonetheless, the accusation has in turn led to fantasies that the Templars had some sort of grisly and/or magical relic, a real or mechanical head with oracular or divinatory powers. Possible identities for this head have included the severed head of John the Baptist or the head of Christ. Such a relic would disprove the resurrection and ascension, and Christ's divinity, and thus undermine the founding myth of Christianity; this would relate to the bloodline-of-Jesus theory and to some Gnostic readings of Christianity. Alternatively, the head is said to have been a cunning mechanism crafted from bronze, linking the Templars with the medieval scholars and magi Albertus Magnus and Roger Bacon, who were also said to possess such marvels.

The story of the Templars' head seems to be the conflation of several different ideas. Accusations of devil worship were part of the larger charge of witchcraft and Satanism that was often levelled at heretics, and fit with the pattern of slanders aimed at the Templars. The magical talking head was a common rumour in medieval times; the special association of the Templars with 'head worship' may be linked to their possession and veneration of the relics of St Euphemia and another female martyr, which included their heads. These relics were not secret and, though gruesome, not that unusual.

The name Baphomet, which seems to echo the Masonic use of strange passwords such as the notorious 'Jahbulon' (see page 163), may also be linked to a misunderstanding. The Austrian writer Joseph von Hammer-Purgstall, in his spurious 1818 book *The Mystery of Baphomet Revealed*, claimed that Baphomet was the Templars' name for the hermaphrodite goddess Achamoth, whom they worshipped with orgies in continuation of her ancient cult. In the 19th-century occult demi-monde, Baphomet later became associated with a horned half-goat, half-human demon with breasts and a phallus. In practice, Baphomet was a French (specifically Provençal) translation of Mohammed, and the accusation that the Templars used it as a sacred name was probably part of the wider accusation that they had conspired with the forces of Islam to betray the Crusader cause.

## KEEPING SECRETS?

In summary, the Templars were probably not a secret society in any meaningful sense of the term, any more than the Cistercians or any of the other military monastic orders, such as the Knights Hospitaller of St John. If they had picked up Gnostic practices and beliefs during their time in the Orient, they would have had good reason to keep them secret, but this is a big 'if', and there is no real evidence to back up such speculation.

# NEO-TEMPLARS

| TYPE | Fraternal, esoteric, occult, political |
|---|---|
| EXISTED | 1740s–present |
| RELATED TO | Freemasonry, Rosicrucians, occult secret societies |
| GOALS AND CONCERNS | Chivalric ideals; self-improvement; esoteric and occult research; right-wing racist fantasies |

Only 60 Templar knights were actually executed, and outside of France there was little appetite for their persecution. Although the order was dissolved by papal fiat, most of the people and property remained. As for the legendary treasure of the Templars, its extent was probably exaggerated and there is evidence that the order was struggling to stay afloat towards the end. Philip IV may have acquired extensive properties, but his dreams of loot unbounded were probably disappointed. Many of the personnel joined other military orders, primarily the Knights Hospitaller and the Teutonic Knights, although in Spain and Portugal sympathetic monarchs created successor bodies – the Order of Montesa and the Order of Christ – which were essentially the Templars by other names.

Portugal's Order of Christ provides a link with the supposed maritime powers of the Templars, for it was heavily involved in the voyages of discovery of the following centuries, and ships bearing the red cross on a white field would eventually carry Columbus to the Americas. Does this prove some sort of hidden Templar succession? In practice, there was nothing secret or mysterious about these successor orders.

## LEGENDS OF PERPETUATION

A survey of Masonic and quasi-Masonic groups reveals that the Knights Templar seemed to have survived up to the

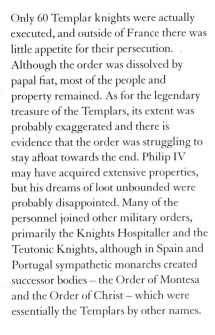

*Late 15th-century Portuguese tile depicting a ship with sails marked with the emblem of the Order of Christ – also the Templar cross.*

Nau redonda - 1498.

TEMPLARS AND NEO-TEMPLARS

modern day. For instance, the *Ordo Supremus Militaris Templi Hierosolymitani* (Sovereign Military Order of the Temple of Jerusalem or OSMTH) claims to have members from over 40 nations and boasts of official recognition from the United Nations. The OSMTH, as it usually known, is just the tip of the iceberg; there have been dozens if not hundreds of groups claiming to be Templars over the last two centuries, many claiming descent from the medieval Templars despite the apparent gap of 400 years between the dissolution of the order and its 'reappearance'. Are these Neo-Templar groups genuine? Can they really trace their descent to the original Templars?

Notwithstanding the spurious links between alleged Templar survival, the Sinclair family and the Freemasons in Scotland, the truth is that there is no evidence of any direct link between original and Neo-Templars, and all claims on the matter are a mixture of wishful thinking, historical fantasy and recycling of unfounded claims and inaccurate sources. These pseudo-historical fictions are technically known as Legends of Perpetuation.

*The Scottish-born Chevalier Andrew Michael Ramsay, whose fantasies about Masonry's chivalric origins proved enormously influential.*

The starting point for Neo-Templar Legends of Perpetuation is the Chevalier Andrew Ramsay, the 18th-century Jacobite whose ability to meld contemporary politics with inspirational myths was to have such a far-reaching impact on the development of Freemasonry and secret societies in general (see pages 146–149) for a full discussion of Ramsay, Jacobite politics and Freemasonry). In brief, Ramsay was a supporter of the exiled House of Stuart who saw Freemasonry as a tool to build support for a Jacobite rebellion (an attempt to retake the British throne for the descendants of James II). He wrote a celebrated oration in 1736 in which he claimed that Freemasonry was a continuation of the chivalric tradition of the knightly orders of the Crusades. Ramsay had in mind the Knights Hospitaller, but the Templars, with their rich heritage of myth and legend, grabbed the imagination of his audience much more effectively.

Ramsay's oration formed the basis for the creation of higher degrees in Masonry, one of which was Knight of the Temple. As justification for these, and to lend historical weight to the 'mission' of the Freemasons, Legends of Perpetuation linking Templar survival in Scotland to the genesis of the Freemasons were created. The legend

the result that the two sets of legends became entwined. For instance, the 18th-century German Masonic group the Order of the Golden and Rosy Cross (OGRC) claimed that its rite had been passed down from 1st-century Alexandria via the Templars, who in turn had been initiated by an ancient Rosicrucian society in the 12th century.

Some Legends of Perpetuation even involved forged documents, such as the Charter of Larmenius. Apparently a charter giving authority over a secret Templar continuation, it recorded that in 1324 Jacques de Molay had passed the succession over to Johannes Marcus Larmenius. The Charter had been signed by the 22 subsequent Grand Masters, eventually turning up in the hands of Bernard Raymond Fabré-Palaprat (1773–1838), who used it as the basis for his own Order of the Temple (the organization from which the Order of the Solar Temple, or *Ordre du Temple Solaire* or OTS – see pages 206–208 – traced its descent). A different Legend of Perpetuation claimed that de Molay had passed the succession to Pierre d'Aumont, the Temple Prior of Auvergne, who had escaped to Scotland

of the Templars thus became bound up with the creation of new rites in Freemasonry, and demand led to the proliferation of rites and degrees claiming connection to the Knights Templar. At the same time, the Freemasons were developing similar legends about the Rosicrucians, with

and passed on a secret tradition that was only revealed in 1754 when Baron von Hund established the Rite of Strict Observance (see page 149).

## CONSPIRACY THEORIES

Some elements of the Templar mythos developed from anti-Masonic conspiracy theorists (see pages 144–151 on anti-Masonry). The late 18th and 19th centuries saw a backlash against the perceived revolutionary nature of the Freemasons and other secret societies by the forces of reaction, and conspiracy theorists invented or borrowed fictions about the Templars to support their tales of grand conspiracies stretching across history. The 1796 book *The Tomb of Jacques Molay* by Charles-Louis Cadet de Gassicourt linked the Freemasons to both the French Revolution and the Templars, claiming that the Revolution was part of a plot to gain revenge on the French state for crushing the knightly order. Cadet de Gassicourt was the first to link the Templars to the Assassins. Joseph von Hammer-Purgstall's 1818 book on Baphomet (see page 83) elaborated the Templar myth with secret traditions of Gnosticism and sex magic.

Although these works were attacks on Neo-Templars, the fantastical histories they invented were later seized upon by the founders of occult Neo-

Templar groups. The *Ordo Novi Templi* (Order of the New Temple or ONT – see page 200) was a proto-Nazi group founded in 1903 that took its inspiration from these pan-historical legends, and that played an influential part in the developing brew of pseudo-history, pseudoscience, mysticism and virulent racism that shaped Nazi ideology (see pages 198–200). In 1906 a very different group, the *Ordo Templi Orientis* (Order of Oriental Templars, or OTO), was set up to practise a system of sex magic not dissimilar to the fantasies of von Hammer-Purgstall. Under the leadership of Alesteir Crowley, the OTO would become notorious and influential (see pages 196–197).

Today the myth of the Knights Templar is highly evolved and intertwined with almost every aspect of New Age, occult, esoteric and alternative belief. The medieval order is linked to the Freemasons, magic, ancient wisdom, Gnosticism, the Atlanteans, fertility cults, secret history, revolutionary politics, the Illuminati, the Rosicrucians. the Assassins, the Holy Grail, the Ark of the Covenant, lost gospels, mystery religions, the Cathars, Rosslyn Chapel, the discovery of America and much else besides. Yet there is little or no evidence to support these claims.

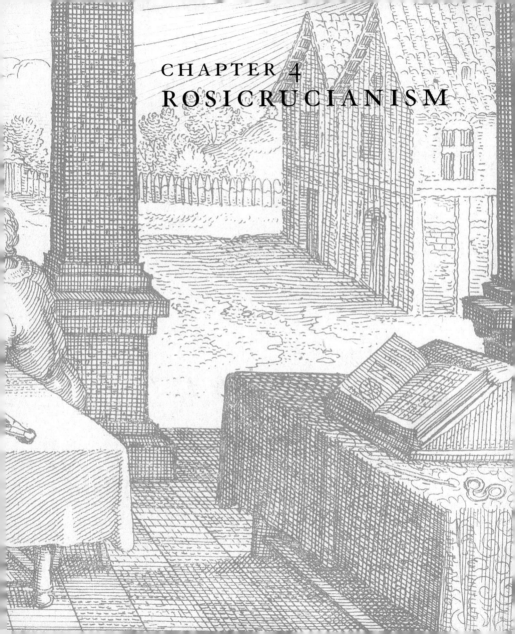

# CHAPTER 4
# ROSICRUCIANISM

# THE ROSICRUCIANS

| | |
|---|---|
| TYPE | Esoteric, mystical, occult, religious, fraternal |
| EXISTED | 1614–present |
| RELATED TO | Freemasonry, Order of the Golden and Rosy Cross, *Societas Rosicruciana* (Soc Ros), Ancient Mystical Order Rosae Crucis, *Fraternitas Rosae Crucis*, Hermetic Order of the Golden Dawn, *Ordo Templi Orientis*, *Ordo Novi Templi*, Order of the Solar Temple |
| GOALS AND CONCERNS | Reformation of society, culture and religion according to reason and Hermetic wisdom; self-improvement |

The Rosicrucians, or the Brotherhood of the Rosy Cross, are supposedly a hugely influential secret society of Western intellectual elite who have existed since the late Middle Ages and played an active part in successful and attempted revolutions in America, France and much of the rest of Europe. But from the beginning they were a fiction, and if they did come to exist it was through a strange process whereby the fiction created its own reality. Today there are a number of quasi-Masonic and/or occult societies of more or less secret nature that use the word 'Rosicrucian' in their titles.

## THE ROSE AND THE CROSS

'Rosicrucian' comes from the Latin for 'rose' and 'cross', words and images rich in symbolism. The Christian symbolism of the cross is obvious, but the rose also has particular Christian significance, as a symbol of divine love and illumination, and of the Virgin Mary. Both elements also have wider significance. The cross is an ancient solar symbol and has numerical/ geometrical significance. It can represent the four elements and/or the intersection between heaven and earth, God and man, male and female. The rose can represent the female genitals and

*This line engraving from 'Summon Bonum' by Robert Fludd, 1629, shows the Rosicrucian symbol of the rose and cross.*

therefore the female principle; love, purity and beauty; the passage of time; and secrecy (the Latin phrase *sub rosa* denotes 'in secret'). The rose has also been used to represent the Holy Grail, and the colour most associated with the rose means that it is also a symbol of blood. Red crosses have been used as the symbol of various organizations, including the Knights Templar.

## THE ROSICRUCIAN MANIFESTOS

The existence of the Rosicrucians was announced to the world in 1614 with the publication in Germany of a document called the *Fama Fraternitas Rosae Crucis* (*Discovery or Report of the*

Allgemeine vnd General

# REFORMATION,

der gantzen weiten Welt.

Beneben der

# FAMA FRA

## TERNITATIS,

Deß Löblichen Ordens des
Rosenkreutzes / an alle Gelehrte
vnd Häupter Europæ geschrie-
ben :

Auch, einer kurtzen RESPONSION
von dem Herrn Haselmeyer gestellet / welcher
deßwegen von den Jesuittern ist gefänglich ein-
gezogen / vnd auff eine Galleren ge-
schmiedet :

Itzo öffentlich in Druck verfertiget
vnd allen trewen Hertzen communiciret
worden.

Gedruckt zu Cassel/ durch Wilhelm Wessell/

ANNO M. DC, XIV.

*The title page from the first edition of* Fama Fraternitatis, *which was published in 1614 in Germany.*

*Brotherhood of the Rose Cross*), or to give its full title *The Fama Fraternitas of the Praiseworthy Fraternity of the Rosy Cross, written to all the Learned and Rulers of Europe.* The following year another document appeared, the *Confessio Fraternitas* (*Confession of the Fraternity*), and in 1616 another German printer published *The Chymical Wedding of Christian Rosenkreutz.* Collectively these three documents are known as the Rosicrucian Manifestos.

According to the Manifestos, the Rosicrucian Fraternity had been founded by a German nobleman in the early 15th century, who had taken the allegorical name Christian Rosenkreutz. Having travelled the East in his youth and acquiring secret knowledge (see below), he had gathered eight disciples to pass on and spread his teachings, which amounted to a wholesale revolution in every field of human endeavour that would usher in a new, utopian age. After the death of Rosenkreutz in 1484 at the age of 104, his disciples had been charged with finding, initiating and training their own successors, but the Fraternity had been kept secret, as the world was not deemed ready to hear its tumultuous message. The rediscovery of Rosenkreutz's tomb in 1604, however, signalled that the time had come to reveal the existence of the Fraternity, hence the production of these manuscripts. The latter had allegedly been circulating in manuscript form since that date, and were only then being published. The Manifestos included a rousing call to arms to the intellectual and political elite of Europe, who were encouraged to apply for membership of this revolutionary band of brothers, though only those worthy would be granted admittance.

## CHRISTIAN ROSENKREUTZ

The key figure in this fantastical tale was the knight Christian Rosenkreutz (referred to in the initial document only as C.R.). The story went that he was born in 1378 to an impoverished family of German nobles, had grown up in a monastery and then travelled to the East as a teenager. Arriving in Damascus, he had been directed to the city of Damcar in Yemen, home of the wise, and after studying medicine, mathematics and alchemy there for three years, he had travelled to Egypt and Fez, in Morocco, where he had been schooled in magic and Kabbalah. Eventually, filled with Oriental wisdom and theosophy (knowledge of the sacred truths behind all religions – see below), Rosenkreutz had returned to Germany only to find that he was ridiculed and shunned for his unorthodox beliefs.

Setting up headquarters in his old monastery as the College of the Holy Spirit, Rosenkreutz founded his secret Fraternity in 1408. He taught its eight members how to study the hidden forces of nature, master the arts of alchemy and medicine, harness the power of natural magic for all mankind and promulgate the Rosicrucian philosophy (see below). Every year he would meet up with his disciples at the College of the Holy Spirit, and between times they would travel the land healing the sick and pursuing their studies. When he died in 1484 he was buried in a seven-sided vault, and when this was opened in 1604 his body was found to be uncorrupted. Clutched in his hand was a parchment bearing the testimony of the Rosicrucian Brotherhood.

The third of the Manifestos detailed a series of adventures and tests that Rosenkreutz had supposedly undergone, but it was clearly intended as a dense allegory, combining alchemical symbolism with a structure similar to John Bunyan's *Pilgrim's Progress*, published 1678–1684. In alchemy, elements and the alchemist himself undergo various processes of trial and transformation so that they are purified and elevated. Similarly, in *The Chymical Wedding*, Rosenkreuz undergoes spiritual self-discovery and purification.

## THE ROSICRUCIAN AGENDA

The Rosicrucian message electrified the learned circles of Europe with its potent blend of magic and revolution. So what exactly was this message? It had several related and interdependent elements: natural magic and the application of knowledge (close parallels today would be science and technology); restoration of ancient wisdom and religion; transformation of society and religion; reforming and utopian ideals.

Natural magic, as understood by the Rosicrucian scholars of the early modern period, was more scientific than supernatural. It was believed that through understanding and mastering the hidden forces of nature, they could be manipulated, controlled and harnessed. The same is true of modern science. But the difference is that early modern magi, as practitioners of natural magic were known, believed that these hidden forces included correspondences between the stars and things and events on Earth (so that astrology could be used to forecast and control those things), or natural sympathies between elements that seemed to have things in common (for instance, since walnuts resembled the brain, they could be used to treat brain maladies). (See page 60 for more on the principles of magic.)

Beliefs such as these were a departure from the philosophy that held sway at this time. Magi wanted to extend their knowledge and establish new philosophies. Above all they wanted to put their knowledge to good use for the benefit of mankind. Accordingly, they were renowned for constructing cunning devices, and indeed the tomb of Christian Rosenkreutz was reputed to be full of mechanical marvels, recalling the

*An illustration from Robert Fludd's* Utriusque Cosmi Historia, *1617–1624, showing an astronomer and an astrologer.*

brazen head said to have belonged to the Templars (see pages 80–83).

As well as finding out new things, Rosicrucian scholars of the period believed that they could restore the old ways. It was commonly thought that before Noah's flood more perfect forms of religion, philosophy and society had existed, and the goal of the Rosicrucian was to restore mankind to this more perfect state, and in doing so approach nearer to God.

Religion – and, despite the claims of its enemies, Christianity in particular – was at the heart of the Rosicrucian project. The Rosicrucian message was a mystical one with a Gnostic-style focus on personal experience of the divine and a personal approach to spiritual transformation. Transformation was a key concept. Just as alchemy tried to achieve the ultimate transformation that would turn ordinary mercury into the Philosopher's Stone, so the Rosicrucians wanted to elevate man and mankind to a similar level of purity and magical ability.

The end result would be a utopian vision, in which man and society would

*Woodcut of 1618 by Theophilus Schweighardt Constantiens, showing a mobile 'Temple of the Rose Cross', ideal for spreading the teachings of the fraternity. Note Noah's Ark stranded on Mt Ararat in the background.*

be reformed: an all-encompassing reformation that would include religion, philosophy, the arts, technology, commerce and government. This meant overturning the established order, and especially the established religion – the Catholic Church and the papacy – so the Rosicrucian message was revolutionary and essentially Protestant. Not surprisingly, it aroused hostility from government and Church alike.

## SOURCES OF ROSICRUCIANISM

Rosicrucianism had a huge impact because it brought together several streams of thought – streams that had been running underground, but which were now brought out into the open (see pages 58–60, the Secret Stream). Since the rediscovery of the *Corpus Hermeticum* in the Renaissance, scholars had been increasingly excited about the possibility of tapping into ancient wisdom above and beyond what was authorized by the Church. Alchemy and Kabbalah were part of this; both seemed to be schools of ancient wisdom that had been kept alive not through the Church but through Jewish and Islamic mystics and scholars.

By relying on these non-Christian sources, Hermetic scholars were opening themselves up to new ideas about the nature of religion and religious authority. These religions appeared to be different and antagonistic, but what if they were expressing the same fundamental truths? What if there was more to religion than what was taught by the Church? Ideas like this were one aspect of a new philosophy called theosophy, which had been developed by German visionary Jakob Boehme (1575–1624). Boehme in turn was a major influence on Rosicrucian philosophy. He stressed the role of direct experience in learning about and approaching the divine, with many parallels with Gnosticism, so that Rosicrucianism also had a distinctly Gnostic flavour.

The Rosicrucian Manifestos also reflected the work of several important Hermetic scholars of the preceding centuries, most prominently the English sage Dr John Dee (1527–1608). Dee had amassed a huge library of books and travelled all over Europe making contacts with other scholars. Although primarily renowned as an astrologer – a service he performed for Queen Elizabeth – Dee was also deeply involved in gematria, alchemy, Kabbalah and magic. He used a crystal ball to speak to angels, and travelled to Bohemia to warn the Holy Roman Emperor to mend his ways. His writings and research covered many fields, from mathematics and logic to geography and calendar reform, and he believed in the power of Hermeticism to usher in a new world. In many ways he was the model of a Rosicrucian, and it has been suggested that he was the real Christian Rosenkreutz and/or that he founded the Rosicrucians. There is no evidence for this, but it is likely that his work formed the basis for much of the Rosicrucian Manifesto, and it is significant that the second manifesto – the *Confessio* – was published alongside an essay based on Dee's 1564 book *Monas Hieroglyphica*, an occult masterpiece about symbols and ancient wisdom. Dee had also been a strong influence on the Elizabethan poet Edmund Spenser, whose epic *The Faerie Queene* (published 1590–1596) features none other than a Knight of the Red Cross. Both Dee and Boehme were important in the formation of Protestant theology and philosophy, and their probable contributions to Rosicrucianism underline how the announcement of the secret society should be seen in the context of the religious tensions and developments of the period.

*An anonymous painting of Dr John Dee, painted in 1594. He was an English mathematician, astronomer, astrologer, geographer and occultist.*

# THE REAL ROSICRUCIANS

Scholars all over Europe were excited by the arrival of the Manifestos and the 'coming out' of this revolutionary brotherhood. Its daring call to arms echoed the belief of many Hermeticists and Christian (particularly Protestant) mystics that a watershed in human history was fast approaching, and they were desperate to answer that call and sign up to the Fraternity. At the same time, reactionary forces were alarmed and angered by this dangerous mix of the occult and the anarchic, and there were many attacks on the Rosicrucians, whereby they were branded as troublemakers as well as devil worshippers. But despite the publication of the Manifestos, the Rosicrucians did not emerge from the shadows, but remained invisible and incommunicado. Public – and published – pleas for membership from the likes of physician and alchemist Robert Fludd (see pages 106–107) produced no response from them. Who had written the Manifestos, and were they really members of a secret brotherhood? Did the Rosicrucians even exist at all?

## LITERARY MANHUNT

Clues to the authorship of the Manifestos were present in the form of their co-publications: the first two had been published in pamphlets alongside other documents. In 1614 the *Fama* had been preceded by the *Universal and General Reformation of the Whole Wide World*, a German translation of part of *News from Parnassus*, written by the Italian Traiano Boccalini in 1612. The passage involved was a satire on the grand schemes drawn up by so-called wise men for the reformation of the world. In 1615, as discussed above, the *Confessio* was accompanied by *A Short Consideration of the More Secret Philosophy*, an essay based on John Dee's *Monas Hieroglyphica*. The messages of these co-publications are contradictory: the presence of the *Reformation* suggests that the *Fama* was itself satirical in intent, but the Dee-inspired *A Short Consideration* points to the serious and scholarly underpinnings of the Rosicrucian project.

The *Fama* was also accompanied by a third piece, which put the whole project into chilling context. 'A short reply sent by Herr Haselmayer, for which he was seized by the Jesuits and condemned to a galley', was a genuine letter written by German physician Adam Haselmayer, who had read a manuscript copy of the *Fama* in 1611 and published an enthusiastic open letter of response in 1612. His punishment for supporting the anti-Catholic sentiments of the *Fama* was to be sentenced to five years as a galley slave. The Rosicrucian affair was not just a game: openly supporting the Fraternity was playing with fire.

The authorship of the first two Manifestos remains unknown, but the authorship of *The Chymical Wedding* offers strong clues. It is generally accepted that it was written by German writer Johann Valentin Andreae (1586–1654), who admitted as much in his autobiography, claiming that he had written it in 1602 or 1603 as a 'youthful literary trifle', intended as a satire on the contemporary mania for the occult and esoteric. He may have lifted the rosy cross motif from either his own family's coat of

*Protestant theologian Johann Valentin Andreae, probable author of the Rocisrucian Manifestos, from a copper engraving after 1648.*

arms, or that of his theological hero Martin Luther. In later life Andreae was a respectable Lutheran theologian in Württemberg, keen to play down his role in creating one of the most notorious revolutionary schemes of all time. But as a young man he had moved in progressive circles, studying at Tübingen University where he was part of a group centred on Dr Tobias Hess, a physician, lawyer and alchemist. The most likely scenario is that the Rosicrucian Manifestos started as an intellectual game or exercise for the Hess circle, and that Hess, Andreae and others jointly wrote the *Fama* and the *Confessio*. Their intention was probably partly satirical, partly inflammatory and partly purely philosophical. Whether they ever intended their creation to take on a life of its own is impossible to say, but this is what happened (there are distinct parallels with the Masonic frauds of Leo Taxil, the so called Taxil-Schwindel – see pages 170–172).

Later in life Andreae would dismiss the Rosicrucian affair as a comedy and a folly. However, his other significant literary production, the 1619 utopian

*Frederik V of the Rhine Palatinate by Robert Dunkarton (1744–c.1817). Frederik was known as the Winter King because of the short period for which he ruled Bohemia.*

vision *Christianopolis*, in which Christian ideals and natural philosophy inform the structure and conduct of a model society, suggests that he was serious in his commitment to a programme of social, cultural, moral and religious reform.

If the Manifestos were little more than a literary parlour game, why were they published and disseminated? One possibility is that the Rosicrucian Manifesto was actively pushed because it served someone's political ends. The early 17th century was a period of tension and instability in Central Europe as the Catholic Habsburgs vied with the Protestant princes of Germany for control. The succession to the throne of Bohemia was in contention around the time of the Manifestos, and their essentially Protestant message of reform matched the ambitions of the Protestant prince Frederick V of the Rhine Palatinate, who had designs on the previously Catholic, Habsburg-controlled kingdom. Rosicrucianism served as useful propaganda for Frederick and his camp, with the Manifestos as a rallying cry for the forces of Protestantism to line up behind his power grab. The ploy did not succeed: Frederick seized the Bohemian crown in 1619, but was forced out by Catholic armies, the dispute having triggered the Thirty Years War that devastated Central Europe.

# ROSICRUCIAN DEFENDERS

The Rosicrucian Fraternity may have begun life as the fictional creation of Andreae and his Tübingen circle, but they quickly began to take on a life of their own. Leading scholars of the occult and the Hermetic wrote articles and books in their defence. Michael Maier (1569–1622) was a German physician, diplomat and alchemist who wrote in support of the Rosicrucians, and although he denied that he belonged to the Fraternity, he seemed able to write in detail on their organization and principles.

Similarly, the English physician and alchemist Robert Fludd (1574–1637), a friend of Maier's, was one of the leading apologists for the Rosicrucian movement. Rebutting an attack launched by a Continental physician, Andreas Libavius, Fludd wrote a short *Apologia compendiaria* in 1616 and a longer *Tractatus apologeticus* in defence of Rosicrucianism the following year. Although he specifically stated that he had only heard of the Fraternity for the first time through the publication of the Manifestos, Fludd seemed to know a lot

about them and had travelled extensively on the Continent in previous years. Suspicions that he himself was a Rosicrucian were strong enough for him to be summoned by James I to explain himself, and he wrote two more tracts explaining his support for them. These further highlighted the similarities between the Rosicrucian philosophy and his own, which stressed Christian virtue in combination with theories of cosmic mystical harmony that harked back to Plato and Pythagoras (see page 137). It was also notable that the Manifestos specified that would-be recruits should be sexually abstinent, and Fludd claimed to be a virgin.

Perhaps Maier and Fludd were examples of actual members of the elusive Fraternity? Certainly their opponents accused them of this (an accusation risked by any natural philosopher who deviated from orthodox thinking, as the great French philosopher René Descartes would later discover), but in fact there is no evidence that this was the case. Both men specifically denied it, and Fludd's

*Robert Fludd 1574–1637: chemist, astrologer and mystic. He defended Rosicrucianism and may have had a hand in its creation.*

'Apologies' include pleas to be admitted to the brotherhood. And why would he make such pleas if he were already a member? It is more likely that one or both men had been in correspondence with the Tübingen circle and were in on the joke from the start, viewing their own contributions as a way to move the project along and further spread the Rosicrucian teachings.

# THE INVISIBLE COLLEGE

According to the Manifestos, the eight original disciples of Christian Rosenkreutz were known as the 'Invisibles' or the 'Invisible College', because they pursued their revolutionary ideals in absolute secrecy, their existence unknown to the world. In England in the 17th century, a real-life brotherhood of scholars steeped in alchemy and natural magic took shape in apparent echo, or direct application, of the Rosicrucian ideal, and like their supposedly fictional forebears they were known as the Invisible College.

## FRANCIS BACON

The story of the Invisible College starts with Sir Francis Bacon (1561–1626). An Elizabethan lawyer and Jacobean statesman, Bacon was the pre-eminent philosopher of science of his time, not because of his own scientific discoveries but because of the project he developed for scientific advancement and the role of science in society. In this period,

*Painting by Paul van Somer of Sir Francis Bacon (1561–1626), philosopher and statesman.*

however, the word science was not in use, and what Bacon actually discussed was something very similar to the Rosicrucians – the use of natural philosophy and natural magic for applied ends. At times his work reads much like the Rosicrucian Manifestos. In his 1605 book *The Advancement of Learning*, for instance, he describes 'a fraternity in learning and illumination'.

In his posthumously published *New Atlantis* (1626) Bacon describes a utopian society run by an institution called Salomon's House, which is similar to both the Rosicrucian ideal and more specifically to Andreae's utopia Christianopolis. In fact, Bacon may well have corresponded with Andreae and his circle, and have influenced, and been influenced by, the Rosicrucian Manifestos. This has led to claims that Bacon was actually the secret master of the Rosicrucians, but in practice there were important differences between his project and the Rosicrucian one. Bacon believed that science should be an open, public process, and he was explicitly opposed to secret societies and hidden knowledge.

*Portrait of Elias Ashmole, English antiquary, 1689, by John Riley (1646–91). Ashmole was an astrologer and alchemist, early member of the Royal Society and Freemason. His diaries include some of the earliest verifiable mentions of Freemasonry, and also mention the founding of a Rosicrucian lodge. Despite his interest in these heterodox movements, Ashmole was no revolutionary – during the Civil War he was a staunch Royalist.*

## THE ROYAL SOCIETY

Bacon's work helped encourage the network of correspondence between natural philosophers in 17th-century England that came to be called the Invisible College. Despite the sinister name, this was in fact an informal group dedicated to principles and practices that had a distinctly Rosicrucian flavour, pursuing alchemy, Kabbalah, mathematics, natural philosophy and magic for the good of all mankind, and with the eventual aim of reforming society. Inspired by Bacon, and also by Dee, Fludd, Maier and others like them, the Invisible College eventually founded

a formal society, which in 1660 gained the seal of royal approval from Charles II and became the Royal Society. Thanks to men like Robert Boyle, Robert Hooke and Isaac Newton – all assumed by conspiracy theorists to have been members of the Rosicrucian Fraternity – the Royal Society would become the birthplace of the Scientific Revolution. In some ways, thanks to their influence on Bacon and other English scholars, the Rosicrucians could be seen as the midwives of that revolution. This is different, however, from saying that the Invisible College and the Royal Society were actually Rosicrucian institutions or were set up by Rosicrucians.

## PSEUDO-ROSICRUCIANS

At least one important member of the Invisible College, and an early member of the Royal Society, was a Rosicrucian of sorts. The antiquarian Elias Ashmole (1617–1692) recorded in his diary that in 1646 he and several others, including the astrologer William Lilly (1602–1681), founded a Rosicrucian lodge in London. This is the first recorded instance of an actual Rosicrucian fraternity as opposed to a fictional one, but it is almost certainly also the first example of a pseudo-Rosicrucian brotherhood. Ashmole had recently been initiated into the Freemasons (see page 135), and it seems

likely that he and the others started their own Masonic lodge in London and described it as Rosicrucian because they sympathized with the Rosicrucian agenda they had learned about, not because of any actual chain of initiation by real Rosicrucians. In so doing, Ashmole, Lilly and the others were foreshadowing what would happen in the 18th century, when Masonic pseudo-Rosicrucians became commonplace.

The next instance of what were probably pseudo-Rosicrucians was in 1710, when Sigmund Richter, writing under the pseudonym Sincerus Renatus, published a *Perfect and True Preparation of the Philosophical Stone, according to the Secret of the Brotherhoods of the Golden and Rosy Cross*. Richter gave a list of 52 'Laws of the Brotherhood', revealing, for instance, that there must be no more than 63 members, that Catholics could be admitted and that 'when the brethren meet they shall salute each other in the following manner: The first shall say, *Ave Frater!* The second shall answer, *Roseæ et Aureæ*. Whereupon the first shall conclude with *Crucis*.' Whether Richter actually founded such a brotherhood at this time or it remained a fantasy is unclear, but it became a reality in the 1750s as part of the Rosicrucian flowering in Freemasonry.

# THE ORDER OF THE GOLDEN AND ROSY CROSS

| | |
|---|---|
| TYPE | Esoteric, occult, mystical, political |
| EXISTED | c.1750–c.1805 |
| RELATED TO | Freemasonry, *Societas Rosicruciana* (Soc Ros), Hermetic Order of the Golden Dawn |
| GOALS AND CONCERNS | Esoteric and occult study; reactionary political agenda |

The same process that saw the Knights Templar co-opted by Freemasonry, and particularly by the Jacobite movement within Freemasonry, resulted in the recruitment of Rosicrucianism to the Masonic cause. As discussed on pages 144–146, the early and mid-18th century saw the emergence of a Jacobite strain within Freemasonry, as supporters of the exiled House of Stuart attempted to redirect French Freemasonry in favour of their cause. Just as these Jacobite Freemasons had seen a natural connection between the Templars and the Stuart cause, so they perceived some Jacobite connection with the Rosicrucians. James I, founder of the Stuart line of British kings, had been an avid student of the occult, although mainly in terms of catching and killing

witches. Charles II had both sponsored the Royal Society and taken a keen interest in alchemy; according to one theory, he died as the result of poisoning from an alchemical experiment.

When the Scottish degrees of Freemasonry appeared in the 1740s and '50s, they included in their number Rosicrucian titles. For instance, the 2nd degree of the Royal Order of Scotland, a rite founded in 1750 at The Hague in Holland, is the Rosy Cross; Masons who attain this degree are known as Rosicrucian Knights. There is no evidence of any genuine connection between the Royal Order of Scotland and the Rosicrucians.

*Portrait of King Charles II (1630–85) who was known to be an avid alchemist.*

## POWER BEHIND THE THRONE

In Germany there was a demand for more occult and esoteric flavour to be injected into Freemasonry, and one way to meet this demand was by inventing Rosicrucian degrees and orders. One of the most popular and influential was the *Orden des Gold und Rosenkreuz*, the Order of the Golden and Rosy Cross (OGRC), founded in the 1750s by German alchemist Herman Fichtuld and based in part on the writings of Sincerus Renatus (see page 111). Candidates had to be Master Masons, and once admitted they could pass through nine degrees: Junior, Theoreticus, Practicus, Philosophus, Adeptus Minor, Adeptus Major, Adeptus Exemptus, Magister and Magus. Unusually, members of the Order were expected to pursue serious academic and practical study of the esoteric and occult, and even to engage in actual alchemical experiments.

Masonry was widely associated with liberal, freethinking and revolutionary movements, but the OGRC represented a very different school of thought. It was aligned with conservative and reactionary elements in German culture, and attracted aristocratic members, culminating in the extraordinary coup of recruiting the Prussian crown prince Frederick William in 1781. When his father, Frederick the

Great, died in 1786 and he ascended the Prussian throne, members of the Order attained high rank and became influential at court, informing the cultural and social programme of the state. Given the relentless tide of anti-Masonic propaganda and conspiracy theorizing accusing secret societies of fomenting revolution, it is ironic that on one of the few occasions where a secret society has genuinely got its hands on the levers of power, its programme was reactionary and conservative.

The OGRC lost its influence on the death of Frederick William in 1797, and although it continued to exist for a few more years, it faded from view and appears to have disintegrated during the Napoleonic era, which saw Europe racked by war and political upheavals. But its legacy was far-reaching. Its structure and esoteric pursuits were hugely influential on the 19th-century Rosicrucian order *Societas Rosicruciana in Anglia* (Soc Ros or SRIA – see pages 117–119), and through that on the Hermetic Order of the Golden Dawn (HOGD – see pages 184–187). Both of these took their degree structure and much of their occult content from their German forebear.

The OGRC had an elaborate Legend of Perpetuation. It had allegedly been founded by a 1st-century CE

Egyptian magician named Ormus who converted to Christianity, and had adopted the symbol of the red cross. Ormus combined ancient Egyptian lore, including Hermeticism, alchemy and so on, with Christian and theosophical mysticism. Joining forces with the Essenes – a Jewish sect believed to have practised Gnosticism and been a significant influence on early Christianity – he had founded the Order of the Rose Cross. The Order had been brought to Europe, either in the time of King Arthur or by the Templars, who had been initiated in the Holy Land before coming to Scotland to found an early version of Freemasonry and initiate the king of England.

The OGRC was by no means the only Rosicrucian order to emerge within Freemasonry in the 18th century. The rich heritage of mystery that the Rosicrucians represented was tapped by many seeking to enrich Freemasonry (and themselves), including notorious figures such as Alessandro di Cagliostro and the Comte de St Germain, two probable charlatans who claimed to be immortal.

*Portrait of King Frederik William II of Prussia (1786–97) by Anton Graff, painted in 1792. Such high-powered members allowed the OGRC great influence in society.*

# SOCIETAS ROSICRUCIANA

| | |
|---|---|
| TYPE | Occult, esoteric, mystical |
| EXISTED | 1866–present |
| RELATED TO | Freemasonry, Order of the Golden and Rosy Cross, Hermetic Order of the Golden Dawn |
| GOALS AND CONCERNS | Occult and esoteric study; self-improvement |

The 19th century saw a widespread resurgence in the popularity of all things occult and esoteric. Secret societies were at the forefront of this movement, and Rosicrucianism, with its mixture of Christian mysticism and magical and alchemical exploration, was an attractive way in for many people, offering a strange combination of respectability and unorthodoxy.

## ZANONI

Rosicrucianism received an extra boost from the success of the 1842 novel *Zanoni* by eminent Victorian novelist Edward Bulwer-Lytton (1803–1873). Neglected today, Bulwer-Lytton was second in popularity in the 19th century only to his friend Charles Dickens, and his novels dealing with the esoteric and

occult were enormously influential. Many assumed he was presenting thinly veiled reality, and as with the original Rosicrucian Manifestos, his fictions had a tendency to create their own reality.

*Zanoni* is the story of the eponymous immortal Rosicrucian adept (an adept is someone highly trained and skilled in occult practices), who surrendered his humanity in ancient Babylon in 2000 BCE so that he could master the occult arts. When he falls in love, his humanity returns, but with it his mortality, and he sacrifices himself to save his wife and child from dark forces during the French Revolution. His visit to the guillotine was the model for the fate of the protagonist of Dickens' *A Tale of Two Cities*. *Zanoni* includes much detail about the organization, history and

*Edward Bulwer-Lytton, leading English novelist of the 19th century. He coined the immortal opening line: "It was a dark and stormy night."*

beliefs of the Rosicrucian Fraternity, and Lytton was widely assumed to be highly placed in the real life Fraternity, an assumption that became self-fulfilling in 1871 when he became Grand Patron of the pre-eminent British Rosicrucian order, the Soc Ros.

## THE GERMAN CONNECTION

One of the most influential Rosicrucian societies was founded in 1866 by Freemason Robert Wentworth Little (1840–1878), who was working as a clerk at the English headquarters of Masonry, Freemasons' Hall in London. Following a pattern that recurred repeatedly in the history of esoteric Masonic orders, Little supposedly came across an intriguing packet of papers in the dusty vaults of the Hall, and approached Kenneth Mackenzie (1833–1886), an expert on matters Masonic and occult, for help in deciphering them. The papers apparently detailed the rites of a defunct Rosicrucian society, and by a happy coincidence Mackenzie claimed to have been initiated into a similar society on an earlier visit to Germany (although there is no record of one existing at this period). If the papers genuinely existed, they might perhaps have related to the Order of the Golden and Rosy Cross (OGRC – see pages 112–115), as the society that Little then founded, the *Societas Rosicruciana in Anglia* (Soc Ros or SRIA), had many points of similarity, including its hierarchy of degrees.

## 'A PENCHANT FOR OCCULTISM'

The Soc Ros claims to be more than just a side-degree of Masonry ('The Society is not merely another degree of Freemasonry... and it exists outside of the normal "workings" of the Craft', according to the website of its American branch), but Little limited the membership of his new society to Master Masons. He almost certainly took his inspiration from the constitution of the OGRC, which explains: 'Masonry has deteriorated on its own part and has passed almost beyond recognition... all this notwithstanding it remains the preparatory school of the Rosy Cross and from this source only can the Order itself be recruited.' Many quasi-Masonic esoteric societies follow similar reasoning: only those whose minds have been prepared by Masonic training are ready for the greater revelations that they offer.

Like its German forebear, the Soc Ros had a scholarly aspect, with members expected to undertake serious study into the occult and esoteric. Little's own interest in these matters was said to stem from his study of the works of the great French magus Eliphas Lévi (see pages 178–179). Historian of the esoteric, Ellic Howe dismisses the Soc Ros as 'A small coterie of Master Masons with a penchant for occultism', but it would go

*Freemasons' Hall in London, headquarters of the United Grand Lodge of England. This magnificent Art Deco building was opened in 1933; an earlier version was the workplace of Robert Wentworth Little, who claimed to have discovered in its dusty bowels the rites of the Soc Ros.*

on to become extremely influential when three of its members, including its Supreme Magus William Wynn Westcott, founded the Hermetic Order of the Golden Dawn (HOGD) using the Soc Ros as a model (see pages 184–187).

During Westcott's tenure, the Soc Ros expanded and produced significant offshoots. First was the *Societas Rosicruciana in Scotia*, the Scottish branch, members of which set up a branch in America in 1880 as the *Societas Rosicruciana in Civitatibus Foederatis*, or the Rosicrucian Society of the United States, members of which in turn set up in 1909 the *Societas Rosicruciana in America* (known as the SRIA). The various Soc Ros bodies are organized into colleges, and there are around 58 of these around the world today, mostly in Britain.

# AMERICAN ROSICRUCIANS

| TYPE | Occult, esoteric, mystical, magical |
| --- | --- |
| EXISTED | 1694–present |
| RELATED TO | Rosicrucians, Freemasonry, *Ordo Templi Orientis*, Order of the Solar Temple, Priory of Sion |
| GOALS AND CONCERNS | Occult and esoteric study; self-improvement; magic; profit; Egyptology |

In modern times Rosicrucian societies have flourished most in America, where Rosicrucianism seems to have been particularly popular, perhaps because of the strongly Christian framework in which it explores occult and esoteric topics. American Rosicrucianism can trace its roots back to the Colonial era when German settlers in Pennsylvania brought Rosicrucian ideas with them as early as 1694.

## RANDOLPH'S HISTORY OF LOVE

American Rosicrucianism has been defined by charismatic but often problematic figures. The first of these was the remarkable Paschal Beverly Randolph (1825–1875), a mixed-race anti-slavery campaigner who became a well-known trance medium and spiritualist, able to communicate with the spirits of the dead. Randolph travelled the world investigating all things occult and esoteric, almost certainly becoming a Mason in the process.

In 1857 Randolph founded the Third Temple of the Rosie Cross in San Francisco, and although it became defunct during the Civil War, he continued to develop a new and daring system of magic, using hashish, scrying mirrors and, above all, sex magic to further his occult powers. In 1874 he published his most famous book, *Eulis! The History of Love: Its Wondrous Magic, Chemistry, Rules, Laws, Modes, Moods and Rationale; Being the Third Revelation of Soul and Sex.* In this he explained a complete system of sex magic, in which

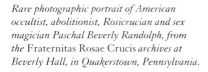

*Rare photographic portrait of American occultist, abolitionist, Rosicrucian and sex magician Paschal Beverly Randolph, from the* Fraternitas Rosae Crucis *archives at Beverly Hall, in Quakerstown, Pennsylvania.*

exploration of the sexual act and orgasm could improve health, enable telepathy and spirit communication, bring wealth and happiness and produce direct experience of the divine.

That same year he founded new Rosicrucian orders in Nashville and San Francisco, proclaiming himself Supreme Hierarch, Grand Templar, Knight, Prior and Hierarch of the Triplicate Order of Rosicruciae, Pythianae and Eulis. Afflicted with depression, he committed suicide a year later in 1875.

*A specacular lenticular cloud display over Mount Shasta, northern California, USA.*

Randolph's legacy was eventually inherited by R. Swinburne Clymer (1878–1966), who in 1922 brought together a number of small societies under the banner of the *Fraternitas Rosae Crucis* (Fellowship of the Rosy Cross or FRC), based on Randolph's own Brotherhood of Eulis. The FRC still exists and is also known as the Beverly Hall Corporation.

## ANCIENT MYSTICAL ORDER ROSAE CRUCIS

Clymer and his FRC engaged in a long and bitter feud with the most successful of American Rosicrucian organizations, the Ancient Mystical Order Rosae Crucis (AMORC), set up in Florida in 1925 (or possibly earlier, in New York; sources differ) by H. Spencer Lewis (1883–1939). Lewis was a keen occultist who had earlier headed a lodge of the *Ordo Templi Orientis* (Order of Oriental Templars, or OTO

– see pages 196–197) in New York, and who claimed to be the inheritor of ancient wisdom going back to the pharaoh Akhenaten. AMORC established the lucrative practice of offering correspondence courses in occult and esoteric topics, which became the model for many modern Rosicrucian and esoteric societies. Lewis had been an advertising executive and used his skills to build AMORC into an international success story, opening branches in France and forging links with German societies, eventually attracting over 250,000 members. He used the Order's growing income to build a college and planetarium at its headquarters in San Jose, California, along with a highly respected Egyptian museum that houses an important collection of ancient artefacts.

Lewis himself developed a fascination with the lost continent of Lemuria (imagined by Madame Blavatsky and the Theosophical Society – see pages 180–183) as a counterpart of Atlantis, where previous races of humans had acted out millions of years of history before our own era. This led to the bizarre belief that Lemurian superbeings in magically powered flying saucers lived within California's Mount Shasta, and AMORC sponsored several expeditions

to the area in the 1930s to hunt for secret cities below the mountain.

## WARRING FACTIONS

Clymer and Lewis each claimed to be the only true representatives of the Rosicrucians in America, with sole authority, and their outsized egos put them on a collision course. When Clymer alleged that Lewis was a phoney whose only interest in Rosicrucianism was as a moneymaking vehicle, Lewis hit back and a vicious feud ensued. Eventually, Clymer took Lewis to court in an attempt to be awarded sole use of the term 'Rosicrucian'. The court decided that it was in the public domain and could be used by anyone.

All this seems a long way from the popular image of how a secret society might be expected to conduct itself – that is, by skulking in the shadows and keeping a low profile, rather than advertising in magazines and fighting in court. Indeed, between sex magic, unedifying court battles over titles and correspondence courses in Kabbalah, it seems that modern American Rosicrucianism has strayed a long way from the original, deeply Christian, utopian message of moral, cultural and social reform envisaged by the original authors of the Rosicrucian Manifestos.

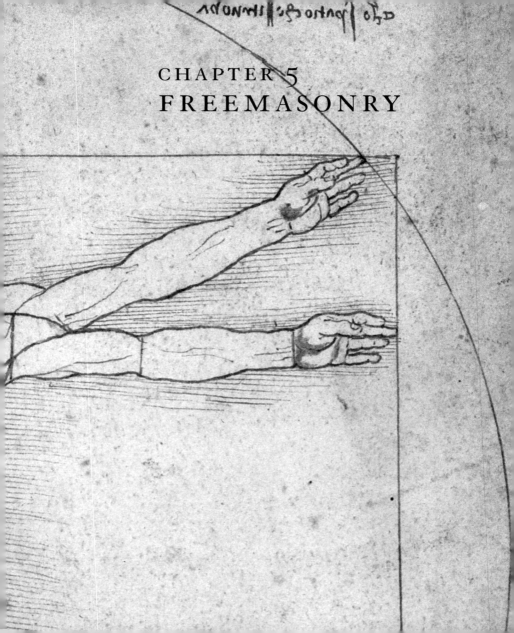

# CHAPTER 5
# FREEMASONRY

# THE FREEMASONS

| TYPE | Fraternal, mystical, esoteric |
| --- | --- |
| EXISTED | 17th century–present |
| RELATED TO | Neo-Templars, Rosicrucians, most occult and esoteric orders, Priory of Sion, P2 (Propaganda Due), Illuminati |
| GOALS AND CONCERNS | Personal growth; fraternal bonds; philanthropy |

The Freemasons, also known as the Masons and the Craft, are a fraternal order dedicated to spiritual and moral improvement and self-exploration, fostering brotherly love, and philanthropy. They are possibly the oldest and definitely the most popular and successful secret society in the world today, and are the ancestors of almost all non-criminal Western secret societies that are currently in operation. Membership is open to all men who believe in a supreme being or divine principle of some sort, although at times some Masonic organizations have practised discriminatory recruitment policies. Members meet as lodges, which consist of up to a few hundred members, and the lodges in one state, province or country, such as Maryland, British Columbia or England, are then organized under the jurisdiction of a Grand Lodge.

Freemasonry probably started in Britain at some point in the 17th century, although its origins are shrouded in mystery and confusion and it claims to be much older. The first undisputed recorded mention dates back to 1646 and the first recorded meeting of Masonic lodges was in 1717.

## OPERATIVE AND SPECULATIVE

Freemasonry is also sometimes known as speculative Masonry, to distinguish it from operative masonry. The latter refers to the work of actual stonemasons – artisans who dress and carve stone, specifically freestone masons, the most skilled type of mason who works blocks of 'free' or soft stone, which can be carved into intricate patterns. Alternatively, the 'free' is said to be an English corruption of the French *frère macon*, 'brother mason'. The distinction between speculative Masons (those who are initiated into an order of Masons but do not actually practise masonry as a profession) and operative ones implies something specific about the origins of Freemasonry – that the former derived from the latter.

Freemasonry is characterized by a hierarchy of grades and degrees, by initiation and other rituals, and by its use of symbolism and allegory, both visual or decorative and in its legends and lore. As well as using myths and legends for symbolic purposes, Freemasonry has a long history of inventiveness and speculation about its own origins and practices. These have combined with myths and legends created and perpetuated by those hostile towards and/or suspicious of Freemasonry, to generate a great deal of confusion, half-truths and outright fictions. In fact, anti-Masonry has become a significant movement in its own right, with its own history and lore, which have fed back into the practice of Freemasonry and produced new variations (see pages 169–173).

*The George Washington Masonic National Memorial in Alexandra, Virginia, USA. It was modelled after the Lighthouse at Pharos in Alexandria, one of the Seven Wonders of the Ancient World.*

# BELIEFS AND GOALS OF FREEMASONRY

With millions of members (see page 151), Masonry inevitably means many different things to many different people within the brotherhood. In addition, people outside it, especially anti-Masons, hold a range of views about its beliefs and goals, most of which are false.

## ADMISSION CONDITIONS

The Freemasons only admit men, although the modern era has seen the establishment of quasi-Masonic orders open to men and women, some of which are more or less officially associated with Masonry. Like initiates

to the ancient mysteries of Eleusis (see pages 30–41), prospective Masons are expected to be men of good character with 'clean hands' – that is, not guilty of any major offences. They must also believe in God, at the very least in the sense of believing that there is a Supreme Being or, as the Masons would prefer to phrase it, a Supreme Architect of the Universe.

## DEISM

The idea of a Supreme Being is at the heart of Masonry, which is deist to its core. Deism is a philosophy of religion that holds that a supreme being of some kind created the universe, but which rejects most of the revelation, authority, dogma and supernaturalism of organized religion. Deists believe that reason on its own is sufficient for discovering religious and moral truths, including how to be a moral person and how to experience and get closer to the divine – both core concerns in Freemasonry. Deists also believe that all religions essentially express the same truths, although they may have built up layers of superstition, dogma, myth and legend that either

*This painting shows an initiation ceremony in a Viennese Masonic Lodge during the reign of Joseph II, 1784. It is believed that Mozart is the figure shown seated on the extreme left.*

obscure or illuminate those truths. Because of its deist principles, Freemasonry does not discriminate against non-Christian religions that share belief in a supreme being or principle; since this encompasses most forms of faith in world religion, Freemasonry is open to almost everyone. The most significant group excluded by this criterion is, of course, atheists, which is ironic given that Freemasonry has been accused almost from its beginning of being atheistic.

Following on from this deist principle, Masonry has traditionally encouraged freethinking, in the sense of open-mindedness and tolerance of different religions, philosophies and moral systems. This in turn has supported a generally progressive and liberal approach to thinking about society and culture, and Masonry shared similar utopian ideals to early Rosicrucianism, and indeed probably derived them from exactly that source. Despite this apparent emphasis on both religion and politics, Masonry actually bans discussion of religion or politics at lodge meetings. It is important to bear in mind the distinction between a particular religion or political persuasion and religion or politics in general as an approach to spiritual and moral improvement.

RELIGIOUS, MYSTICAL AND OCCULT SOCIETIES

## FRATERNITY

Perhaps the most widespread suspicion of the Craft is that it is corrupt, in the sense of providing unfair assistance to its members, so that, for instance, a Masonic judge would let someone off lightly if they were a fellow Mason, or one Mason might give a job or contract to another Mason when he did not really deserve it. This probably stems from the fraternal aspect of Masonry, which places great stress on boosting fraternal feeling between members, and indeed between all men, including providing mutual support. Freemasons would argue very strongly that this does not extend to anything illegal or underhand.

## SACRED ARCHITECTURE

Freemasonry holds that in a universe created by a Supreme Architect, eternal and divine truths are embodied in the geometry and architecture of that universe, so the best way to discover and understand those truths is through the study of geometry and architecture. This belief essentially explains why Masonry is called Masonry, and offers strong clues as to its origins in Hermeticism and esoteric concepts of sacred geometry, rather than actual, operative stonemasonry (see pages 154–158).

In Freemasonry, symbolism and ritual based on these ideas of sacred geometry and architecture are used to explore spirituality and mysticism. Symbolic images and actions can have an archetypal resonance; that is to say, they resonate with elements of deep psychology, stirring sensory, intellectual and emotional responses beyond the reach of normal awareness. Freemasonry uses such responses as a way to invoke direct experience of the mystical and spiritual, and perhaps even of the divine. In this sense, it draws upon the Gnostic tradition of direct personal experience of the divine, and parallels can be seen between aspects of Masonic belief and aspects of Gnosticism. More generally, however, Masonry incorporates many elements of the Hermetic tradition, and although it may not be an occult society, it is definitely an esoteric one.

*Leonardo da Vinci's* Vitruvian Man. *Vitruvius' 1st century masterwork,* De architectura, *set out the principles of sacred geometry and profoundly influenced Renaissance and Hermetic thought about man, nature and the role of God as the supreme architect of the cosmos after its rediscovery in 1414. Da Vinci's famous drawing shows how the human body encodes key geometric principles that also inform architecture.*

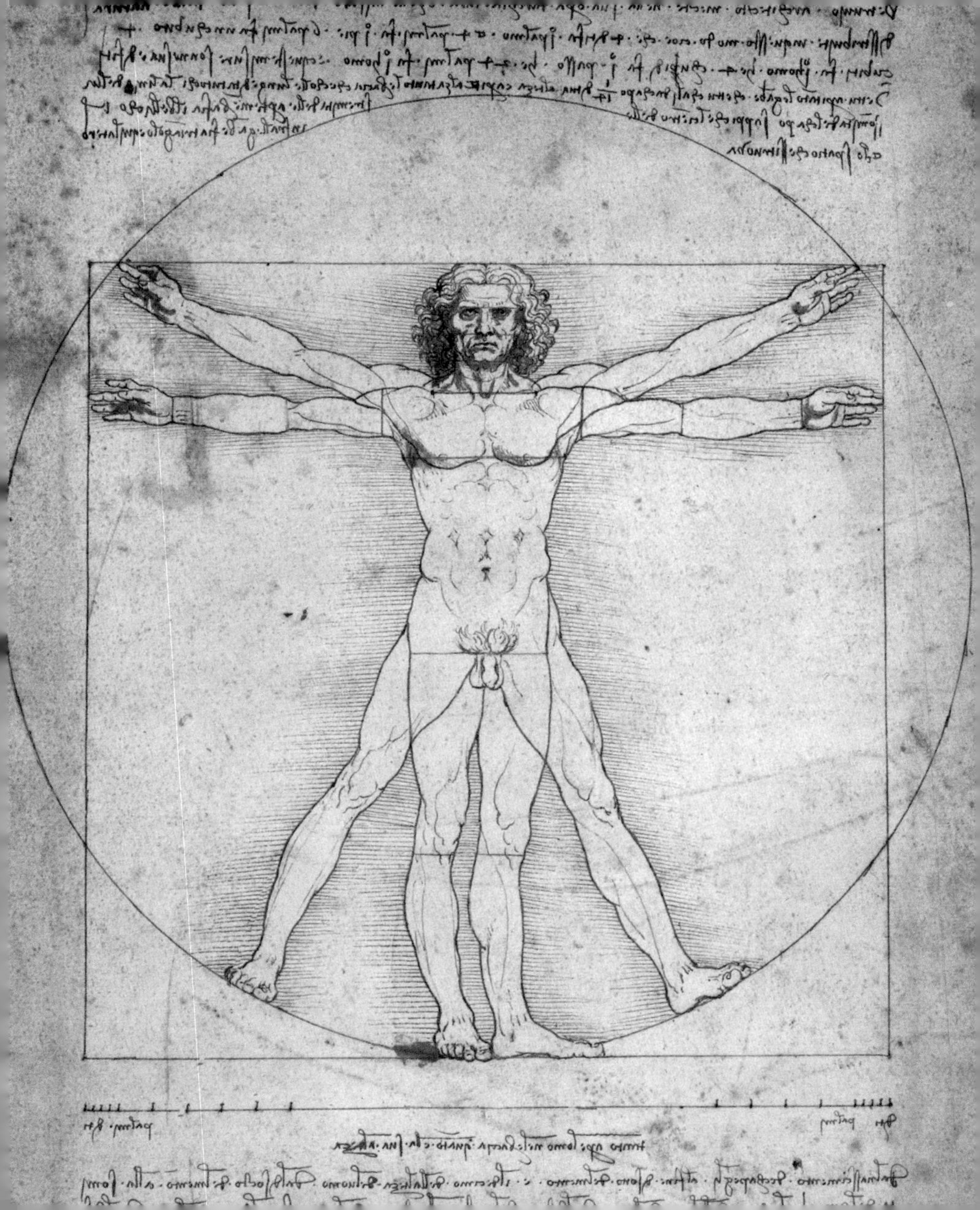

# DEGREES AND RITES
# OF FREEMASONRY

One of the most exotic and intriguing aspects of Freemasonry is the range of mysterious titles that Masons can win for themselves as they progress further and deeper into the secrets of the Craft. These vary from the most basic level, or degree, known as Entered Apprentice, up to the highest degrees with fantastical names such as Grand Elected Knight Kadosh, Knight of the Black and White Eagle. Strange titles like this have helped to increase the allure of the Craft, and also to strengthen the inaccurate but popular association between Masonry and the occult.

Today there are many different sets or systems of these degrees, known as rites, in world Freemasonry. Different regions and countries may use different rites, while others are used at the same time in the same regions, and even by the same Masons. This helps to confuse non-Masons and maintain the air of impenetrable mystery around the Craft.

The term 'the Craft' technically refers only to the basic system of three degrees: Entered Apprentice, Fellow Craft and Master Mason. But on top of

these basic three degrees, a huge and complex set of different and sometimes competing rites exists, two well-known examples being the York Rite and the Ancient and Authentic Scottish Rite. To confuse matters further, each rite may be administered by a different organization, so that a single man might be a Master Mason, answering to a Grand Lodge, a Holy Royal Arch Mason of the Scottish Rite, answering to a Chapter, a Knights Templar Mason, answering to a Commandery, and a Knight of the Ancient and Accepted Scottish Rite, answering to a Supreme Council.

In the early 20th century there were over 2,000 different rites. Most of these are now defunct, or practised by only a handful of Masons. The different rites and degrees are intimately bound up with the history of Freemasonry, so to understand them it is necessary to travel back in time.

*Many emblems of Masonry are depicted in this lithograph, c.1870–1880. The all-seeing eye, ark, beehive, lamb, globes atop the columns, square and compass, trowel and anchor can all be seen.*

# THE ORIGINS OF FREEMASONRY

The history of the Craft is so contentious that there is not even agreement on which elements are contentious. Most sources agree that the first undisputed mention of Freemasonry comes in the journal of the 17th-century antiquarian Elias Ashmole (1617–1692). Ashmole was an English astrologer, alchemist and historian who became deeply interested in old books, coins and other artefacts, eventually donating his collection to the University of Oxford in 1683 as the Ashmolean Museum. On 16 October 1646 he noted that he had been admitted to a Masonic lodge at Warrington; later in life he recorded his attendance at a lodge held at Masons' Hall in London in 1682. Ashmole was a man of many parts, but operative stonemasonry was not among his talents, so it is apparent that speculative Masonry was up and running by the mid-17th century and well established enough less than 30 years later to have its own Hall.

*A stonemason at work from the 9th-century* Gospel Book *of Archbishop Ebbo of Rheims. Medieval ideas of health and safety at work were very different from modern ones.*

## MEDIEVAL ORIGINS

Masonic sources claim that there are much older references to masonry that suggest a clear evolution from operative to speculative Masonry (see, for instance, the Old Charges, pages 138–143), and it is generally assumed that Freemasonry developed from the tradition of medieval craft guilds. Many characteristics of Freemasonry are prefigured in the medieval guilds, including the basic hierarchy of degrees, the fraternal and philanthropic functions, the elaborate origin myths and the systems of secret words and signs.

In the Middle Ages the different crafts were arranged into a system of guilds – organizations that protected the interests of their members, collected money as a sort of proto-welfare system to pay for funerals and support widows and children of dead members, for instance, oversaw training and maintained standards. Typically, the guilds were run by master craftsmen, assisted by highly trained journeymen, who might move about working under different masters and who took on apprentices to serve as

labour while they were trained up. Guilds often claimed descent from legendary and biblical figures and times, and protected their trade secrets with oaths, signs, passwords and handshakes.

More specifically, much of the terminology of the Freemasons can be traced back to stonemasons' guilds. Medieval stonemasons – especially freestone masons – were highly skilled craftsmen who combined the roles that would today be performed by architects, engineers and artists. The palaces, castles and, in particular, the cathedrals of the Middle Ages were the greatest undertakings of their era. Teams of masons would move from one great project to another, and while on site they would eat, sleep and work together in a lodge. Unskilled labourers, or cowans, were excluded from the lucrative monopoly held by the guild, and to prevent them from infiltrating the lodge, learning trade secrets and taking advantage of guild benefits, the masons might place a guard, or tyler, at the door of the lodge, and would use passwords and secret handshakes to distinguish

*The Parthenon in Athens. Studies show that the temple façade and floorplan incorporate golden ratios and the 'golden rectangles' derived from the golden ratio principle. This ratio appears in nature in the guise of the Fibonacci Sequence.*

true masons. In Freemasonry the role of Tyler is a ceremonial title, and the Tyler is supposed to stand outside the door to the lodge, 'being armed with a drawn sword to keep off all intruders and cowans to Masonry'.

## MASONS OR MAGI?

According to the Masonic view of their own history, the operative master masons of the Middle Ages, as highly skilled and qualified professionals, would have been well versed not just in the practical tenets of geometry and architecture but also in their symbolic and esoteric aspects, and indeed the rich symbolism embodied in the great Gothic cathedrals confirms this. The operative masons knew, for instance, about the golden ratio, supposedly discovered by Pythagoras. The golden ratio, approximately 1.618, also known as the golden section, the golden mean and the divine proportion, is the ratio between two quantities where the ratio of the sum of the quantities to the larger quantity is equal to the ratio of the larger quantity to the smaller one. Algebraically, it is expressed as: $a+b$ is to $a$ as $a$ is to $b$. This ratio, which supposedly is found throughout nature and in music, featured heavily in Classical art and architecture (for instance, governing the proportions of the façade and statues of the Parthenon), and is said to underlie the aesthetic appreciation of beauty. Since Pythagoras it has been invested with mystical properties, and in Freemasonry contemplation of the golden ratio is supposed to help lead to revelation of the divine.

The Masonic assumption is that operative masons developed the philosophy of their craft to such a high degree that they became esoteric sages, using these divinely inspired principles to elaborate a moral and mystical system that became Freemasonry. Eventually, they opened their brotherhood to those non-masons they considered sufficiently advanced to benefit from this system, and speculative Masonry was born.

This account of Masonic origins is open to question because of a lack of evidence. An equally or possibly more plausible account is that speculative Masonry owes little to operative masonry beyond its evocative terminology, and much more to the increasing popularity of Hermeticism. The enthusiasm for esoteric learning that led to the Rosicrucian Manifestos and subsequent outpouring of interest could easily have led to the formation of a society based around the concepts of sacred geometry and architecture as a metaphor for esoteric wisdom, while offering a genial atmosphere of male conviviality. The 17th century saw a great many clubs and

societies founded; most were short-lived, but the Freemasons had hit upon a winning combination. To the fad for architectural esoterica they added the attractions of ritual and theatre, all played out within a safe, private environment free from the religious divisions that were tearing Europe – and England in particular – to pieces.

## THE OLD CHARGES

The known history of Freemasonry properly begins on 24 June 1717 when four London lodges gathered together at the Goose and Gridiron Tavern in St Paul's Churchyard to form the first Grand Lodge and elected Anthony Sayer as the first Grand Master. The formation of the Grand Lodge marked a time of consolidation and regularization for what had presumably been a loose, informal network of lodges. In 1723 a committee headed by James Anderson published *The Constitution of Freemasons*, sometimes known as Anderson's Constitution. This Constitution brought together rules and traditions previously set out in old documents held by individual lodges, generically known as the Old Charges.

*Early 19th-century goose and gridiron emblem from a tavern sign. A similar emblem may have marked the first known gathering place of Masonic lodges in 1717.*

The Old Charges include documents that apparently extended the origins of the Masons back to the early Middle Ages. For instance, the Regius Manuscript, also known as the Halliwell Manuscript, is supposedly a poem from 1390 that traces the origins of Masonry to the ancient Greek geometer Euclid and to ancient Egypt. It dates its introduction to England to the reign of the Anglo-Saxon king Athelstan, from 924 to 939 CE: 'In tyme of good kynge Adelstonus day'. It sets out the precepts of Masonry, including a number of 'points', including:

> The third point must be severely,
> With the 'prentice know it well,
> His master's counsel he keep and
> close,
> And his fellows by his good
> purpose;
> The privities of the chamber tell
> he no man,
> Nor in the lodge whatsoever
> they do;
> Whatsoever thou hearest or seest
> them do,
> Tell it no man wheresoever you
> go;
> The counsel of hall, and even of
> bower...

The Old Charges also included a colourful account of the mythical origins of Freemasonry in biblical times. Supposedly, the sons of the biblical patriarch Lamech invented geometry and all the other sciences, and sought to protect them against disaster by inscribing their wisdom inside two hollow pillars, one of marble to withstand fire and one of bronze to withstand flood. When the biblical Deluge came, the marble pillar was lost but the bronze one survived and was found by Hermes Trismegistus. He passed on its secrets to the Egyptians, and from there to ancient Babylon where masons built the Tower of Babel, adopting secret hand signals to communicate with one another after the confusion of languages. King Solomon restored the wisdom of the ancient Craft to its highest perfection and employed 80,000 masons to build his Temple, which was equipped with two pillars, named Boaz and Jachin, in replica of the ones from before the Flood. Solomon employed Hiram Abiff as the chief architect of the Temple, but Abiff was murdered when he refused to disclose his secret passwords. This mythical history, especially the tale of Hiram

*Medieval illumination showing the Tower of Babel, with stonemasons at work, including freestone masons in the foreground.*

Abiff, is of great importance in Masonry, referred to in many symbols and passwords and re-enacted in important rituals. The Temple of Solomon, believed to represent the order of the universe in physical form and to encode divine wisdom in its architecture, is also the focus of intense interest in Masonry.

The problem with the documents that make up the Old Charges is that they are generally not well attested until relatively late, in the 17th and 18th centuries, and there is scepticism about whether some or even any of them are genuine. Given Freemasonry's undistinguished record of fabricating antiquity, this scepticism is justified.

## MODERNS AND ANTIENTS

The Grand Lodge of England quickly extended its authority to cover over a hundred English lodges, and Irish and Scottish Grand Lodges were set up in 1725 and 1736 respectively. Masonry soon spread overseas, with lodges in France by the 1720s and in America by the 1730s. In 1751, however, there was a crisis as a group of five lodges, intending 'to revive the Ancient Craft upon true

*A portrait of Master Mason the Duke of Montagu (c.1688–1749), Master General of the Ordnance.*

Masonical principles' formed a breakaway group calling itself the Antients, on the basis that the 'Moderns' had fallen away from the ancient principles and practices of the Craft. The Moderns and the Antients formed rival Grand Lodges and feuded until 1813, when they agreed to form the United Grand Lodge of England (UGLE).

By this time Freemasonry had changed enormously from its 17th-century origins. Where originally there had been only two grades or degrees – Entered Apprentice and Fellow Craft – a third, Master Mason, was added in the early 18th century, followed by an amazing proliferation of degrees over the course of the next 150 years (see pages 144–151). Also, whereas the Craft had originally been a club for the educated middle classes and minor gentry, it quickly began to attract the upper classes. It is significant that whereas the first Grand Master was a 'mere' gentleman, within four years he was replaced by the Duke of Montagu, and by the time of the formation of the UGLE, both Antients and Moderns were headed by royal princes. Although egalitarianism is supposed to be a guiding principle of the Masons, the role of Grand Master has featured a disproportionate number of dukes and princes, and even the occasional king.

# RISE AND FALL OF FREEMASONRY

Although the Craft specifically bans discussion of politics at lodge meetings, Freemasonry originated from and developed against the background of great political, social and religious upheavals, and these have very strongly affected its evolution. England during the 17th century went through a terrible Civil War, regicide (the execution of Charles I), a period of rule by fanatical Puritans (who banned Christmas, for instance), constant anti-Catholic hysteria and the Glorious Revolution of 1688, in which the Catholic-sympathizing James II was deposed in favour of the Protestant William and Mary. The 17th century was also the period of the great witch-hunts, which saw suspicion of all things magical and occult boil over into terror, hatred and persecution. Men like Dr Dee – the sort of men who built the intellectual and philosophical foundations of Freemasonry – had to defend themselves against accusations of witchcraft and Satanism. In this context, the unorthodox, even heretical, beliefs at the heart of Freemasonry, including the apparently harmless belief that Protestants and

Catholics could be brothers and share the same approach to religious philosophy, were dangerous and vulnerable. This is one reason why Freemasonry may have embraced a high degree of privacy, maybe even secrecy.

## GORMOGONS AND JACOBITES

The early 18th century, when Freemasonry really took off, saw yet more religious and political turmoil. The Act of Settlement of 1701 transferred the British throne to the Protestant House of Hanover, to prevent it from falling once more into the hands of the Catholic House of Stuart. The Elector of Hanover became George I in 1714, acceding to the throne instead of James Stuart, the son of James II, later known as the 'Old Pretender'. His son, Charles Edward Stuart, Bonnie Prince Charlie, would become known as the Young Pretender, and they and their supporters were called Jacobites. After the Act of Union of 1707 merged Scotland and England into a single kingdom, the Jacobite cause came to encompass the movement for Scottish

independence. Thanks to historic links between the two countries, French Catholic sympathy for the Jacobite cause translated into support for Scottish Jacobite exiles and the development of a distinctive Scottish-French alliance.

Masonry soon became caught up in the struggle between the Jacobites and Hanoverian Britain. One of the earliest Grand Masters of the Grand Lodge of England was Philip, Duke of Wharton (1698–1731), a leading Jacobite. He became Grand Master in 1722, but when Anderson's Constitution was adopted in 1723, he resigned in protest at its commitment to 'obedience to the civil government', which he interpreted as

*French anti-Masonic postcard of the 20th century. Anti-Masonry was a common theme of the reactionary movement in France.*

tacit support for the Hanoverian cause. The Constitution also banned religious and political talk within lodges.

The following year Wharton set up the Ancient Noble Order of the Gormogons, placing a newspaper advert announcing the new society, claiming that it had been founded 'many thousand years before Adam' by Chin-Quaw Ky-Po, the first emperor of China. Freemasons were warned that they had to renounce the Craft before they could join. Wharton and his

145

Jacobite backers saw the Gormogons as a kind of Jacobite Freemasonry, hoping to build support for the cause of the Old Pretender, and they engaged in a campaign of anti-Masonic propaganda. Wharton, an appalling alcoholic, died in 1731 and the Gormogons soon disappeared, but this was only the first stage in a long struggle for the soul of Freemasonry.

## CHEVALIER RAMSAY'S ORATION

A turning point in the evolution of Masonry came in 1737 with the delivery of a speech, or oration, that has become legendary in the annals of the Craft. Freemasonry was becoming increasingly popular in France during the 18th century. Whereas in England it was more a middle-class pursuit, and therefore associated with the Protestant, Hanoverian establishment, in France it was popular with the upper classes, who were Catholic and might be sympathetic to the Jacobite cause if properly motivated.

It was against this background that an obscure Scottish convert to Catholicism, who had served as tutor to the young Charles Stuart in Rome, was initiated into Freemasonry in 1729. Andrew Michael Ramsay (1686–1743), known as the Chevalier because he had been admitted to the Order of St Lazarus of Jerusalem, was appointed Grand Orator of a lodge in Paris, and delivered his landmark Oration on 20 March 1737 (1736 according to some sources, possibly reflecting calendar differences between Britain and France). Copies of it were circulated in the French government and it was published several times. In the speech Ramsay discussed the origins and principles of Freemasonry, claiming that it was born in biblical times and linked to the ancient mystery religions: 'Yes, sirs, the famous festivals of Ceres at Eleusis, of Isis in Egypt, of Minerva at Athens, of Urania amongst the Phoenicians, and of Diana in Scythia were connected with ours. In those places mysteries were celebrated which concealed many vestiges of the ancient religion of Noah and the Patriarchs.'

Crucially, he went on to assert that during the Crusades 'our Order formed an intimate union with the Knights of St John of Jerusalem', and that the warrior-monks of the Crusades had brought Freemasonry back to Britain, and to Scotland in particular. However, Ramsay asserted, 'The fatal religious discords which embarrassed and tore Europe in

*Philip Wharton, 1st (and last) Duke of Wharton, prominent Jacobite and founder of the Gormogons.*

*Portrait of Baron Karl Gotthelf von Hund (1722–1776).*

the 16th century caused our Order to degenerate from the nobility of its origin.' In other words, the Reformation and Protestantism were linked to the decline of Freemasonry. He may not have stated it openly in his Oration, but Ramsay was effectively calling for a renewal and restoration of Freemasonry by returning it to its roots in the Catholic warrior orders of the Crusader era.

Contrary to legend, Ramsay did not claim a link between the Masons and the Templars, or found new degrees of Masonry, but he did plant the idea of a link between Masonry and the chivalrous medieval orders, with overtones of a Jacobite, Scottish–French, Catholic agenda. These ideas were to germinate into a revolution in Freemasonry.

## THE EVOLUTION OF FREEMASONRY

Although the immediate impact of Chevalier Ramsay's Oration is not clear, the sentiments he expressed seemed to kick-start the effort to make Freemasonry in France a tool for the Jacobite cause, by stressing its links with a Scottish, Catholic chivalric tradition. Scottish–French Jacobites probably created the first of the higher degrees added to Freemasonry. Up until this point Masonry had been restricted to the three basic degrees of Apprentice, Fellow and Master, but now Master Masons could be initiated into a higher degree, the Royal Arch, administered by a separate body from the lodge that controlled the basic degrees. Later, this body would become the Royal Arch chapter. The Royal Arch spread quickly to England where it was first recorded in 1744, and became popular throughout Masonry, though its place in the complex scheme of degrees and rites (see page 132) varied by country.

Jacobite-influenced higher degrees proliferated as the Jacobites prepared for an assault on the British mainland led by Charles Stuart, which culminated in the Battle of Culloden in 1746, ending realistic hopes of a Stuart restoration. The Royal Order of Scotland, for instance, was probably created in France or Holland in the 1740s. Conferring the exotic degrees of the Heredom of Kilwinning and the Rosy Cross, the Order claimed to be descended from Knights Templar who had sought refuge in Scotland and fought alongside Robert the Bruce at Bannockburn in 1314. Although this Legend of Perpetuation was entirely bogus, the connections between the Templars, the Rosicrucians and the Freemasons were now established and they have lasted – and strengthened – to this day.

After the Battle of Culloden had crushed the Jacobite Rising of 1645–1646, there were even more exiled Jacobites in France and further high degrees sprang up to service them. In 1754 the Rite of Perfection was established at Clermont and introduced 22 degrees, stressing the Templar connections and claiming that every Freemason was effectively a Templar. Influenced by this new development, German Mason Baron Karl Gotzhelf von Hund (1722–1776) established the Rite of Strict Observance, which used a simple system of seven degrees that became enormously popular throughout Europe. Von Hund claimed that the Rite of Strict Observance was based on ancient wisdom preserved by the Templars but kept secret until then. He asserted that these secrets had been revealed to him by a circle of Unknown Superiors, who would eventually come forth and reveal yet more secrets of world-changing significance. The Rite included practical elements of Kabbalah and alchemy, and von Hund claimed that its members would learn the secret of the Philosopher's Stone, and therefore become immortal.

Eventually, von Hund's refusal to reveal the identity of the Unknown Superiors, or any more of their secrets, led to his demotion and the disbanding of the Rite, but its influence was huge, doing much to introduce occult and esoteric elements into Freemasonry and inspiring the creation of new rites such as the Order of the Golden and Rosy Cross (OGRC – see page 112–115). Even the story of the Unknown Superiors was to be repeated in the origin myths of future societies and organizations. For instance, both the Hermetic Order of the Golden Dawn (HOGD) and the Theosophical Society claimed similar sources of authority (see pages 181 and 185). Freemasonry came to be seen as the 'preparatory school' for a whole range of mysteries and occult societies, with over 2,000 rites and orders created by the early 20th century.

## POPULARITY AND DECLINE

All the basic ingredients of modern Freemasonry were now in place, and the Craft continued to increase in popularity

around the world. It was wildly successful in America, and many of the founding fathers of the American Revolution were Masons (see pages 164–167). It was in America that the Ancient and Accepted Scottish Rite, also known as the Scottish Rite, was founded and, alongside the York Rite, became one of the two major systems of Freemasonry practised today. In 1775 Prince Hall, a black American of West Indian origin, was initiated into the Craft, but found segregation and racist attitudes in mainstream Masonry. He went on to help set up a system of African American lodges known as Prince Hall Masonry that spread to every state in the USA.

Worldwide, Masonic membership grew to a high of around 8 million in 1900. How many of these were genuinely interested in Gnostic-style philosophies of personal revelation or esoteric aspects of sacred geometry? Probably relatively few. In America, for instance, Masonic lodges and chapters

*US President Warren Gamaliel Harding (1865–1923) taking part in a Shriners' parade. Shriners, The Ancient Arabic Noble Order of the Mystic Shrine for North America, are often recognized by the red fez that is worn by members.*

were often able to use their considerable incomes to provide luxurious amenities for their members, making them attractive to people who simply wanted to use the facilities. To maintain and expand their income, some American lodges started to fast-track new initiates by promoting them through all three initial degrees in a single day without having to do more than sit through a token lecture.

Many other prospective Masons were attracted by the charitable work undertaken by Masonic lodges, particularly under the auspices of the Shriners. The Ancient Arabic Noble Order of the Mystic Shrine was founded in New York in 1871 as a Masonic drinking club, and quickly became wildly popular. From 1888 it began to focus less on drinking and more on fundraising, supporting a massive programme of hospital building and child healthcare.

For various and complex reasons, including bad or derisive publicity, changing tastes and fashions, attacks by anti-Masons, decline in religious observance and the growth of alternative leisure pastimes, the Freemasons have suffered a long, slow decline in membership. There are fewer than two million Masons worldwide today and sources differ over whether membership is increasing or declining.

# RITUAL AND SYMBOLISM OF FREEMASONRY

The air of mystery surrounding Freemasonry is partly due to the vows of secrecy that Masons are supposed to observe. For instance, as part of the oath, or Obligation, that a Master Mason has

to swear, he promises 'that my breast shall be the sacred repository of... secrets', while up until 1986 Entered Apprentices had to swear a particularly blood-curdling oath:

> I most solemnly swear and sincerely promise and swear, that I will always hail, ever conceal, and never reveal, any of the arts, parts or points of the hidden mysteries of ancient Freemasonry... under no less a penalty than that of having my throat cut across, my tongue torn out by its roots, and buried in the rough sands of the sea at low water mark, where the tide ebbs and flows twice in twenty four hours, should I ever knowingly or willingly violate this my solemn oath or obligation...

Similarly gruesome oaths accompanied the next two degrees. The Fellow Craft had to swear to keep the secrets of Masonry, 'Binding myself under no less penalty than that of having my left

*A 1723 engraving by Bernard Picart showing a newly elected member being sworn in at a Freemasons meeting for the Reception of Apprentices.*

breast torn open, my heart plucked out, and given as a prey to the wild beasts of the field and the fowls of the air...', while the Master Mason swore to 'Bind myself under no less a penalty than that of having my body severed in twain, my bowels taken from thence and burned to ashes, the ashes scattered to the four winds of heaven, so that no more trace or remembrance may be had of so vile and perjured a wretch as I...'

These oaths have now been toned down, so that the Entered Apprentice's oath, for instance, now refers to 'the dangers which traditionally would have awaited you... the physical penalty at one time associated with the obligation of a Mason, that of having your throat cut across...' In the eyes of many, however, the damage has been done. Fundamentalist Christians, for instance, argue that taking a vow that appears to condone murder is blasphemous. Conspiracy theories argue that the bloodthirsty vows are representative of the true face of Masonry – a murderous and bloody one. This has allowed them to draw links between Masonry and, for instance, the horrible murders of Jack the Ripper, who slashed the throats of his victims and disembowelled them, or between Masonic forces and the mysterious death of Roberto Calvi, a banker with links to the Vatican and to organized crime, found hanging under Blackfriars Bridge in London in 1982 (see page 219).

Masons argue that this is all a terrible misunderstanding, and that like most of the practices of the Craft, the gruesome oaths are purely symbolic. Symbolism is at the heart of Freemasonry; the elaborate rituals, the paintings, carvings and objects, the strange words and phrases, the Masonic regalia – all these are rich in symbolism

## TOOLS OF THE CRAFT

Freemasonry borrows freely from operative masonry, and many of the terms it uses are words relating to the stonemason's craft or the medieval guild. For instance, Freemasons are said to 'work' different rites and degrees, just as operative masons worked stone. It borrows even more directly in the symbolic tools that are presented to Masons at each grade: the apron, the 24-inch gauge and gavel, the plumb, square and level, and the trowel.

During their initiation, new Masons are presented with an apron of white lambskin, with a triangular flap across the top. Operative masons wear aprons to protect their clothes from rock dust and sharp edges; in speculative Masonry the apron serves a quite different

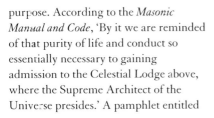

purpose. According to the *Masonic Manual and Code*, 'By it we are reminded of that purity of life and conduct so essentially necessary to gaining admission to the Celestial Lodge above, where the Supreme Architect of the Universe presides.' A pamphlet entitled

*Master Mason's painted leather apron, 18th century. Note the Masonic symbolism, such as the two pillars labelled J (Jachin) and B (Boaz), alluding to both the named pillars of the Temple and the bronze and marble pillars of the sons of Noah.*

*To the Lady and Family of a Mason* explains in more detail:

> During the ceremonies of his initiation, each Mason is presented with a white apron. It is, to him, an emblem of innocence and the badge of a Mason. It has, in all ages, been cherished by the rich, the poor, the high and the low. It is his for life. He will never receive another one and has, therefore, been cautioned to take it home and instructed in its care. While perfectly satisfactory for him to do so if he desires, he need not bring it to Lodge, as linen aprons are provided for his use at meetings.

As a Mason progresses through the grades and degrees, so his apron becomes more decorated. Master Masons who have served as the Worshipful Master of a lodge can have a blue trim on their apron, and an emblem on the flap. Office holders at a Grand Lodge decorate their aprons with gold braid and embroidered emblems. Each degree in a system such

*A seal showing the compass and set square that are practical tools for operative masons and symbolic ones for speculative Masons.*

as the Scottish Rite comes with its own symbolic apron design. Given that many Masons work several rites and may progress through hundreds of different degrees, the cost of accumulating different aprons can be high.

The Entered Apprentice is presented with a 24-inch gauge (a folding, extendable ruler) and a gavel (a small mallet). Operative masons use gauges to measure the dimensions of the blocks they are working; speculative Masons use theirs to measure out time, symbolically at least. The gauge reminds the new Mason that there is a time for everything, and also that their lives are finite and they must use their time carefully to improve themselves. The gavel relates to the symbolic representation of the new Mason as 'rough ashlar'. This denotes an unworked block of stone from the quarry, which needs to have its rough edges and sides chipped, chiselled and ground into smoothness so that it becomes a perfect ashlar – a perpend ashlar or a broached thurnel. The gavel is for symbolic use by the Entered Apprentice as he begins the long task of self-improvement, metaphorically chipping away his own rough edges. According to the *Masonic Manual and Code*, the 'common gavel' teaches 'the more noble and glorious purpose of divesting our hearts and consciences of all the vices and superfluities of life, thereby fitting our minds as living stones for that spiritual building, that "House not made with hands; eternal in the heavens.'"

At the Fellow Craft level, the Mason is presented with the plumb, square and level. In operative masonry these tools help measure out lines and angles and ensure that masonry is straight and level. For speculative Masons, according to former Lodge Master Theron Dunn, they serve to 'remind us to square our actions by the square of virtue, to walk uprightly in our several stations before g-d and man, and by the level, that we are travelling upon that level of time toward that undiscovered country.'

Master Masons are presented with a trowel, a tool normally used to spread cement. The Master metaphorically spreads the cement of brotherly love and affection, to unite the individual stones (the individual Masons within the lodge) into a single structure. These tools are considered to be the 'Jewels of Masonry', alongside the trestleboard or tracing board, a board decorated with the symbols of Masonry. Supposedly, the trestleboard dates back to the time of Hiram Abiff, the legendary founder of Freemasonry, who used a wax tablet to mark out instructions for his masons working on the Temple, and then erased them to protect his secrets. Later Masons would scratch out

their symbols on the dirt floor of the lodge and then ceremonially erase them. Today the trestleboard is a permanent record of the symbols, but lodge meetings are still ended with the phrase, 'Nothing further remains to be done, according to ancient custom, except to disarrange our emblems'. There follows a ritual re-enactment of the erasure process known as Squaring the Lodge, in which the Masons march around in straight lines and right angles.

## PASSWORDS

In medieval times, according to the origin theory of Masonry, stonemasons were itinerant workers and would therefore expect to encounter new faces at each job. To ensure that they did not reveal their secrets to outsiders, they developed a set of secret signs and passwords to distinguish genuine members. A more colourful origin of the secret signs and words of the Masons was suggested by the Chevalier Ramsay (see pages 146–148):

> We have secrets; they are figurative signs and sacred words, composing a language sometimes mute, sometimes very eloquent, in order to communicate with one another at the greatest distance, and to recognize our brothers of

*Masonic tracing board, decorated with symbols of death (to remind Masons that life is fleeting and ethical living is therefore all the more important), masonic tools, a representation of the entrance to the inner sanctum or adytum, the Holy of Holies of the Temple, other esoteric symbols and one of the Masonic 'secret' scripts. From* The Text Book of Freemasonry *published by William Reeves of Charing Cross Road c.1928.*

whatsoever tongue.

These were words of war which the Crusaders gave each other in order to guarantee them from the surprises of the Saracens, who often crept in amongst them to kill them... They agreed

*A Masonic seal of the Grand Lodge of Pennsylvania emphasizing fraternal bonds.*

upon several ancient signs and symbolic words drawn from the well of religion in order to recognize themselves amongst the heathen and Saracens. These signs and words were only communicated to those who promised solemnly, and even sometimes at the foot of the altar, never to reveal them.

Each degree of initiation is marked by the ritual instruction of secret words and 'signs of recognition', including special handgrips. On initiation as an Entered Apprentice, the candidate is given the word 'Boaz' (the name inscribed on one of the pillars of the Temple of Solomon, in the biblical origin myth of Freemasonry). He is then shown a sign that, according to a guidebook to Masonry, 'alludes to the penalty of the Entered Apprentice's obligation', made by drawing the right hand rapidly across the neck in imitation of the dire warning about 'having my throat cut across'. The secret handgrip is made by 'pressing the thumb against the top of the first knuckle-joint of the fellow Mason, the fellow Mason also presses his thumb against the first Mason's knuckle'. As the candidate is not yet a Mason, he is instructed in the sign and word through a dialogue between the Worshipful Master (WM) of the lodge and the Senior Deacon (SD), who stands in for the candidate. The dialogue runs like this:

WM: Brother Senior Deacon.
SD: Worshipful Master.
WM: I hele.
SD: I conceal.
WM: What do you conceal?
SD: All the secrets of a Mason in Masonry, to which this token alludes.
[At this time, the candidate is shown the grip of an Entered Apprentice]
WM: What is that?
SD: A grip
WM. Of what?
SD: Of an Entered Apprentice.
WM. Has it a name?
SD: It has.
WM: Will you give it to me?
SD: I did not so receive it, neither will I so impart it.
WM: How will you dispose of it?
SD: Letter it or halve it.
WM: Letter it and begin.
SD: You begin.
WM: Begin you.
SD: A.
WM: B.
SD: O.
WM: Z.
WM: [Directing his words to the candidate] Boaz, my Brother, is the name of this grip, and should always be given in the customary manner, by lettering or halving.

LE GENIE DU COMPAGNONNAGE FAISANT LE TOUR DU GLOBE.

When lettering, always commence with the letter 'A'.

At the next stages of initiation, there are passwords to enter the grade and secret words for use by members of that grade. So, in addition to new handgrips and signs, the password for becoming a Fellow Craft is 'Shibboleth' (a biblical term that has come to mean a password or sign of good faith), and the secret word is 'Jachin'. The password to Master Mason is 'Tubal Cain' (one of the sons of Lamech, said to have invented metalworking), and the secret word is 'Machaben' (variant spellings of which are common). The meaning of Machaben is unclear, but it has been translated as relating to rotten flesh, and this would seem to link up with the theme of the initiation ceremony for Master Masons, which concerns the murder and burial of Hiram Abiff.

## JAHBULON

One particular password, 'Jahbulon', has caused controversy because anti-Masons claim that it is blasphemous and possibly Satanic. Jahbulon is the secret word of

*Chart showing Masonic signs of recognition, Masonic insignia and other aspects of Masonic symbolism and ritual, with the all-seeing eye of the Supreme Architect at the top.*

the Holy Royal Arch degree (see page 132), available to Master Masons and, in many rites, a necessary precondition before going on to work side degrees. According to anti-Masons, such as Stephen Knight, author of the influential 1984 book *The Brotherhood*, the word is made up of syllables referring to Yahweh, the Judaeo–Christian god Baal, the fertility god of the ancient Canaanites, and Osiris, the ancient Egyptian god of the underworld. It is therefore the name for a compound deity worshipped by the Masons in mockery of the Christian god, proving that they are basically Satanic.

The Masons claim that this is nonsense. Initiation into the Holy Royal Arch involves a detailed explanation of where the word comes from, describing it as a compound word formed from Chaldean, Syriac and the Egyptian words for god and aspects of god: 'The various significations of the words may thus be collected: I am and shall be, Lord in Heaven or on High.' Given that the initiation also involves a lecture on the need to be humble before god, the mercy of the Divine Creator as the route to salvation and various other mainstream Christian sentiments, it seems misleading to claim that there is anything Satanic about the word or its use.

# THE FREEMASONS IN HISTORY

An amazing range of famous names through history were Freemasons, including Christopher Wren, Mozart, Benjamin Franklin, Napoleon, Joseph Smith and Brigham Young (founders of the Mormon Church), George Washington, Mark Twain, Oscar Wilde, Harry Houdini, Edward VII, Winston Churchill, Harpo Marx, Duke Ellington and Sugar Ray Robinson. Freemasons have come from every walk of life. Right from the start, however, the Masons were accused of being much more than a fraternal society dedicated to self-improvement.

In an era of religious and social upheaval, there was widespread fear of groups plotting to cause regime change, and the Rosicrucian Manifestos (see pages 93–95) seemed to demonstrate that there truly were secret societies dedicated to wholesale, revolutionary reform of society. When two hugely significant revolutions, the American and French, actually came to pass during the late 18th century, there were many who saw the hidden hand of the Freemasons at work.

## THE AMERICAN REVOLUTION

The high level of membership of the Craft among the Founding Fathers has led to widespread speculation that the Freemasons orchestrated the American Revolution of 1775–1783, when the North American colonies of Britain fought a war to gain their independence. George Washington and Benjamin Franklin were both high-level Masons, along with over half of Washington's staff in the Continental Army and eight signatories of the Declaration of Independence and 15 signatories to the US Constitution. After Washington, a further 14 Presidents were Masons, including Andrew Jackson, Theodore Roosevelt, F.D. Roosevelt, Harry Truman and Gerald Ford. In practice, there is no evidence that the Masonic affiliation of the Founding Fathers played a significant part in their revolutionary politics, let alone that

*George Washington officiating at a lodge meeting. Washington was an enthusiastic Mason but refused requests to become Grand Master of Masonry in America.*

*This painting shows an artist's impression of the Boston Tea Party, 16 December 1773, Boston, Massachusetts.*

Masons planned the Revolution. In fact, many of the higher echelons of American Masonry favoured remaining loyal to the King and opposed independence.

It is well documented that secret societies *were* involved in stoking revolutionary feeling, organizing resistance and provoking hostilities. The Committees of Correspondence helped to coordinate a unified response among the colonists during the build-up to the War, and later formed the core of the Continental Congress. The Sons of Liberty, based in Boston, escalated the

conflict by plotting acts of civil and armed defiance, possibly including the Boston Tea Party of 1773, and helped to organize the militia who became the Continental Army.

It is widely believed that Masonic influence among the Founding Fathers spilled over into areas such as the design of Washington DC and the iconography and mottoes of the new state, most notably the Great Seal of the United States and the dollar bill. The eye emanating rays of light on top of a truncated pyramid is generally supposed to be a Masonic symbol. In practice, Masons were not directly involved in designing the Great Seal, and the eye and the pyramid may not have been a

Masonic symbol at the time, although it is now. Symbols with an esoteric background were part of the intellectual climate, so it is not surprising that those people charged with choosing symbols for their designs would pick them.

Some buildings in Washington DC had their foundation stones laid in Masonic ceremonies. For instance, George Washington used a Masonic trowel to lay the cornerstone for the Capitol, and the same trowel was used to lay the cornerstone for the Washington Monument in a ceremony presided over by Mason President James K. Polk. There is, however, no evidence that this was part of some dark plan. It is more likely that, schooled in the positive symbolism of the trowel as a Masonic tool, the presidents performed what they believed to be symbolically appropriate acts.

## THE FRENCH REVOLUTION

There is far less evidence of Masonic involvement in the French Revolution of 1789. Although many of the educated middle class who provided the intellectual foundation of the Revolution were Masons, so were many of the aristocrats who were destroyed. The link between Masonry and the Revolution goes back to the 1790s, with the publication of two books that have become greatly influential in the mythology of secret societies.

Abbé Augustin Barruel (1741–1820) was a Jesuit (an organization that has suffered its own share of smears) whose *Memories Towards a History of Jacobinism* was published in four volumes in 1797 and 1798. Also in 1797, Edinburgh University Professor John Robison (1739–1805) published *Proofs of a Conspiracy against all the Religions and Governments of Europe carried on in the Secret Meetings of the Freemasons, Illuminati, and Reading Societies, collected from Good Authorities*. Both told a similar tale in that the French Revolution had been orchestrated by the Freemasons, who were in turn a front for the Bavarian Illuminati (see pages 266–267). The latter were in turn part of a secret plot going back at least to the time of the Knights Templar, who had brought down the French government in revenge for the murder of Jacques de Molay more than 400 years earlier. According to Robison (an ex-Freemason), the Illuminati, working through their Masonic dupes, were also responsible for the American Revolution. Both books were filled with fictions, inaccuracies and speculation, and have been thoroughly discredited. For instance, according to the *Encyclopaedia Britannica*, *Proofs of a Conspiracy* 'betrays a degree of credulity extremely remarkable'.

# ANTI-MASONRY

Almost as old as records of Freemasonry are records of anti-Masonry, a movement that denounces Masonry as corrupt, subversive, dangerous, blasphemous or Satanic, and often of being guilty of all of these. Political anti-Masons accuse the Craft of nepotism, subverting justice and the law, corrupting institutions and even plotting the downfall of governments and ways of life. Religious anti-Masons do not like the Masonic principles of deism, freedom of conscience and religious equality, and accuse it of being heretical, anti-Christian, Gnostic, atheistic or Satanist. As early as 1698 a pamphlet printed in London warned 'all Godly people' that the Masons 'are the Antichrist which was to come leading them from fear of God', and conservative Christianity has been at the core of anti-Masonry ever since.

The secrecy of the Masons prompted suspicions of immorality as early as the 1720s, and they were accused of heavy

*Portrait of Pope Clement XII. Catholicism has been opposed to Masonry from the start, and Clement was the first to issue decrees against it.*

drinking, homosexuality, ritual flagellation and drunken orgies. The religious unorthodoxy of the Masons and their rapid spread across Europe, coupled with the association between the Protestant House of Hanover and Masonic roots in Britain, aroused the hostility of the Roman Catholic Church. In 1738 Pope Clement XII issued a bull denouncing Masonry and excommunicating Catholics who joined up.

## ILLUMINIZED MASONRY

Anti-Masonry became a serious international movement after the 1780s. The unmasking of the Bavarian Illuminati (see pages 266–267) sparked widespread fear amid claims by reactionary forces that they presented a genuine threat to the established order, claims that seemed to be realized in the outbreak of the French Revolution. Writers like Augustin Barruel and John Robison (see page 267) developed elaborate conspiracy theories in which the Illuminati had taken control of the Freemasons and used them to orchestrate the French Revolution, and were now planning revolutions in every other nation. 'Illuminized Masonry', as it became known, rapidly became the bugbear of the conspiracy community and has remained so in one form or another up to the present day. Concern over Illuminized Masonry spread quickly to the United States, where Masonry had been increasingly powerful and respected. Even George Washington, a lodge master and keen Mason, was moved to comment on the danger it posed.

## THE ANTI-MASONIC PARTY

America's love–hate relationship with the Craft soon boiled over into a fully-fledged political movement. Masonry had become identified with power and status and was increasingly seen as a corrupt social club for personal advancement. Populist sentiment against what was perceived as elitism was easily stoked, especially by conservative church ministers who disliked the religious philosophy of the Masons. In the 1820s and '30s the anti-Masonic movement, mainly based in the Northeastern States, gave rise to the Anti-Masonic Party, a genuine third force in American politics that was sparked into life by the William Morgan affair of 1826. Morgan (1774–1826) had been preparing to

publish an exposé of the Craft when he disappeared, and Masons were arrested and accused of his abduction and murder. When they were let off with light sentences by a judiciary also thought to be riddled with Masons, there was public outrage. Modern Masons cast doubt on the whole affair, suggesting that Morgan was a crook who ran away to avoid bad debts.

The following year the Anti-Masonic Party was formed, and in 1832 it fielded a candidate for President, William Wirt. Eventually, the party ran out of steam and disbanded in 1843, but not before winning Senate, Congressional and gubernatorial seats. The attacks caused a decline in Masonry, but as it rebounded after the Civil War, so did anti-Masonic alarm, culminating in the presidential campaign of General John Wolcott Phelps in 1880.

## THE TAXIL SWINDLE

The next chapter in anti-Masonry took place back in Europe. The 19th century was a period of complex political and religious tensions, particularly in France where the liberal forces associated with the Revolution contended against the reactionary forces associated with the monarchy, the upper classes and the Catholic Church. The establishment, especially the Church, used anti-

RELIGIOUS, MYSTICAL AND OCCULT SOCIETIES

Masonry as a propaganda weapon against enemies, and the papacy issued several condemnations of Masonry. In 1885 noted pro-Masonic, anti-Catholic writer Leo Taxil, the pseudonym of Gabriel Jogand-Pagès, c.1854–1907, apparently had a change of heart and was reconciled with the Church. He soon began publishing exposés of what he claimed was a secret order within the Freemasons, known as the Palladian Order. He claimed that the Palladians practised debauched Satanism as well as plotting to overthrow all nations and the Catholic Church, and they were led by Albert Pike, the most influential figure

*Fanciful depiction of the fate of William Morgan, menaced by Masons angry at his supposed betrayal. In fact no one knows what happened to Morgan after his disappearance; he may even have faked his own death.*

in American Masonry. According to Taxil, Pike had proclaimed that Lucifer was god, and led the Palladian Order from a base in South Carolina. Taxil's lurid revelations were wildly popular, and he caused even more of a sensation in the 1890s when he began to publish the amazing confessions of Diana Vaughan, Grand Priestess of the Palladian Order, who he claimed was descended from a medieval demon. In 1895 Vaughan published her *Memoirs of an ex-Palladist*, which revealed the obscene worship of Satan and orgies that Palladian Freemasons indulged in. It was a massive bestseller and confirmed the suspicions of anti-Masons everywhere. But in 1897 Taxil revealed it had all been a huge hoax. He had invented Vaughan, the Palladians and the Satanism as a way to test the gullibility of the public and the Catholic Church. Despite his confession, what became known as the Taxil-Schwindel (from the German for 'hoax') is still quoted as fact by anti-Masons today.

## THE PLOT THEORY
## OF HISTORY

The success of the Russian Revolution in 1917, in which the Bolsheviks successfully took over the most autocratic state in Europe, sparked a fresh wave of fear about conspiracies and secret societies. Masons were blamed even though the Communists ruthlessly suppressed Freemasonry.

The woman who did more than anyone to stoke these fears was British fascist Nesta Webster (1876–1960). After a psychotic episode, Webster had come to believe she was the reincarnation of a French aristocrat, and wrote a series of books linking the French Revolution to 'Illuminized Masonry'. Her 1924 book *Secret Societies and Subversive Movements* set out the 'plot theory' of history, claiming that throughout history a Jewish–Satanic–Communist conspiracy had been attempting to destroy Christianity and overthrow civilization. Although she recycled the same lies and distortions as past writers and added many of her own, the book became immensely influential. Her theory was picked up by the Nazis, who persecuted Freemasons as well as Jews and others during the Holocaust, and later by both the Far Left and the Far Right. Modern-day conspiracy theorists still accuse Freemasonry of being a front for the Zionist–Bolshevik–Satanic Illuminati plot to institute the New World Order.

*Lurid cover art for* The Mysteries of Freemasonry, *by 'Leo Taxil', pseudonym of Gabriel Jogand-Pagè. Note the Masons worshipping Baphomet in the background.*

CHAPTER 6
# OCCULT SECRET SOCIETIES

# PATHS TO PERSONAL AND SPIRITUAL DEVELOPMENT

The magic and alchemy practised by the learned men of the 16th and 17th centuries (see page 60) mostly died away with the Scientific Revolution and the Enlightenment, but were not entirely forgotten. A few scholars and eccentrics kept alive what became known as the Western esoteric or Hermetic tradition, passing on the secrets of alchemy, Kabbalah, gematria, Tarot, astrology, mythology and all the other mysteries of the occult. In the late 19th century, these mysteries would flower once more with the creation of new societies centred on the study of the occult.

The term 'occult' is often confused with dark and sinister practices, or at least practices that are deemed to be dark and sinister by mainstream religions and the mainstream media, such as witchcraft, Satanism and necromancy (summoning up the spirits of the dead). In fact, 'occult' simply means 'hidden', and can be used more or less interchangeably with 'esoteric' or 'Hermetic'.

'Magic' is another poorly understood term. Thanks to children's books and

fairy tales, magic is linked in the popular imagination to the ability to shoot fireballs out of your fingertips or turn people into frogs. In fact, there are many different kinds of magic, including religious magic, such as the use of scraps of paper with lines from the Bible or Koran as charms, and folk magic, for example folk remedies for curing warts by rubbing them with a toad.

Occult secret societies that practise magic tend to have a sophisticated and technical view of it as the art and science of effecting change through the exercise of will, by exploiting natural but mysterious and occult connections between things, for instance between the stars and events on Earth, or between elements and diseases. The magic they practise, sometimes known as 'magick', a spelling introduced by Aleister Crowley (see page 194), involves what are known as psychophysical practices – actions, words and thoughts that change the consciousness of the magician to allow him or her to perform magic. Occult secret societies developed elaborate systems of psychophysical practices,

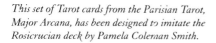

*This set of Tarot cards from the Parisian Tarot, Major Arcana, has been designed to imitate the Rosicrucian deck by Pamela Coleman Smith.*

using regalia, tools such as wands and swords, symbols like the pentagram, preparation and purification routines, incantations, readings, lists of names of beings to invoke and dramatic rituals.

Although magicians practise both white magic (helpful, positive, healing) and black magic (negative, selfish, harmful), the real aim of most occult societies has been personal and spiritual development. According to a modern society, the Ordo Stella Matutina (OSM), 'our mission... is to commit ourselves and others to challenge students to their full learning potentials; to develop each individual's mind, body, and soul; and to inspire students to become productive members of our global society'.

# ELIPHAS LÉVI

The most influential 19th-century writer on magic was French journalist and ex-priest Alphonse Louis Constant (1810–1875), who wrote occult works under the pseudonym Eliphas Lévi. The men and women who would later found occult secret societies all acknowledged their debt to him, both for providing their central theory of magic and for spreading the word about it. Dr William Wynn Westcott, co-founder of the Hermetic Order of the Golden Dawn (HOGD – see pages 184–187), acknowledged that it was 'through his adeptship [training and skill in occult practices] that the occultism has been popularized'. Aleister Crowley considered himself to be the reincarnation of Constant, having been born the same year that the Frenchman died.

## FROM PRIEST TO MAGICIAN

Constant trained as a priest with an unorthodox abbé, who taught a mystical and Gnostic-tinged variety of Catholicism and was deposed as a result. Constant was ordained as a deacon in 1835 but grew disillusioned with seminary life and quit

the priesthood when he fell in love. He spent time dabbling in revolutionary politics while working as a journalist and was in and out of jail. In 1852 he met the visionary Polish mathematician and occultist Józef Hoene-Wroński (1778–1853), who inspired his interest in the occult and in trying to bring together the Western mystery tradition, Christian mysticism and the scientific and rational ideals of the time.

In 1855 Constant published his hugely influential *Dogme et Rituel de la Haute Magie*, later published in English as *Transcendental Magic: Its Doctrine and Ritual*, which pulled together many different streams of occult thought. Taking as his pen-name the Hebrew version of his first two names, Constant combined Kabbalah, Hermeticism, Rosicrucianism and alchemy, linking the cards of the Tarot pack to the secrets of Kabbalah. In the Cabalistic Tree of Life there are 10 *sephiroth* or aspects of God, and these are connected by 22 paths. Constant linked the 22 major arcana of the Tarot to the 22 paths, and developed complex systems of

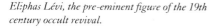

*Eliphas Lévi, the pre-eminent figure of the 19th century occult revival.*

correspondence between these and other aspects of nature and the occult.

Constant lived for a while in London, where he met Edward Bulwer-Lytton (see page 116) and performed a

magical rite summoning the spirit of 1st-century CE sage Apollonius of Tyana. On his return to Paris he lectured on the occult to a growing band of followers, developing a sophisticated philosophy that attempted to reconcile the occult, Christianity and science, with magic as the key to their unification.

# MADAME BLAVATSKY AND THE THEOSOPHICAL SOCIETY

Eliphas Lévi gathered together the many different strands of the Western mystery tradition and produced a working whole from them, but the occult picture was not yet complete. The East had its own mystery traditions, dozens if not hundreds of them, stretching back thousands of years. The 19th century was a time of enthusiasm for all things exotic and ancient, especially if they were Oriental, from the tombs of ancient Egypt to the mystical powers of Indian gurus to the temples of Tibet. One woman was responsible above all others for introducing these elements to the West and for making them part of occult culture: Madame Helena Petrovna Blavatsky (1831–1891), founder of the Theosophical Society.

## FROM RUSSIA WITH LIES

Much of Madame Blavatsky's biography is shrouded in mystery because she made so many extraordinary claims. However, it is believed that Blavatsky, née von Hahn, was born in what is now Ukraine to an aristocratic and literary Russian family, spending parts of her childhood

*Photograph of Russian-born American theosophist, Helena Petrovna Blavatsky 1831-1891. This photograph was taken the same year that she co-founded the Theosophical Society with Henry Olcott.*

at military outposts in remote southern Russia where her grandfather was an administrator. Here she first encountered Tibetan Buddhism, which made a great impact on her, and her esoteric education was further encouraged by reading the library of her great-grandfather, a Rosicrucian Freemason, and by Prince Aleksandr Golitsyn, also a Mason.

After a brief failed marriage in 1849, she travelled to Istanbul and Cairo, and studied with a Coptic magician. She travelled the world in the 1850s and practised psychic gifts that she believed she had demonstrated since childhood. During this period, Blavatsky later claimed, she visited Tibet and studied with 'ascended masters' or Mahatmas, the guardians of ancient wisdom whose esoteric powers made them immortal. These mysterious instructors recall the Unknown Superiors of von Hund (see page 149).

In the 1870s she returned to Cairo and set up shop as a medium and clairvoyant, forming the *Société Spirite* to explore the occult and attract financial support. Accusations of fraud, which would follow her throughout her life, led the *Société* to close and she emigrated to New York in 1873. Here she gained many more followers with her amazing powers, which apparently included clairvoyancy, mediumship, telepathy, levitation and the ability to materialize objects out of nowhere. After another brief marriage she became an American citizen.

## THE THEOSOPHICAL SOCIETY

In New York Blavatsky gained a new disciple, lawyer and journalist Henry Steel Olcott. Olcott, a keen spiritualist (someone who believes in contact with the spirits of the dead), was impressed with Blavatsky's psychic powers and her incredible tales of travels to exotic places and contact with ascended masters. In 1875 Blavatsky began to produce a series of letters, purportedly from these mysterious 'adepts', although some of these were later claimed to be forgeries written by herself. Armed with apparent authority from these adepts, she and Olcott founded the Theosophical Society, to explore the secret esoteric wisdom common to all religions and philosophies.

In 1877 Blavatsky published her first book *Isis Unveiled: A master key to the mysteries of ancient and modern science and theology*. This explored possible links between Old and New World civilizations that proved descent from a common prehistoric civilization, and mixed together Eastern religion

with pseudoscience and occultism. Blavatsky's 1888 book *The Secret Doctrine* explored the popular topic of Atlantis, claiming that her secret masters had taught her the true epic history of human evolution, stretching back millions of years across the lost continents of Atlantis and Lemuria. Apparently, there had been a number of stages in human civilization, with some 'root races' that had been corrupt, evil and degenerate, while others –

*Photograph of Henry Steel Olcott and Helena Petrovna Blavatsky printed in 'Histoire Authentique de la Societe Theosophique' by Olcott, 1908.*

offer a way to combine the increasing power of science, especially Darwin's exciting new theory of evolution, with the timeless truths of religion and philosophy, new revelations about spiritualism (a craze that was sweeping the world), promises of reincarnation and secret wisdom from the Orient. The Society started branches around the world, shifting its headquarters to India, although Blavatsky was caught up in another controversy in 1885 when an investigator for the Society for Psychichal Research concluded that she was a fraud and that the ascended masters did not exist. She left India and moved around, eventually settling in London, where she died in 1891, supposedly gasping as her last words: 'Keep the link unbroken! Do not let my last incarnation be a failure.'

Her influence has been immense, and much of 20th-century New Age thought can be traced back to Blavatsky's Theosophy. Her writings on the occult, human evolution and Atlantis would also be profoundly influential on the darker side of occult secret societies (see pages 198–201).

notably the white-skinned ones – had been noble and wise.

The success of her books and her own personal charisma helped to spread Blavatsky's exotic blend of materials. The Theosophical Society seemed to

# THE HERMETIC ORDER OF THE GOLDEN DAWN

| | |
|---|---|
| TYPE | Occult, mystical, magical |
| EXISTED | 1888–1903 |
| RELATED TO | Freemasonry, Rosicrucians, magical and Hermetic orders |
| GOALS AND CONCERNS | Theory and practice of magic; personal growth through magic; exercise of magical power |

In 1887, London coroner Dr William Westcott (1848–1925) claimed he was browsing a bookstall when he came across a curious manuscript, written in code. In another version of the tale, Westcott claimed to have been given it by a Mason, the Reverend A. Woodford, who had it in turn from 'a dealer in curios'. When Westcott deciphered it, he discovered instructions for rituals of an occult society called the Golden Dawn. Westcott was a Freemason and leading member of the Rosicrucian order *Societas Rosicruciana in Anglia* (Soc Ros or SRIA). Recruiting two other members of the Soc Ros, Dr William Robert Woodman (1828–1891) and Samuel Liddell MacGregor Mathers (1854–1918), he decided to set up his own version of the Golden Dawn, inventing a history for it and getting Mathers to draw up a detailed set of rituals. Together they created a new society that brilliantly synthesized knowledge and traditions from across the ages: the Hermetic Order of the Golden Dawn (HOGD, or simply Golden Dawn).

*Painted symbol of the HOGD, combining motifs of Rosicrucianism (crucified figure with his rose-red heart), alchemy (solar and lunar symbols) and magic, along with sacred names of power and colours corresponding to the four terrestrial elements and the realm of spirit.*

The true author of what is known as the Cipher Manuscript was almost certainly Kenneth Mackenzie, the Masonic scholar who had helped 'interpret' the founding documents of the Soc Ros, which originated in similar circumstances to the HOGD. Just as the Soc Ros had evidently drawn on the traditions and structure of its precursor, the German Order of the Golden and Rosy Cross (OGRC), so the Golden Dawn drew heavily on the Soc Ros.

Within the pages of the Cipher Manuscript, claimed Westcott, he also found a letter apparently giving the name and address of one Fräulein Sprengel, high adept of *Die Goldene Dämmerung*, a German version of the Order referred to in the Manuscript. Contacting Sprengel, Westcott gained authorization to set up a new temple of the Order in England, and in 1888 he duly produced a Charter of Warrant for what he called the Isis-Urania Temple of the HOGD. Isis was an Egyptian goddess who had enjoyed her own mystery cult in ancient times, while Urania was the muse of astronomy/astrology, representing both the natural magic of divination and the spirit of reason. In fact, Westcott had invented Sprengel to lend his creation the authority it needed to attract Masons.

# DAUGHTERS OF
# THE GOLDEN DAWN

| | |
|---|---|
| TYPE | Magical, occult, mystical |
| EXISTED | 1900–present |
| RELATED TO | Hermetic Order of the Golden Dawn |
| GOALS AND CONCERNS | Theory and practice of magic; self-improvement; religious devotion |

In 1897 the authorities learned that Westcott, a respected coroner, was also the Chief Adept of an occult society that practised elaborate ritual magic. He was pressured to resign from the Order he had started, and Mathers, who was by now living in Paris, became the de facto head of the Order. Back in England, however, other highly placed members were charting their own course for the Order, and Mathers and his English deputies soon fell out. In 1900 matters came to a head when the English Golden Dawners refused to admit Aleister Crowley to Adeptus rank after Mathers had backed him. This was followed by a row over the Sprengel letters which had by now been revealed to be forgeries, resulting in Mathers' expulsion.

## ALPHA ET OMEGA AND STELLA MATUTINA

In same year a new Golden Dawn temple, named Alpha et Omega, was founded in London, its members declaring loyalty to the expelled Mathers. In 1903 the Alpha et Omega group officially split from the HOGD to become the first of several 'daughter' societies that spun off that year. A year earlier the official HOGD had been hit by a sex scandal and it split into a group focused on magic, who founded the Stella Matutina Society, and a group more focused on Christian mysticism, led by the esoteric scholar A.E. Waite (1857–1942). Initially, Waite called his new version the Independent and Rectified Rite of the Golden Dawn, but by 1916 it had become the Fellowship of the Rosy Cross.

In 1919 psychotherapist Violet Mary Firth, later known as Dion Fortune (1890–1946), joined the Alpha et Omega temple in London (now under the leadership of Moina Mathers (1865–1928), Macgregor having died the year before. Fortune would go on to become a prolific writer on magic and the esoteric, and in 1922 set up her own society, the Fraternity of the Inner Light. During World War II she and her circle claimed to have fought a magical Battle of Britain alongside the real one, helping to beat off the Nazis through occult workings. Also in 1922, another prominent younger member of the Alpha et Omega, Paul Foster Case (1884–1954), was expelled from the Order and went on to create his own secret society in America, the Builders of the Adytum (in ancient temples, the *adytum* was the inner sanctuary or holy of holies), or BOTA. BOTA is still active in the USA, offering a correspondence course for beginners to learn the theory of the occult, and a group called Pronaos for advanced students wishing to practise actual rituals.

The most prominent member of the Stella Matutina was the writer Israel Regardie (1907–1985), who joined in 1933 and in 1937 began publishing many of the secrets of the HOGD in his four-volume work, *The Golden Dawn*.

*A sketch produced in Paris in 1899, depicting Moina Mathers (1865–1928) in the role of the High Priestess Anari.*

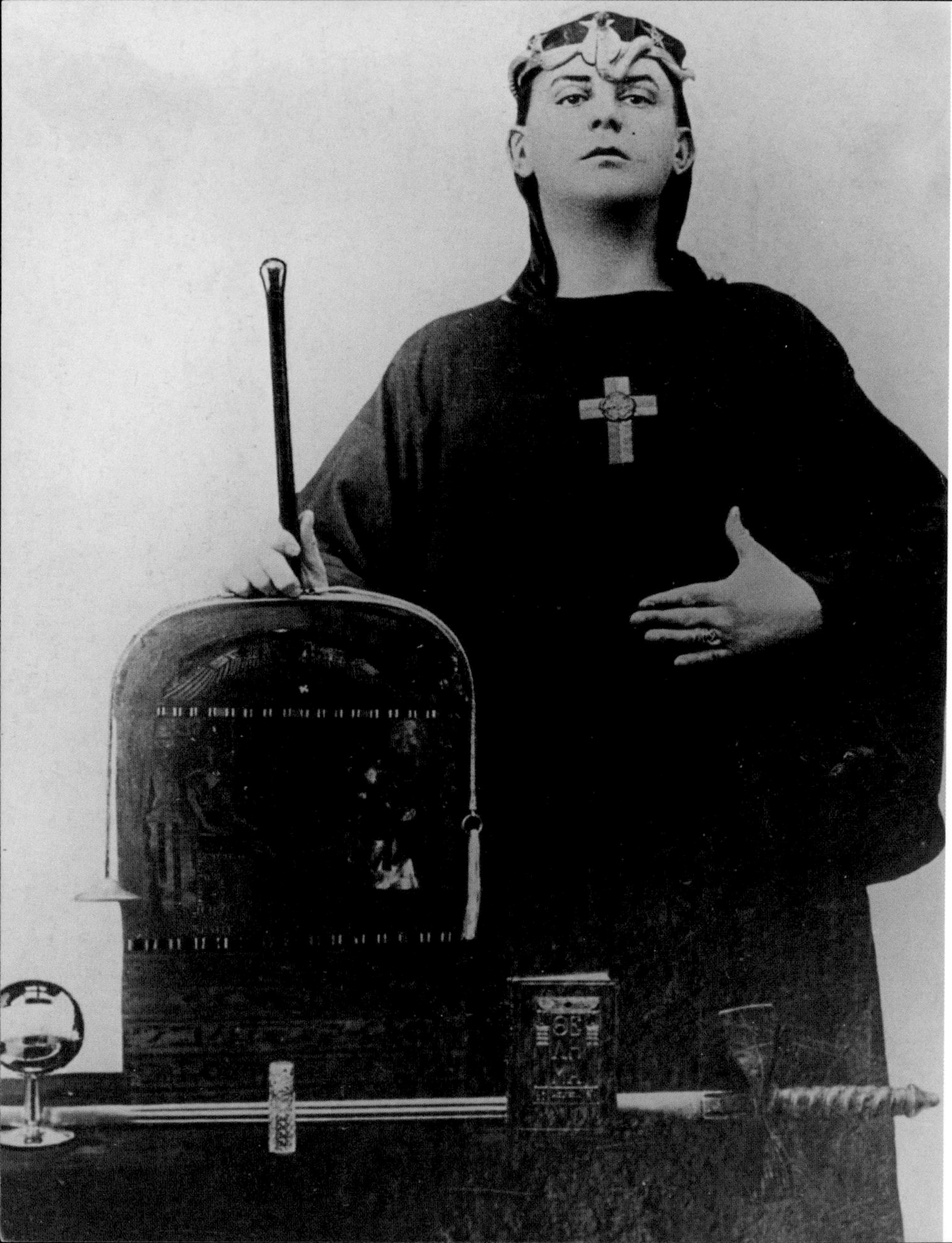

# ALEISTER CROWLEY

Perhaps the most sensational figure in the story of secret societies in the 20th century was English magician, poet, scholar, mountaineer and drug addict Aleister Crowley (born Edward Alexander, 1875–1947). Crowley was important in the history of at least three occult secret societies: the HOGD (see pages 184–187), *Argenteum Astrum* (the Silver Star, or AA) and the *Ordo Templi Orientis* (Order of Oriental Templars, or OTO – see page 196), although only the second of these was founded by him.

## THE GREAT BEAST

Born to wealthy religious fundamentalists, Crowley's dark side emerged early in life, causing his mother to call him the Great Beast – a nickname he became proud of in later life. Intelligent and gifted but also spoiled and wayward, Crowley was studying at Cambridge University when he had a revelation in 1897 that the magical tradition was the only path worth pursuing. At this time he also

*A young Aleister Crowley, dressed for a magical ritual, displaying a variety of occult instruments.*

changed his name to Aleister, dabbled in poetry and came into his inheritance, spending it recklessly.

In 1898 he joined the HOGD, taking the magical name Perdurabo ('I will endure'), and using all his gifts to proceed through the grades with startling speed. Mathers was deeply impressed with the dynamic young man, but the poet W.B. Yeats, another prominent Golden Dawn member, thought that Crowley might be insane. After locking himself away in a Scottish mansion while he attempted to summon his guardian angel in a ritual (known as an evocation) designed by Mathers, Crowley returned to London to insist that the HOGD admit him to the Second Order. London members opposed this, but Mathers supported his young protégée, sparking a crisis that would eventually split the HOGD.

## THE NEW AEON

Crowley meanwhile had lost interest in the Golden Dawn and in 1900 began travelling the world, following the pattern set by Blavatsky and others.

Wandering the Middle and Far East in search of secret teachings, ancient wisdom and enlightenment is a familiar theme throughout the history of secret societies and the mystery tradition, stretching back to Jesus – Christian folklore has him travelling to India and perhaps even as far as Japan – and beyond. In Mexico Crowley took up mountaineering and developed his powers of visualization and concentration, essential skills for performing magic. Using the magical system of Renaissance magus John Dee, Crowley attempted new evocations and came to believe that he was the reincarnation of Edward Kelley, the alchemist and con man who helped Dee with his researches into angels and the occult. It is telling that Crowley identified more with the corrupt and fraudulent Kelley than with Dee himself. In 1902 Crowley made the first attempt to scale K2, the world's second-highest peak, but in later years his mountaineering reputation would suffer when he was accused of leaving members of his party to die in the Himalayas.

In Cairo in 1904, Crowley believed that spirits and gods had dictated supernatural revelations to him, resulting in his *Liber Legis* (*Book of the Law*), and his conviction that he was to usher in a New Aeon of human history, and a new religion that would supersede Christianity, based on what he called the Law of Thelema: 'Do what thou wilt shall be the whole of the Law'. The concept of will is central to the modern practice of magic.

Back in England, Crowley published some of the secret rituals of the HOGD, sparking a feud with Mathers, and in 1909 he founded his own secret society, *Argenteum Astrum*, which he used as a vehicle to explore sex magic. In sex magic the energy of sexuality and the orgasm is used to generate magical power. His exploits attracted the attention of Theodor Reuss, co-founder of the *Ordo Templi Orientis* (Order of Oriental Templars, or OTO), who in 1912 asked him to head up the English branch with which Crowley's name would become closely associated. Around this time Crowley may also briefly have joined the Freemasons.

## THE 'WICKEDEST MAN IN THE WORLD'

By the 1920s Crowley had long since exhausted his inheritance and his remaining decades were increasingly characterized by money troubles and his quest to extract cash from his supporters.

*Aleister Crowley, shown wearing highland dress, with the Scarlet Woman, Alostrael (Leah Hirsig) in 1921. Alostrael is holding their baby, Poupee, who sadly died shortly afterwards.*

He spent World War I in America writing pro-German propaganda, and in 1920 moved to Sicily where he rented a farmhouse and called it the Abbey of Thelema, hoping to attract disciples off whom he could live. Here he practised sex magic and took drugs, but was expelled by the Italian authorities in 1923 after a man died (probably from food poisoning). At this time Crowley was dubbed the 'wickedest man in the world' by the English journal *John Bull*, and he spent the rest of his life as a tabloid hate figure.

The same year saw the death of Reuss, and Crowley appointed himself head of the whole OTO, but this caused a schism in Germany where the OTO divided into pro- and anti-Crowley factions. Back in England, Crowley declined into poverty and drug addiction. But he still managed to spread his Thelemic gospel through overseas branches of the OTO (especially in America) and in a number of influential books, including his 1929 *Magick in Theory and Practice*, and his 1944 *Book of Thoth*, written to accompany a new version of the Tarot he had helped to create. He died in 1947, a heroin addict reduced to living in a boarding house.

## CROWLEY'S MAGICK

Today there are many occult secret societies and thousands of practising

magicians around the world, and many of them use Crowley's system of magick, or variants of it. He introduced the 'k' to distinguish his new brand of magic from the pre-modern versions. In practice, Crowley derived most of his system from the Golden Dawn system created by Macgregor Mathers, which in turn was based on Eliphas Lévi's combination of the elements of the Western mystery tradition, including Rosicrucianism, Hermeticism, alchemy, Kabbalah, Tarot, the writings of Dr Dee and other sources. To this mix Crowley added aspects of the latest psychological theories, such as Freudian psychoanalysis.

Although Crowley has become infamous for his scandalous behaviour, dubious morality and his readiness to play up to the Satanic image painted by the popular press, he was not a Satanist and neither the OTO nor Thelemic magick are Satanic or involved in black masses. In fact, Crowley's esoteric research and writings are still well respected by magicians and scholars alike.

*Portrait of Aleister Crowley as 'The Student' taken from* Equinox *Vol. 1 No. 3, 1910. In the background Egyptian stele can be seen.*

o what thou wilt shall
e the whole of the Law

# ORDO TEMPLI ORIENTIS

| | |
|---|---|
| TYPE | Occult, mystical, magical |
| EXISTED | 1905–present |
| RELATED TO | Freemasonry, Rosicrucians, magical and Hermetic orders |
| GOALS AND CONCERNS | Theory and practice of magic; sex magic; personal development |

Austrian industrialist Carl Kellner (1851–1905) and German journalist and former opera singer Theodor Reuss (1855–1923) were Freemasons with a shared interest in the occult, and particularly in sex magic. Kellner was a member of the Hermetic Brotherhood of Light, an occult secret society that had been founded in America and had probably absorbed some of the teachings of Paschal Beverly Randolph (see pages 120–122), and both men were involved in the Theosophical Society (see pages 181–183). Keen to start an occult society to pass on their secrets to the Masonic elite, they got their rituals and their charter from the head of the esoteric Masonic order, the Rite of Memphis and Misraim. Although they obtained their charter in 1902, the *Ordo Templi Orientis*

(Order of Oriental Templars, or OTO) was not formally founded until 1905, shortly after Kellner had died.

The first OTO lodge was based near Monte Veritas in Switzerland, the headquarters of Europe's avant garde, bohemian community. Members could progress through nine degrees, with the secrets of sex magic reserved for the ninth. When Reuss heard about Aleister Crowley and his secret society *Argenteum Astrum*, he recognized the charismatic figure he needed to attract recruits further afield. Crowley, however, proved to be a divisive figure, attempting to take over the OTO and make it a vehicle for his Thelemic doctrine. He and Reuss ended up running rival branches, and both set up lodges in America, which contended for supremacy. In 1915 Reuss

*Photograph of Theodor Reuss, occultist, journalist and singer, who succeeded Carl Kellner as the leader of the Ordo Templi Orientis (OTO).*

issued a charter to H. Spencer Lewis, who later went on to found the Ancient Mystical Order Rosae Crucis (AMORC – see pages 122–123). Allied to Crowley, Southern California's Agape Lodge flourished briefly in the 1940s under Jack Parsons (see pages 202–205).

After Reuss's death in 1923, Crowley attempted to assert his control over the Order's base in Germany, but succeeded only in provoking a schism, resulting in divisions that still affect the OTO today,

and which have led to court battles. An American branch, known as the Caliphate OTO, was started in the 1970s by Grady Louis McMurty (1918–1985), who visited Crowley briefly in 1943 and claimed to have been handed the succession. Under his leadership it has become one of the largest occult secret societies in the world. Meanwhile, in Britain, Crowley's disciple Kenneth Grant started the Typhonian OTO, which contests the Caliphate supremacy.

RELIGIOUS, MYSTICAL AND OCCULT SOCIETIES

# ORDO NOVI TEMPLI
# AND THE NAZIS

| TYPE | Occult, esoteric, political, mystical |
|---|---|
| EXISTED | 1907–1938 |
| RELATED TO | Neo-Templars, Cistercian order |
| GOALS AND CONCERNS | Perverted chivalric ideals; anti-Semitism; German nationalism; racial purity |

There are many myths and fantasies about the Nazis and the occult. Examples include the belief that Hitler wanted to obtain the Spear of Destiny – the alleged weapon used to pierce the side of Jesus while he was being crucified – for the purposes of dark magic, and that the Nazis used a form of occult energy known as vril to power flying saucers that would emerge from the hollow centre of the Earth at secret polar bases. Myths aside, the occult was important in the formation of the Nazis, both the organization itself and, more importantly, its ideology and mythology.

*Poster advertising a calendar produced by the Nazi's Office of Racial Policy. Aryan fantasies like this were rooted in the pseudoscientific anthropology of Theosophy and its offshoots.*

## ROOT RACES

In the late 19th century, Madame Blavatsky's Theosophical Society popularized the notion that human evolution was a story stretching back millions of years, played out on lost continents like Atlantis and Lemuria, in which 'root races' of humanity engaged in a Darwinian struggle for survival and supremacy. According to her 'root race' theory, physically, morally and spiritually pure races, who were light-skinned, were opposed by corrupt and degenerate races, who were dark-skinned. Ultimately, she argued, the light-skinned races would have to destroy the dark-skinned ones in order to bring about a new dawn for humanity and a new stage in spiritual and psychic evolution. In some versions of this root race theory, the light-skinned races came originally from lost lands in the far north called Hyperborea and Thule. At the same time, Blavatsky tapped into public interest in more recent prehistory. Linguistic and archaeological evidence seemed to show that the Indo-European races could all be traced back to a group of peoples known as the Aryans who had emerged in Central Asia, and she linked this to her claims that ascended masters in Tibet were overseeing human history and development with their advanced psychic gifts.

Meanwhile, in Europe, and particularly in Germanic regions, other cultural forces were developing. In the Masonic community, interest in the Templars was extended to another order of medieval warrior monks, the Teutonic Knights, who had followed a rigidly racist, anti-Semitic code. There was growing interest in the pre-Christian roots of Northern European culture – paganism, the Norse religion and runes – which crystallized into the Volkische Movement, a belief in the oneness and destiny of the Germanic *volk* (folk).

## ARIOSOPHY

Esotericists in Germany combined all these elements into a new mythology called Ariosophy, in which the German *volk* were the inheritors of an ancient tradition going back millions of years to when their ancestors had used occult and psychic powers to battle with degenerate dark-skinned races. Ariosophists believed that the Germanic peoples were still fighting this battle against their enemies the Jews, who in turn had engineered a vast, history-spanning conspiracy to conquer the planet.

Jörg Lanz (1874–1954) was a leading Ariosophist, a former Cistercian monk kicked out of his order for 'surrender to the lies of the world and carnal love', according to a register in Heiligenkreuz

OCCULT SECRET SOCIETIES

Abbey, who added the suffix 'von Liebenfels' to his name to make it more aristocratic. He developed a bizarre version of this Theosophical history of humanity, claiming that the ancient mystery cults had perverted humanity through deviant sex with degenerate dwarf races, but that the Aryan races could recapture their ancient psychic and occult birthright. In 1907 von Liebenfels started a secret society, the *Ordo Novi Templi* (Order of the New Temple, or ONT) to restore the traditions of the lost medieval orders and create a sort of Aryan religious order. Based in a castle, members of the Order followed a monastic-style rule, with hymns and prayers, and advanced through the hierarchy according to tests of racial purity.

Von Liebenfels also helped to start the Guido von List Society, a fan club for the work of the eponymous Germanic novelist and mystic (1848–1919). List had developed an alternative history in which an ancient Germanic caste of priest-kings known as the Armanen had passed on their secret knowledge through the Templars, Rosicrucians and Freemasons. In 1908 the von List Society gave rise to the super-secret *Höhere Armanen-Orden* (Higher Armanen Order), which shared most of its members with the ONT and explored occult aspects of Aryan and *volkische* ideology.

## THE THULE SOCIETY

Another Ariosophist secret society, the *Germanenorden* (Order of Germans), was founded in 1912 by right-wing anti-Semites who believed the best way to counter the supposed Jewish conspiracy was to launch a counter-conspiracy. In 1917 the Munich lodge of the *Germanenorden* set up the *Thule-Gesellschaft*, or Thule Society. It was claimed that this Society, named after the mythical northern homeland of the Aryans, was a scholarly study society, but it helped to raise a militia force to support the fascist aims of the *Germanenorden*. In 1919 members of the Thule Society set up a new party, the *Deutsche Arbeiterpartei*, and the following year, under the direction of its new leader Adolf Hitler, it was renamed as the *National Sozialistische Deutsche Arbeiterpartei*, or the Nazi Party. Although he was not thought to have been an actual member of any of the occult secret societies, Hitler was an associate of the Thule Society and an avid reader of the journal of the ONT, and was heavily influenced by Ariosophy and the occult societies. Ironically, the Nazis forced the closure of all secret societies when they came to power.

*Hubert Lanzinger's allegorical 'Der Bannerträger' (The Standard Bearer) portrait of 1938, showing Hitler as an armoured knight in the Teutonic tradition.*

# JACK PARSONS AND
# THE AGAPE LODGE

A strange chapter in the history of secret societies in America was the extraordinary story of Jack Parsons (1914–1952), rocket engineer and magician. Parsons helped invent the technology that took man to the Moon and powered the missiles of America's nuclear arsenal. He was also a practising magician who headed an *Ordo Templi Orientis* (Order of Oriental Templars, or OTO) lodge (see page 196), engaged in magical battle with foes and claimed to have summoned a deity who would usher in the New Aeon of Thelema.

## ROCKET MAN

Parsons grew up in Pasadena, California, where he pursued twin childhood interests – reading fantasy and blowing things up. After working with an explosives company and becoming expert at mixing his own explosives, he joined up with rocket scientists from the nearby California Institute for Technology to design and test real rocket engines. In 1939 he helped to develop rockets – or jets – that would help aeroplanes to take off from

shorter runways, and after America joined World War II he and his colleagues founded the Jet Propulsion Laboratory (JPL), which became the world's premier research institute for rocketry and space exploration. Parsons personally pioneered development of the solid rocket fuel used in space shuttle booster rockets and nuclear missiles such as Polaris.

In 1939 Parsons was taken along to a Thelemic Mass – a theatrical ceremony with religious and Masonic elements – at the Agape Lodge of the OTO, then in Los Angeles. He had been interested in magic and the occult since reading fairy tales as a boy, and later he had attempted to develop psychic powers and read widely on esoteric topics including at least one book by Aleister Crowley (see page 192). After initial hesitation, Parsons and his wife joined the OTO in 1941, and he quickly became deeply involved in the bohemian lifestyle of parties, drugs and sex centred on the Agape Lodge (named after the Greek word for 'divine love').

## BLACK MAGICK WOMAN

Charismatic and good-looking, with a successful career in rocketry, Parsons was an exciting figure. Crowley, overseeing matters from London,

*Jack Parsons (far right) and other members of the 'Suicide Squad' of rocket pioneers with one of their early test rockets, in 1936.*

realized that his new recruit could help to bring in many more (along with their money), and in 1942 made Parsons the head of the Agape Lodge. The rocketeer moved the Lodge into his mansion in Pasadena, setting up a 1960s-style counterculture commune years ahead of its time. He also plunged deeper into the world of sex, drugs and magick, leaving

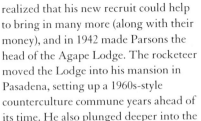

his wife for her much younger sister and practising challenging and disturbing spells with strange results. It was claimed, for instance, that Parsons had to chase away an evil brown cloud with a sword.

His lifestyle was affecting his rocket career – at rocket launch tests he would sing and dance the 'Hymn to Pan', written by Crowley, while the drugs and late nights made him erratic. In 1944 he was forced out of the JPL and turned his attention entirely to magick, attempting more and more complex and dangerous 'workings' with his new accomplice, science-fiction writer L. Ron Hubbard (1911–1986), who had come to live in the commune. Parsons wrote to Crowley that Hubbard was 'the most Thelemic person I have ever met and is in complete accord with our own principles', but Crowley thought they were performing black magick beyond their abilities.

In 1945 Parsons and Hubbard went to the Mojave Desert to perform a long and difficult 'elemental working', intended to summon an elemental being

*American religious leader and science-fiction novelist L. Ron Hubbard, who founded the controversial Church of Scientology, outside his home in East Grinstead, England, in the 1960s.*

in human form, and when they got back to the Lodge an exotic redhead, Marjorie 'Candy' Cameron, was waiting for them. Parsons believed he had succeeded, and moved on to the even more challenging 'Babalon working', his attempt to summon the deity Babalon, whose arrival would usher in the New Aeon on Thelema. Eventually, he claimed to have succeeded, believing that somewhere in the world the Babalon child had been born.

By this time, however, Hubbard had betrayed him, running off with his money and his girl. Parsons chased them to Miami, where they had sailed away on a yacht, and cast a spell that he claimed caused a storm and blew Hubbard's mast off. Nonetheless, Parsons had lost all his money, while Hubbard went on to found Scientology, claimed by some to have many of the attributes of a secret society, and became a millionaire. After this Parsons declined into mental illness and poverty, picking up prostitutes to engage in sex magick as he attempted to gain the OTO grade of Master of the Temple. In 1952, reduced to working for a special effects company, he died in an accident in a makeshift laboratory in his garage. The OTO in America was not revived until Grady McMurty arrived on the scene in the late 1960s (see page 197).

# THE ORDER OF
# THE SOLAR TEMPLE

| | |
|---|---|
| TYPE | **Mystical, occult, esoteric** |
| EXISTED | **1984–1997** |
| RELATED TO | **Neo-Templars, Ancient Mystical Order Rosae Crucis** |
| GOALS AND CONCERNS | **New Age; eco-apocalypse** |

Notorious for the mass suicide/murder of 72 of its current and former members, the Order of the Solar Temple – in French the *Ordre du Temple Solaire*, or OTS – was a neo-Templar order that combined the occult with an apocalyptic eco-mysticism. Also known simply as the Solar Temple, the OTS could trace its descent from the 19th-century neo-Templar Bernard-Raymond Fabré-Palaprat (see page 88).

## THE NEO-TEMPLAR LINE

Fabré-Palaprat was a French physician and high-level Mason who argued that since the Templars predated the Freemasons, neo-Templars should not simply be side degrees of Masonry, but independent and superior organizations. His Order of the Temple, founded in

1804, even gained the blessing of Napoleon. After his death there were many schisms and splinter groups, but the Order lived on until 1932 when it became the Sovereign and Military Order of the Temple of Jerusalem. This is just one of the many neo-Templar groups descended from or inspired by Fabré-Palaprat's Templars. In the 1990s there were more than 30 such groups. Many of them mixed cod-medieval chivalry with fascist politics, anti-Semitism and pseudo-historical mysticism, in similar fashion to the *Ordo Novi Templi* (Order of the New Temple, or ONT) and the Ariosophists of pre-Nazi Germany (see pages 198–200). In the post-World War II era, their anti-communist stance also meant that they received tacit approval and even support

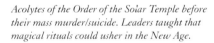

*Acolytes of the Order of the Solar Temple before their mass murder/suicide. Leaders taught that magical rituals could usher in the New Age.*

from Western security and intelligence services (see P2, or Propaganda Due, pages 318–319).

One such right-wing neo-Templar society was the Renewed Order of the Temple (ORT), founded in 1970 and led by French fascist Julien Origas (1920–1983). Belgian doctor and homeopath Luc Jouret (1947–1994) joined the ORT in 1981 and on Origas's death in 1983 he tried to take over as Grand Master, but was kicked out. Before becoming involved in the world of occult secret societies, Jouret was an

important New Age figure – a popular lecturer on homeopathy and spiritual healing. He had built up a following in Montreal, Canada, and Geneva, Switzerland, where he had spoken at the Golden Way Foundation, a New Age organization founded by French watchmaker Joseph Di Mambro (1924–1994), himself a former member of the Ancient Mystical Order Rosae Crucis (AMORC – see pages 122–123).

When Jouret was expelled from the ORT, he and Di Mambro decided to set up a neo-Templar order of their own. That same year Jouret had set up Club Archédia, a New Age secret society, and in 1984 Jouret and Di Mambro drew on the Archédia membership to form their new order, the OTS, which combined New Age and occult concerns in what would prove to be a fatal cocktail.

## THE NEW DIMENSION

The OTS believed in the coming of the New Age, and practised meditation, occult rituals and pseudo-religious ceremonies to help bring it about. Jouret and Di Mambro taught that ascended masters, called the Great White Brotherhood of Sirius – a concept borrowed from Blavatsky's Theosophists (see pages 181–183) – could be invoked through occult rituals, and that members of the group would give birth to messianic cosmic children. The group used some of the trappings of Masonic and Golden Dawn ceremonies, including swords and neo-Templar regalia.

By 1989 the OTS had 442 members, but then things began to go wrong. Members left and demanded back money they had given to the group, and Jouret's teachings took on a darker tone. The Earth would soon become uninhabitable due to pollution, and the Order would use its powers to escape to a higher dimension. One of the suicide notes they would leave explained, 'With a clear mind do we leave this Earth for a Dimension of Truth and Perfection. There, away from obstruction, hypocrisy and hostility, we shall give birth to the seed of our future Creation.'

Preparing for the apocalypse, Jouret made contact with survivalist groups and acquired guns, leading to trouble with the Canadian police; in 1993 he pleaded guilty to firearms offences. In 1994 he and Di Mambro decided to act; members of the Order would commit suicide to ascend to the next dimension, and those who were reluctant would be 'helped' – murdered. At the same time they would take revenge on some who had left the order, particularly Nicki Dutoit and her husband, who had conceived a child against Jouret's orders, a child he believed was the Antichrist.

On 3 October 1994, two members of the Order murdered the Dutoit family at a house in Canada and then killed themselves. Back in Switzerland, 22 people were found dead in a farmhouse, 18 of them arranged like wheel spokes, radiating out from a triangular altar, and 25 more bodies were found in two chalets on 25 October. Of the 52 dead, 37 had been murdered. In 1995, on the winter solstice, 16 more people were killed, and finally on 22 March 1997, the spring solstice, five more, all in Quebec, Canada.

*This burned document is the last note written by Joseph di Mambro. It was found during the investigation into the Solar Temple murder-suicides of 1994.*

OCCULT SECRET SOCIETIES

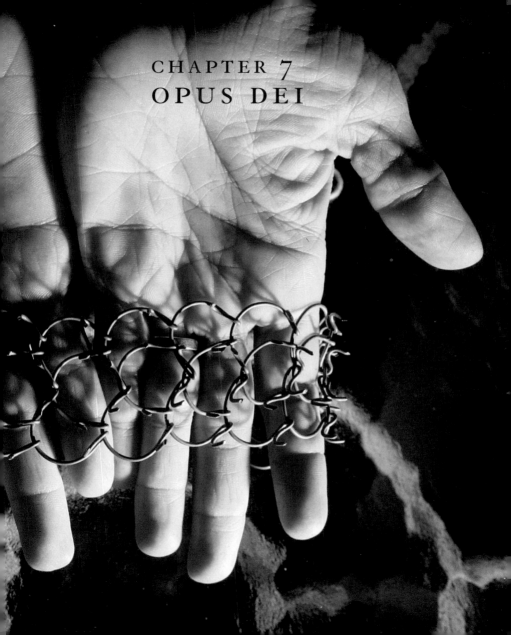

CHAPTER 7
OPUS DEI

# OPUS DEI — AN INTRODUCTION

| | |
|---|---|
| TYPE | Religious, political |
| EXISTED | 1928–present |
| RELATED TO | No direct connections to other secret societies |
| GOALS AND CONCERNS | Religious observance; building power base within Catholic Church; anti-communism; neo-feudal agenda |

Opus Dei, meaning 'God's work', is a Catholic lay order, a transnational organization within the Catholic Church that answers only to the Pope and to its own leaders. Its opponents and conspiracy theorists claim that it is a sinister cult or secret society dedicated to furthering a right-wing political and religious agenda through building up an international network of highly placed individuals in business, politics and other areas of life. The latter are thought to be brainwashed into complete subservience to the fundamentalist, fascist and misogynist principles of the organization's founder, Saint Josemaria Escrivá. According to Opus Dei itself, however, it is not a cult or a secret society, merely a harmless lay order devoted to enhancing the holiness of life in the secular world, and in particular to attaining divine perfection (what the organization calls 'saintliness') in work. Opus Dei mainly recruits professionals and encourages them to follow the group's conservative values in their personal and business lives.

## DIVINE REVELATION

Opus Dei was founded in 1928 when Josemaria Escrivá de Balaguer (1902–1975) had a divine revelation about the relationship between work and holiness, summed up by the verse in Genesis that says that God created man 'in order that he might work'. He felt called to establish an organization that would help laypeople to sanctify themselves through the 'perfect performance' of their daily work. Critics

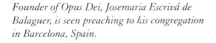

*Founder of Opus Dei, Josemaria Escrivá de Balaguer, is seen preaching to his congregation in Barcelona, Spain.*

of Escrivá claim that his organization is really the result of his experiences in the Spanish Civil War (1936–1939), when he was exposed to anti-Catholic outrages by the Socialists and became a right-wing anti-communist extremist with fantasies of restoring a quasi-feudal order in society. At first the Church regarded Opus Dei simply as a lay society, but later it became a 'personal prelature' of the pope, a unique privilege that exempted it from oversight by any diocese or national body, recalling the favoured status of the Templars before their fall.

Although it was founded in 1928, the organization only came to prominence in the 1950s. From Spain Opus Dei spread to Latin America and around the world, growing to 87,000 members worldwide, 30,000 in Latin America. Of these, 98 per cent are laypeople, not ordained priests, although some of these lay members take vows of poverty, chastity and obedience, and sign over all their possessions to Opus Dei.

213

# THE STRUCTURE OF OPUS DEI

Part of the appeal of Opus Dei is that it recognizes that some people want to be deeply religious without giving up their secular lives, especially their families and careers. Critics claim that this is because the creed of Opus Dei is essentially one of reactionary capitalist elitism, a sort of ministry to the rich and powerful, where money and status will get you into heaven.

## NUMERARIES AND SUPERNUMERARIES

The prelature is organized into four grades, or 'apostolic vocations'. The highest grade is numeraries – highly educated laypeople or priests (they must have a degree) who take vows of poverty, chastity and obedience and give all their money and earnings to Opus Dei. The numeraries run Opus Dei operations, and live in Opus Dei centres, which are strictly segregated by gender. Less-educated people who wish to dedicate their lives to the prelature take similar vows, but can only become associate numeraries. These are generally women, who do all the cooking, cleaning and

clerical work at the Opus Dei centres. Most of the membership is made up of supernumeraries, generally highly educated, successful professionals who take certain vows and follow Opus Dei rules on living and family – very conservative, traditional rules. Finally there are 'co-operators', sympathetic people who are not fully paid-up members. Interestingly, the organization of the prelature parallels that of the Knights Templar.

Critics of Opus Dei claim that not only is its organization deeply sexist and misogynistic but that it is also domineering and authoritarian. Supposedly, Opus Dei centres are run with an iron hand, and associate members can be intimidated and even beaten. This attitude is blamed on Escrivá himself, who was said to have been a fanatical misogynist and a control freak. The prelature seeks to control the thinking of its members, opponents say, pointing to the writings of Escrivá where he appears to order members to be dishonest: 'Do not reveal the secrets of your [apostolic vocation], for the world is

full of selfish incomprehension... I cannot stress enough the importance of discretion...', and warns: 'You shall not buy books without the advice of an experienced Christian.' Critics also say that the hierarchical structure of the organization reflects its right-wing, almost neo-feudal agenda, aimed at maintaining a rigidly stratified social order where everyone knows their place.

*Seminarians come from dioceses all over the world to attend prayer meetings in the Chapel of Opus Dei's seminary 'Sedes Sapientiae'.*

# OPUS DEI — A SECRET SOCIETY?

Conspiracy theorists claim that Opus Dei is effectively a secret society because it conceals its aims, membership, activities, wealth and influence. There is no question that donations by its wealthy supernumeraries and the acquisition of the property of its numeraries has made it stupendously wealthy. But hostile conspiracy theorists say that it has also been involved in shady dealings with the Vatican bank and the laundering of money from organized crime and shady authoritarian regimes and dictators, especially in South America. Meanwhile, critics accuse the prelature of brainwashing people into joining their cult, and point out that Opus Dei has set up schools all over the world to promote its doctrines.

The inclusion of a murderous Opus Dei monk in Dan Brown's 2003 novel *The Da Vinci Code* was responsible for spreading what the prelature argues are myths and gross misrepresentations. For instance, there are no monks in the organization because it is not a monastic order, and it completely refutes claims that it would break the law, let alone murder people. However, mortification – the use of a spiked band called a cilice worn around the thigh and self-flagellation – is a practice recommended by Opus Dei, although it claims that only a very few people actually use this and that it is a perfectly respectable religious observance.

## RIGHT-WING CONSPIRACY

The most serious charge levelled at Opus Dei is that it exists to promote a covert fascist agenda, and there is considerable evidence for this claim. Although at first the fascist authorities in Spain under General Franco were suspicious of Escrivá and his organization, it later became closely allied with it, so that Opus Dei became known as Franco's 'Holy Mafia'. Escrivá's writings suggest that he was an ultra-conservative fundamentalist with fascistic tendencies, and he was obsessed with the crusade against communism. A disgruntled ex-Opus Dei member once accused him of having said, 'Hitler against the Jews, Hitler against the Slavs, this means Hitler against communism.'

In the 1950s Opus Dei members were key ministers in Franco's government and were responsible for the economic modernization of the country. They remained the major force in government until 1973. In Latin America Opus Dei became closely associated with right-wing dictatorships, and even today it wields great influence in the region; supernumeraries include captains of industry, politicians and judges. The failed coup attempt against Venezuelan

*A cilice is a barbed wire-like chain worn around the upper thigh for two hours each day, except for Church feast days, Sundays and certain times of the year. The wearing of the cilice is a particularly controversial practice for Opus Dei, a situation not helped by the lurid portrayal of the masochistic Opus Dei member in* The Da Vinci Code.

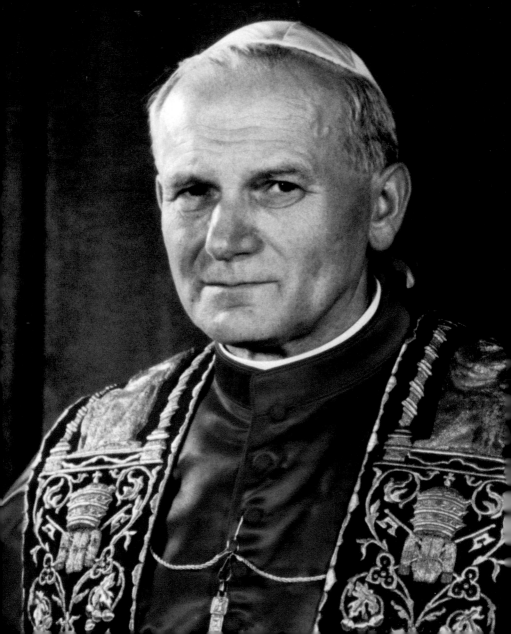

President Hugo Chávez in 2003 was led by an Opus Dei member, and the Ecuadorian military coup d'etat of 2000 was supposedly orchestrated by Opus Dei members. In Spain Opus Dei members control banks and radio stations and run schools, while in Britain and the USA they have included cabinet ministers, Supreme Court judges and FBI heads.

Critics say that Opus Dei has also become disproportionately powerful in the Catholic Church, partly thanks to its close relationship with the former Archbishop of Cracow, Karol Wojtyla, who later became Pope John Paul II. Wojtyla had effectively become a 'co-operator' thanks to the *Centro Romano di Incontri Sacerdotali*, an organization set up by Escrivá in Rome with the specific aim of communicating Opus Dei's agenda to leading members of the Church hierarchy. Conspiracy theorists claim that Pope John Paul II, a staunch opponent of communism thanks to his experiences in Poland and the attempt on his life organized by the Bulgarian secret service, used Opus Dei to help broker a massive loan to the anti-communist Polish trade union Solidarity,

*Pope John Paul II in 1979, shortly after his ordination. As Archbishop of Cracow he had been drawn into the 'orbit' of Opus Dei via their Roman operation, and as pope he would show the group special favour.*

and that as a reward he fast-tracked Escrivá to canonization. The Opus Dei founder became a saint just 27 years after his death – a remarkably short time.

## GOD'S BANKER

Perhaps the most far-fetched conspiracy theory linked with Opus Dei concerns the mysterious death of Roberto Calvi, known as 'God's banker' because of his financial dealings with the Vatican. Calvi was the chairman of Banco Ambrosiano, and according to conspiracy theorists he was involved with the Mafia, Licio Gelli's P2, or Propaganda Due (see pages 318–319) and embezzlement on a massive scale. Although he was briefly jailed in 1981, he was freed pending an appeal, and the following June he was found hanging from London's Blackfriar's Bridge, his pockets stuffed with bricks, murdered with what looked like Masonic symbolism. According to one elaborate theory, Opus Dei were engaged in a Vatican power struggle with P2 and plotted to smear their Masonic rivals by luring Calvi to London, turning him over to Mafia enforcers intent on punishing him for stealing their money, and arranging for the Masonic symbolism. With P2 out of the way, Opus Dei were free to consolidate their role as the power behind the papal throne.

# PRIORY OF SION

| | |
|---|---|
| TYPE | Mystical, esoteric, political, fraternal |
| EXISTED | 1956–present |
| RELATED TO | Ancient Mystical Order Rosae Crucis, neo-Templars |
| GOALS AND CONCERNS | Right-wing, monarchist agenda; pseudo-historical hoax; personal aggrandisement |

The incredible tale of the Priory of Sion has become famous thanks to Dan Brown's massive bestseller *The Da Vinci Code* (2003). The novel tells of a secret society that has operated, in one form or another, since the 7th century CE and which has been the force behind the Cathars, Templars, Rosicrucians and Freemasons. It has supposedly sought to protect from ruthless suppression by the Catholic Church the explosive secret at the heart of Christianity: that Jesus married Mary Magdalene and had children, and that the patriarchal, authoritarian faith of the papacy is a perversion of the true faith – worship of the feminine divine, or the Goddess. Brown's version of the Priory of Sion differs slightly from the story outlined in one of his sources, the non-fiction work

*The Holy Blood and the Holy Grail* (1982), by Henry Lincoln, Michael Baigent and Richard Leigh, which in turn is different from the legend of the Priory of Sion according to the man at the centre of the mystery, Pierre Plantard (1920–2000).

## RETURN OF THE KING

Plantard claimed that although the Merovingian dynasty of the Dark Age kings of France had been cheated of the throne by their palace stewards, who went on to found the Carolingian line, the Merovingian line had lived on. The Priory of Sion was a secret society formed in 1099 in Jerusalem by the Crusader King Godefroy de Bouillon

*The crusader, Godefroy de Bouillon duc de Lorraine, who later became King of Jerusalem.*

(c.1060–1100), pledged to protect the descendants of the Merovingian kings from their enemies the Carolingians. The Priory in turn had founded the Knights Templar as a military wing, and for a while the Grand Master of the Templars was also the Nautonnier ('Navigator') of the Priory. In 1188 the two organizations fell out, and their leadership diverged.

Plantard claimed that the Priory had safeguarded the underground stream of esoteric wisdom in the West, occult secrets that pointed to the future fulfilment of Nostradamus's prophecy that a Great King would one day take the throne of France. He further claimed that his family motto, *Et in Arcadia ego*, was a clue that had also been incorporated by the 17th-century French painter Nicolas Poussin into a picture of an ancient tomb, which pointed to the real tomb of one of the secret Merovingian dynasty, located near Rennes-le-Château in southern France. The last remaining descendant of this dynasty, and the true heir to the throne of France, was none other than Plantard himself.

Proof that this incredible tale was true was said to be found in the French

*Leonardo da Vinci, after a self-portrait. Da Vinci has been widely linked with secret societies and historical mysteries, including the Turin Shroud and the Holy Grail.*

national archives at the Bibliothèque Nationale in Paris, in the form of the *Dossier Secrets d'Henri Lobineau* (*Secret Files of Henri Lobineau*), documents that listed the Grand Masters of the Priory since 1188. The list included many of the most significant names in esoteric/occult history, including alchemists Nicolas Flamel and Robert Fludd, Johann Valentin Andreae of Rosicrucian fame (see pages 103–105), Leonardo da Vinci and Isaac Newton, and French artistic and literary figures including Claude Debussy, Victor Hugo and Jean Cocteau. The last name on the list was, of course, Pierre Plantard. Further proof took the form of medieval parchments supposedly discovered by the parish priest of Rennes-le-Château, Bérenger Saunière, in 1896, linking the Priory of Sion to the mystery of Rennes (see pages 228–229). These parchments contained encrypted clues that led Saunière to uncover the secret of the Priory, which he used to blackmail the Bourbon dynasty of France and become rich.

## THE HOLY BLOOD AND THE HOLY GRAIL

The story of the Priory, the secret Merovingian bloodline and the mystery of Rennes appeared in a 1967 book *L'Or de Rennes* (*The Treasure of Rennes*) by Plantard and Gérard de Sède

(1921–2004), which in turn inspired a series of TV documentaries by Henry Lincoln, co-author of *The Holy Blood and the Holy Grail*. Lincoln added new elements to the story: the real treasure of Rennes – the secret that the Priory had been set up to protect and the true identity of the Holy Grail – was the bloodline of Jesus. According to this version, Jesus had married Mary Magdalene and had a family, and this family had moved to the South of France where they gave rise to the Merovingian dynasty of kings.

The existence of Jesus's biological heirs was a threat to the power and legitimacy of the papacy and the Catholic Church, which depended on the apostolic succession (according to which Jesus had entrusted Peter and his successors with rule of the Church). As a result the Church had attempted to suppress the secret of the holy bloodline and destroy the heirs of Jesus and all those who preserved the secret and protected the bloodline, including the Cathars, Templars and other Gnostic and esoteric groups throughout history.

Meanwhile, the Priory had been working to oppose the Church and prepare for the revelation of the secret, which would usher in a new era in which a sacred Merovingian pope-king would sit on the throne of a theocratic

United Europe. Supposedly, the Priory had created the Rosicrucians, Freemasons and Illuminati to allow it to achieve this.

To prove his argument, Lincoln used the *Dossier Secrets* in the Bibliothèque Nationale and the medieval documents uncovered by Saunière, together with many other clues hidden in the works of Nicolas Poussin and Leonardo da Vinci. At first Plantard went along with the 'expanded' theory and hinted that he might well be the descendant of Jesus, but later he and Lincoln fell out and in 1989 Plantard presented a new aspect to the mystery of Rennes. He claimed that the secret was nothing to do with Jesus or the Merovingians, but actually concerned the occult secrets of geomancy – earth magic – and the harnessing of mystic energies from the landscape around Rennes, in particular a mountain called Rocco Negro, where he owned land.

When Dan Brown came to write *The Da Vinci Code*, he added another dimension to the story, claiming in a preface that his version was factually true. In Brown's version, the Priory of Sion is a mystery cult preserving ancient Gnostic and esoteric secrets, including suppressed gospels, the true identity of Mary Magdalene and the

fact that goddess worship, or at least worship of the feminine principle, was central to the very earliest and truest form of Christianity. He suggested that the Church, and more recently Opus Dei in particular, had been attempting to suppress these 'feminist theology' revelations, revelations that were encoded in some of the works of Leonardo da Vinci, particularly his *The Last Supper* mural, in which the figure conventionally said to be the apostle John is actually a heavily pregnant Mary Magdalene.

*Leonardo da Vinci's mural* The Last Supper, *painted between 1495 and 1498. According to* The Holy Blood, Holy Grail/*Dan Brown school of thought, the figure to the left of Jesus, leaning away from him, commonly identified as the apostle John, is actually a pregnant Mary Magdalene.*

# THE TREASURE OF
# RENNES-LE-CHÂTEAU

RELIGIOUS, MYSTICAL AND OCCULT SOCIETIES

Rennes-le-Château, normally shortened to Rennes, is a village in the Aude province of France, in the foothills of the Pyrenees, in what used to be Cathar territory. Thanks to the success of books like *L'Or de Rennes*, *The Holy Blood and the Holy Grail* and many others, Rennes is now a major tourist destination, attracting tens of thousands of visitors every year to a community with a population of little more than 100.

In 1896 the local priest, Bérenger Saunière (1852–1917), began spending large amounts of money, even though his was an impoverished parish. The church was expensively renovated and redecorated at his expense, and he had a large villa built on land that he acquired, complete with a tower to hold his library. He took up expensive hobbies, threw parties and travelled to Paris, where he mingled with influential figures in politics, culture and the occult. This display of extravagance caused problems with the Church authorities, and he was suspended, but he refused to leave Rennes, where he stayed until his death in 1917.

In the 1950s rumours began to circulate that the key to Saunière's sudden wealth was that he had discovered something hidden within an ancient pillar in his church, something that led him to a Visigothic treasure trove (the Visigoths were a Germanic tribe who had occupied the area at the end of the Roman era). The publication of *L'Or de Rennes* in 1967 added new elements to the tale. The priest had supposedly discovered medieval parchments hidden within the pillar, and once their clues, riddles and cryptograms were solved, they led Saunière to the discovery of the Priory of Sion and the secret of the Merovingian bloodline.

Later books added even more elements to the mystery of Rennes, which is now said to be riddled with tunnels (some of them dug by latter-day treasure hunters) and surrounded by a sacred landscape that may conceal anything from the Ark of the Covenant to the Holy Grail.

In fact, the mystery of Rennes started off as a gigantic hoax. Saunière made his money by illegally selling

masses and was suspended as a result, dying in poverty. The legends were started by restaurateur and pulp-fiction writer Noël Corbu, as a means of attracting visitors to his restaurant in Saunière's old villa, and later attracted the attentions of Plantard and his ring of hoaxers.

*Magdala Tower at Rennes-le-Chateau, a folly built by Abbé Saunière to house his collections of books and stamps. Its name, location and structure have become part of the Rennes mystery/legend.*

229

# TRUE ORIGINS OF
# THE PRIORY OF SION

Despite the claims of Dan Brown that the Priory of Sion is a real secret society, it has been conclusively proven to be a hoax, a bogus secret society created by Pierre Plantard in the 1950s. Plantard himself turns out to have been a convicted con man, a wartime collaborator with reactionary, right-wing, anti-Semitic politics and fantasies about his royal roots.

Just as in Germany the occult tradition merged with fantasies about a mythical history of noble warriors and a strong streak of anti-Semitism, giving rise to Ariosophy and violent fascism, so in France similar forces were at work. Conspiracy theories about the Freemasons, the Jews and the overthrow of the monarchy in the French Revolution blended with occult and neo-Templar fantasies. Plantard was part of this tradition. During World War II he was a collaborator with the German invaders and their puppet Vichy government, and tried to start a number of right-wing action groups to spread his conservative Catholic, pro-monarchist and anti-Semitic politics, including a

quasi-Masonic group called Alpha Galates. He also studied literature from the Ancient Mystical Order Rosae Crucis (AMORC – see pages 122–123), probably including the list of supposed 'Imperators' or Grand Masters of AMORC since the Middle Ages, which he later appropriated for his list of Priory 'Nautonniers'.

## CREATING THE PRIORY

After the war Plantard was briefly sent to jail for selling entry to the degrees of his esoteric order, and later moved to the small town of Annemasse in the Rhône Alps. It was here in 1956 that he and a few friends officially incorporated a new secret society, the Priory of Sion, named after Mount Sion, a hill near the town. Officially, the new secret society was founded as a fraternal order for mutual support, but its real concerns were local politics (specifically the issue of low-cost housing) and Plantard's fantasies about lost ideals of esotericism and chivalry.

*Berenger Saunière (1852–1917), played a central role in Plantard's elaborate fantasies about the Priory of Sion.*

Plantard's parents were both servants, but he had invented for himself an aristocratic background, complete with a family motto, later elaborating it to include Merovingian descent.

The Priory of Sion was not successful and Plantard spent more time in jail in the late 1950s for abuse of minors. In the 1960s he revived the Priory and decided to create a romantic Legend of Perpetuation for it. He had read about a real-life Order or Abbey of Zion, a religious order created during the Crusades and based on Mount Zion

near Jerusalem until 1291, when the Abbey was destroyed by the Saracens. The Order eventually petered out in Sicily in the 14th century. Plantard claimed that this real monastic order was the same as his recent invention, and, after meeting Noël Corbu, the owner of Saunière's old villa, he added the mystery of Rennes to the mix.

To lend credibility to his story, he recruited a friend to help forge the *Dossier Secrets d'Henri Lobineau*, which included a bogus list of former Grand Masters of the Priory, and planted it in the Bibliothèque Nationale in Paris. He also forged medieval parchments containing encrypted riddles, claiming that these were the mysterious documents that Saunière had discovered in his church pillar, and then collaborated with Gérard de Sède on the book *L'Or de Rennes*. His elaborate hoax succeeded beyond his wildest dreams. The success of books like *The Holy Blood and the Holy Grail* convinced millions that he was not only the Grand Master of the Priory of Sion, a super-secret society responsible for the entire occult tradition of Western Europe, but

also the rightful heir to the French throne, and possibly even the physical embodiment of the Holy Grail and a direct descendant of Jesus.

But the success of the myth he had created failed to attract the new members of the Priory of Sion for which Plantard had hoped. When he tried to relaunch the Priory in 1989 as a New Age society based on earth mysteries (such as ley lines and standing stones) in the Rennes area, he made a serious mistake. Issuing a revised list of Grand Masters, he included the recently deceased Roger-Patrice Pelat, a millionaire who had enjoyed close ties to the Mitterand presidency, but was under investigation for insider training. When the supposed link between Pelat and a quasi-Masonic secret society came to the attention of the investigating judge, Plantard was hauled into court to explain. He admitted under oath that he had fabricated the entire story. After this, Plantard faded from view and died in poverty in 2000.

The Priory of Sion lives on in some senses, as a former associate of Plantard is trying to revive it. Sceptics, however, have accused him of simply trying to take advantage of the high-level of 'brand awareness' that has resulted from the huge success of the Dan Brown book and film.

*THE PRIORY OF SION AND THE MYSTERY OF RENNES*

*An illustration showing a distant vista of Mount Zion on the outskirts of the city of Jerusalem, c.1840. This aspect is from the Hill of Evil Counsel.*

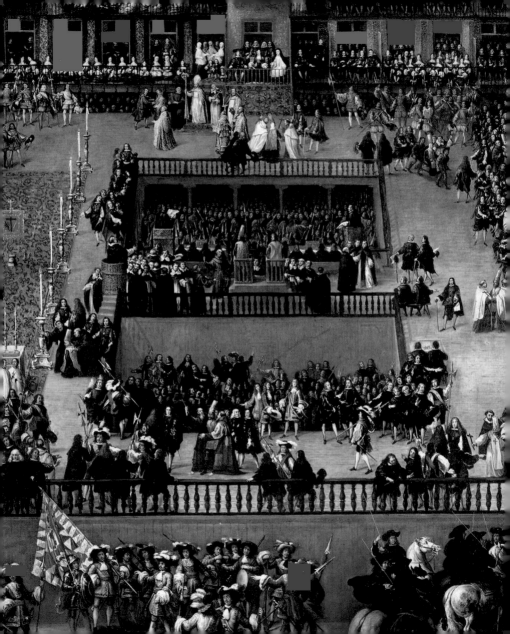

# PART 3
# POLITICAL AND
# CRIMINAL SOCIETIES

The conspiracy theorists' fear is that secret societies keep
secrets because they are up to no good. While many of
the targets of these accusations are undeserving, there
are many examples in history of secret societies that
pursue plots and schemes, either to advance an ideology
or to enrich themselves through criminal conspiracies.
The label 'conspiracy theorist' is often applied
dismissively, indicating crackpots or liars. This book
is no exception, as the term is mainly used when
describing those who advance untenable theories based
on poor or absent evidence. But it is important to
recognize that sometimes conspiracies do take place, and
that there are several instances in history where secret
societies have been at the heart of these conspiracies. But
even here, truth and fiction tend to become hopelessly
entangled, as the stories of the Assassins, the Illuminati,
the New World Order elites and the Mafia each
demonstrate. Time and again conspiracy theories about
secret societies are used to demonize minority groups
and obscure the real drivers of history.

# CHAPTER 9
# THE ASSASSINS

# THE ASSASSINS

| TYPE | Paramilitary, religious, esoteric, political |
|------|----------------------------------------------|
| EXISTED | 1094–1273 |
| RELATED TO | Gnostics, Knights Templar |
| GOALS AND CONCERNS | Esoteric version of Islam; religious and political independence |

'Assassin', meaning a treacherous murderer, or more specifically one who kills for specific ideological, political or financial ends, is a term that comes from the name of a medieval Islamic secret society, the Hashashin or Assassins, once feared throughout Western and Islamic society. The Assassins are regarded by some conspiracy theorists today as the original source of all secret societies.

According to the popular legend of the Assassins, they were a fearsome sect of fanatical killers motivated solely by loyalty to their evil overlord, the Old Man of the Mountains, who dwelled in the impregnable mountain fortress of Alamut, the Eagle's Nest. Possessed of occult power and secret wisdom, he used drugs and cunning ruses to brainwash his followers into slavish obedience, and would demonstrate his command by ordering guards to leap from their watchtowers, which they willingly did. Acolytes of the sect would be sent forth to infiltrate communities and courts, until activated by mind-control techniques, when they would strike without regard to their own survival. The Assassins embraced death, as they believed it meant instant admission to the Gardens of Paradise, a fantasy land revealed to them by the trickery of the Old Man of the Mountains.

With an army of brainwashed killers at his command, the Old Man of the Mountain became feared across the Middle East. Even the mighty Saladin, leading his armies against their mountainous fortress, was scared off when he found an Assassin's dagger on his pillow. Assassins struck at will, murdering Crusader princes and Muslim sultans alike, until they were destroyed by the invading Mongol hordes in the mid-13th century. In the meantime, however, they had allegedly initiated the Knights Templar into their occult secrets, and the Templars brought their legacy to Europe. There, the Assassins flourished in new forms, as the Freemasons and the Illuminati, who still practise advanced mind-control techniques in support of their ultimate goal, the New World Order.

This tale has penetrated to every corner of popular culture, showing up in books, film, literature and games, such as *The Count of Monte Cristo*, *The Manchurian Candidate* and *Assassin's Creed*, and becoming a mainstay of modern conspiracy theory. Scholars dismiss it as a myth born of intra-Islamic feuding, Western ignorance and Orientalist fantasies, but could there be a core of truth to the legend of the Assassins?

*The Mongols besieging a citadel; illustration dating to c.1256. A similar scene attended the end of the Persian Assassins, their mountain fastness crushed by the overwhelming might of the Mongol horde.*

# THE GARDEN
# OF PARADISE

The first reports of a strange Muslim sect known as the Hashishin came to Europe in the 12th century. The travelogue of a Spanish rabbi, Benjamin of Tudela, who travelled across the Middle East and Persia between 1159 and 1173, mentions them by this name. A report from Burchard of Strassbourg in 1175, an envoy of the Holy Roman Emperor to Egypt and Syria, tells of the 'Heyssessini'. William of Tyre (*c*.1130–1185), the first historian of the Crusades, discussed the 'Assissini' of Syria, while William of Rubruck (*c*.1215–1295), an early traveller to China, was the first Westerner to mention 'Axasins' in Iran. By the time Dante Aligheri (1265–1321) came to write his *Divine Comedy*, the name had acquired its connotations of treacherous murder. In Canto XIX of the *Inferno*, Dante describes a criminal who has been buried alive, upside down, as '*Lo perfido assassin*' – 'the wicked assassin'.

*Benjamin of Tudela exploring the Sahara; this 12th-century Spanish rabbi was one of the first Westerners to record the existence of the Assassins.*

The most influential report of the Hashishin, however, came from the travelogue of Marco Polo (1254–1324), who claimed to have visited the ruins of Alamut in 1273. Polo's story of a fabulous garden hidden in the mountains and an enigmatic sheikh who used drugs and deception to indoctrinate his subjects has shaped the image of the Assassins in the Western imagination ever since.

Polo first described how the Old Man of the Mountains 'caused a certain valley between two mountains to be enclosed, and had turned it into a garden, the largest and most beautiful that ever was seen'. The garden was filled with fruit trees, elegant pavilions and gilded palaces; its streams 'flowing freely with wine and milk and honey and water'. Also present were 'numbers of ladies and the most beautiful damsels in the world', singing and dancing, 'for the Old Man desired to make his people believe that this was actually Paradise. So he had fashioned it after the description that Mahommet gave of his Paradise'.

Polo went on to relate that, 'The Old Man kept at his court a number of the youths of the country, from 12 to 20 years of age, such as had a taste for soldiering'. After filling their heads with tales of paradise, he would give them 'a certain potion which cast them into a deep sleep' and then have them brought into the Garden, so that when they awoke they believed themselves to be in that wonderful place. Here they were allowed to live in a state of bliss, until the Old Man required their services, at which point they would be drugged once more, brought to his palace and told, 'Go thou and slay So and So; and when thou returnest my Angels shall bear thee into Paradise. And shouldst thou die, nevertheless even so will I send my Angels to carry thee back into Paradise.' Motivated by this belief, 'there was no order of his that they would not affront any peril to execute, for the great desire they had to get back into that Paradise'.

## OBEDIENT SERVANTS

Polo claimed to have heard the tale from local informants. Like something from the *Arabian Nights*, the story made a deep impression on European listeners with its beautiful *houris*, exotic drugs and religious fanatics, confirming their prejudices about the alien qualities of the Oriental mind. This image of brainwashed, zombie-like

cultists was reinforced by another popular tale, the account of the 1194 visit of Henry, Count of Champagne and titular King of Jerusalem, to the Assassins of Syria.

Henry (1166–1197) was given a tour of his fortress by the Old Man of the Mountains (the name given by Europeans to any leader of the Assassins, lending an air of immortality to the title), who pointed to the white-robed *fida'is* ('ones who sacrifice themselves for the cause' or 'martyrs') guarding the battlements. 'Have you any servants who obey you as well as my men?' he asked, signalling to two guards, who promptly threw themselves to their deaths. 'If you desire it,' the Old Man said, 'all my *fida'is* shall throw themselves down from the battlements in the same way.' The Count went away suitably impressed by the knowledge that it would be unwise to tangle with a man who could command such fanatical loyalty.

Although this story was repeated by several sources and became famous in the West, historians doubt that the incident really happened. A 13th-century writer told the same story of the Assassins in Iran. A similar tale was also later applied to Peter the Great, who allegedly demonstrated the loyalty of his Cossacks in similar fashion to the King of Denmark as they stood atop the Round Tower in Copenhagen.

*Fourteenth-century Persian miniature showing the Garden of Paradise, complete with a stream meandering through flowering trees and groves of cypress to a pool abundant with waterfowl. The Old Man of the Mountains was said to have created a similar garden at Alamut.*

# LEGENDS OF THE HASHISH EATERS

The identity of the mysterious potion that the Old Man of the Mountains used to control his subjects was unknown until the 19th century. European knowledge of psychoactive drugs was still hazy, but they were increasingly identified with the decadent and degenerate Orient, and its alien but thrillingly exotic mindset. In the meantime, all sorts of explanations were propounded for the name of the strange sect. For example, it was suggested that it came from the root *hassa*, meaning 'to kill', or that the headquarters of the Syrian Assassins, the fortress of Masiyaf, was located on the *Jabal al-Sikkin*, 'Mountain of the Dagger', and that the Arabic word for 'dagger' was the real root of the name.

Others pointed to the first Old Man of the Mountains, Hasan i-Sabah, legendary founder of the sect, and conjectured that 'Hashashin' was simply a corruption of his name. Hasan

*Silvestre de Sacy, the French Orientalist who began untangling the complex web of history, legend and myth surrounding the Assassins.*

himself had become a magical figure. It was said that he initiated his *fidai*, or *fedayeen*, in a ceremony where he announced the End of Time and declared his maxim: 'Nothing is true, everything is permitted.'

## SILVESTRE DE SACY

It was not until 1809 that the true root of the word 'assassin' was revealed in a lecture by French Orientalist Baron Antoine Isaac Silvestre de Sacy (1758–1838): 'Nor should there be any doubt, in my opinion, that the word *hashishi*, plural *hashishin*, is the origin of the corruption *heissessini*, *assassini* and *assissini*.' De Sacy was an expert in Middle Eastern languages who had travelled the region in the wake of Napoleon's invasion of Egypt in 1798, untangling the intricate web of Islamic history that had previously been impenetrable to most Europeans. Tracing the schisms between Sunnis and Shi'ites, and then between different sects of Shi'ites, he had uncovered the origins of the Druze, the Ismailis and even the mysterious Assassins.

De Sacy had discovered that the Assassins were in fact an Ismaili Muslim sect known as the Hashashin, a name that derived from their supposed use of hashish, the psychoactive resin of the marijuana or cannabis plant. Hashish, de Sacy explained, was used by the Arabs in place of alcohol, banned under Islam, and 'causes an ecstasy similar to that which the Orientals produce by use of opium'.

In the popular legend of the Assassins, however, the fedayeen were described as carrying out their killings under the influence of the sect's mystery drug, which was essential for turning them into implacable killers. De Sacy pointed out that descriptions of hashish did not equate with this description, as it was usually said to produce 'a kind of quiet ecstasy, rather than a vehemence apt to fire the courage and the imagination to undertake and carry out daring and dangerous acts'. But hashish did match up, de Sacy argued, with the method used by the Old Man of the Mountains to indoctrinate his fedayeen in the first place, making them into 'blind instruments of his will'.

*Austrian writer, Joseph von Hammer-Purgstall (1774–1856). A distinguished Orientalist, von Hammer-Purgstall also entertained lurid fantasies about occult conspiracies, inventing wild tales about the Assassins and Templars.*

## VON HAMMER-PURGSTALL

The Assassin legend was next taken up by Joseph von Hammer-Purgstall (1774–1856), author of the lurid fictions linking the Templars to orgiastic rites of Baphomet (see pages 80–83). In his 1818 *History of the Assassins*, the Austrian writer accused the medieval sect of being 'a union of impostors and dupes', an 'order of murderers' and an 'empire of conspirators', 'able to undertake anything or everything', thanks to their intoxication with hashish. They worked constantly to 'undermine all religions and morality' with their 'doctrine of irreligion and immorality', attempting to spread 'the mysteries of atheism... the freest infidelity and the most daring libertinism'. For von Hammer-Purgstall, the Assassins were the root of all subsequent secret societies, and their evil doctrines had been taken up by 'the Jesuits, the Templars, the Illuminati'.

Von Hammer-Purgstall was a rabid anti-Mason and reactionary monarchist intent on blackening the name of groups he despised by any means necessary. His fictions and wild accusations were taken up enthusiastically by later conspiracy theorists such as Robison (see pages 280–283), and have fed into modern conspiracy culture.

POLITICAL AND CRIMINAL SOCIETIES

# THE CLUB DES HASCHISCHIN

| | |
|---|---|
| TYPE | Mystical, recreational |
| EXISTED | 1844–1849 |
| RELATED TO | Assassins |
| GOALS AND CONCERNS | Recreational drug use, investigation of effects of hashish |

The legend of the Assassins manifested in a strange form in 19th-century Paris, when a short-lived club of bohemians, poets, artists and intelligentsia gathered regularly under the auspices of a mysterious, drug-dispensing leader. Many of the elements of the Assassin legend found an unlikely echo in this counterculture experiment, from the garden of delights to the mystical initiation ceremony.

Yet it was the Club des Haschischin that said far more about Western attitudes to the Orient than about any genuine esoteric secret society. Orientalism – regarded as a fantastical and romantic but caricatured view of Oriental culture and history – was all the rage, and the story of the Assassins played into this.

## THE HOTEL SUITE OF DR MOREAU

In 1836 French physician and psychiatrist Jacques-Joseph Moreau de Tours (1804–1884) visited Egypt for three years, where he researched the use and effects of hashish, or rather of *dawamesc*, the form in which it was taken in that region. Moreau interviewed *hashishin* (drug users), visited their dens and even tried the bitter green paste for himself in order to understand its effects on the mind and body. Unlike modern cannabis,

*Jacques-Joseph Moreau de Tours. Moreau pioneered new approaches to mental illness and the study of psychoactive drugs, prescribing the hallucinogen datura as a psychiatric treatment and experimenting with hashish himself.*

which is usually taken in relatively small doses through smoking, the *hashishin* of the Islamic world typically consumed massive doses by eating the resin or paste with high concentrations of the active ingredient. The effects of cannabis in such high doses include vivid and prolonged hallucinations and intense euphoria.

On his return to Paris, Moreau published a celebrated monograph, *Hashish and Mental Illness* (1845), and began a series of investigations on the effect of cannabis on the European mind by supplying it to friends and other interested parties. Perhaps to put his test subjects at ease, or to conform to their Orientalist expectations or simply for a bit of fun, Moreau staged his experiments in lavish surroundings at the Hotel Pimodan, and the artists and journalists who met there called themselves the Club des Haschischin, or even the Order of Assassins according to some sources.

Writer Theophile Gautier (1811–1872) gave an account of his visit to the Club in 1846, describing a

*Postcard showing the grand exterior of the Pimodan Hotel, c.1900, where members of the Club des Haschishchin met to experiment with drugs.*

mysterious Doctor X, who was dressed in Turkish costume, and dispensed green paste on a saucer with the warning: 'This will be deducted from your share in Paradise'. At other times this doctor – presumably Moreau – was called the Sheikh of Assassins. A wild trip subsequently followed as the drug took hold.

Although the Club has become legendary in artistic and counterculture circles, many of the details about it are hazy. It probably met once a month, but was held at the Hotel Pimodan for only a short period. Membership of the club was said to include most of the celebrated names of the period, including Gautier, Gerard de Nerval, Alexandre Dumas, Honoré de Balzac and Charles Baudelaire.

In fact, Alexander Dumas (1802–1870) made his own contribution to the evolving Hashashin legend. In his book, *The Count of Monte Cristo*, the hero encounters the eponymous Count in full Old Man of the Mountains mode when he is given a mysterious paste to eat. He then experiences a lavish Oriental-style feast, is seduced by beautiful *houris* and wakes up to find it was all, apparently, a drug-induced dream. In the course of the novel the Count executes a cunning conspiracy, like a latter-day Assassin.

# BEHIND THE LEGEND

The true story of the Assassins is one of religious schisms, complex politics and a thousand years of smears and false propaganda about the Islamic sect known as the Nizari Ismailis. According to historian Wladimir Ivanow, 'This subject has been as much hackneyed and surrounded by legends or fairy tales as almost everything in connection with Ismailism.' The Ismaili sect is still going strong – making up a tenth of all Muslims according to one estimate – and they are not happy about this long history of slander. According to the Ismaili Heritage Foundation, 'The history of the Ismailis of Alamut has been always grossly misunderstood in a hideous form.'

## THE REAL ASSASSINS

The name 'Hashishin' that became corrupted to 'Assassin' was a name applied to the sect by their enemies, intended to smear them with a practice despised in Islam – the use of hashish – in a process similar to the vilification of the Bogomils (see page 55). They were also known by their enemies as *malahida* (arch-heretic) or *batiniyya* (an esoteric, or

one who allows personal interpretation to supersede the sacred law of sharia and/or the Koran). They called themselves *ad-dawa al-jadida* ('the new doctrine'), *al-Sufat* ('the pure') or simply fedayeen (from *fida'i* – 'martyrs' or 'those who sacrifice themselves for the cause').

Their origins lay in the complex history of Islamic schisms. Shia and Sunni split soon after Mohammed's death, but then the Shi'ites had many more schisms of their own. After the death of the sixth Shia Imam, Jafar al-Sadiq, there was a dispute over whether the succession should pass to his oldest surviving son, Musa, or to the son of his first son, Ismail, who had died before him. The majority followed Musa, but the group that followed Ismail came to be known as the Ismailis, and also as the Seveners. This was partly because they had followed the seventh imam in direct succession and partly because they taught that the prophets came in cycles

*Detail of a 15th-century line engraving showing Hasan i-Sabah in the castle of Alamut in Persia, giving orders to his followers.*

of seven and stressed the seven pillars of the Islamic faith. The Ismailis became noted for their esoteric take on Islam, with emphasis on the hidden teachings of the Koran and mystical aspects of man's relationship to God.

The Ismaili faith spread across much of the Islamic world under the Fatimids, who by the 11th century controlled an empire stretching from Spain to Yemen. In 1094 a dispute over the Fatimid succession in Cairo led a group of Ismailis under the leadership of Hasan i-Sabah to recognize the infant Nizar as their imam. Hasan was a Persian convert from mainstream Shia, and after escaping the clutches of his rival Mustalian Ismailis, he fled back to his homeland and set up a power base in northern Persia centred on the decrepit old fortress of Alamut in Kazvin. Sources differ over the date of Hasan's capture of Alamut, varying from 1090 to 1097.

## HISTORY OF VIOLENCE

From his fortress at Alamut, Hasan succeeded in setting up a de facto Nizari kingdom in northern Persia. But he was surrounded by enemies. As a Shia he was hated by Sunnis, as an Ismaili by mainsteam Shi'ites and as a Nizari by Mustalians. All the Islamic world was against the Nizari, and it has been suggested that this was one reason for their use of targeted killings; what modern military jargon describes as 'asymmetrical warfare'. Bernard Lewis, author of the landmark 1967 book *The Assassins: A radical sect in Islam*, wrote: 'Hasan found a new way, by which a small force, disciplined and devoted, could strike effectively against the overwhelmingly superior army.'

One of the most immediate threats to the Nizari enclave was the Seljuk sultan Sanjar, originally the sultan of Khorasan, a region of Persia to which the Assassins were beginning to spread their influence. Sanjar raised an army to destroy Alamut, but was dissuaded from his campaign when he discovered a dagger stuck in his bedstead, bearing a message from Hasan:

> Let it not deceive you that I lie far from you on the rock of Alamut, because those whom you have chosen for your service are at my command and obey my direction. One who could fix this poniard in your bed could also have planted it in your heart. But I saw in you a good man and have spared you. So let this be a warning to you.

*Nineteeth-century watercolour depicting Hasan i-Sabah striking an enemy.*

*The fortress of Masyaf in Syria. The Byzantines were the first to build here, but the Ismailis under Sinan constructed the most significant and lasting fortifications in the 12th century, including the throne room, from where the Old Man of the Mountains was said to rule.*

A similar story was later told of how Saladin was persuaded to leave the Assassins in peace, so perhaps this is simply a legend. But the effectiveness of the Nizari methods successfully spread fear across the Muslim world, with the result that their enemies started various 'black legends' about

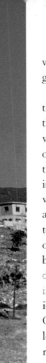

were less likely than other Muslim groups to use hashish.

By the 1130s the Nizari had spread their influence to Syria and established themselves in the Ansariyah Mountains with a number of fortresses, the greatest of which was Masyaf. It was here that they encountered the Crusaders, and there is much evidence that their relationship was often good. According to some accounts they even considered converting to Christianity in 1173 to take advantage of favourable taxation laws, but were blocked by other Christian groups jealous of their prerogatives. The Nizari leader in Syria in the late 12th century, Sinan ibn-Salman, may have been the original Old Man of the Mountains of Crusader legend, but the title was then applied retrospectively to Hasan i-Sabah and other Nizari leaders, or *Dais*.

Since most of what is known about the Nizari comes from their enemies, it is hard to distinguish fact from fiction. They were accused of assassinating a series of high-ranking Muslim potentates and later a few Crusader ones, most notoriously Conrad of Montferrat, King of Jerusalem, killed in 1192. It was widely suspected that they had been hired by Richard I, the Lionheart, of England, who had become involved in the complex politics of the Crusader kingdoms.

them, most prominently the accusation of hashish abuse. They were also denigrated as pork-eating, demon-worshipping apostates (people who have surrendered their religion). In fact, there is evidence that Hasan i-Sabah preached a puritanical gospel of complete abstinence, so the Nizari

# THE END OF
# THE ASSASSINS

*Mongol ruler Hulagu Khan riding with his warriors. Hulagu's horde conquered most of the Middle and Near East..*

The Assassins were said to have been wiped out by the Mongol invasion of the mid-13th century, when a vast Mongol horde under Hulagu Khan, grandson of Genghis, swept down on Persia. In 1256

he arrived at the gates of Alamut with an immense army. According to some sources the Nizari held out until their food ran out, while according to others they surrendered meekly. Alamut was razed to the ground. The Mongols were finally halted by the Mamelukes, but this did not help the remaining Syrian

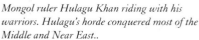

Nizaris, whose last stronghold fell to the Mameluke sultan Baybars I in 1265.

The Nizari Ismailis lived on, however, and can today be found from East Africa to India. They are best known as the Qäsim-Shâhîs, or Khojas, who look to the Aga Khan as their imam. But according to conspiracy theorists, the Aga Khan's Assassin heritage is more than just a historical curiosity, and he is seen as one of the elect bloodline who rule the Illuminati.

In the convoluted and darkly paranoid world of modern conspiracy theory, the Assassins are imagined to have played a pivotal role in the 'plot theory of history', as David Livingstone, author of the 2007 book *Terrorism and the Illuminati: A Three Thousand Year History*, explains:

> The [Illuminati] conspiracy coalesced under Herod the Great, who incepted a series of dynastic relationships, that would cooperate, first, to impose a corrupt version of Christianity upon the Roman Empire, Catholicism, with which they would struggle ever since for supremacy over Western civilization. During the Crusades, these families associated with their

counterparts in the East, members of the heretical Ismaili Muslims of Egypt, known as the Assassins. The basis of this relationship became what is known as Scottish Rite Freemasonry.With Napoleon's conquest of Egypt, these Freemasons reconnected with their brethren in Egypt, sparking a relationship that was pivotal to the development of the Occult Revival of the late 19th century. It produced the Salafi reform movement of Islam, since promoted by Saudi Arabia, and the Nazis of Europe. Together, they collaborated to found the Muslim Brotherhood, a collective of Islamic impostors, operated by the CIA, to foment a Clash of Civilizations, towards implementing a New World Order.

A scenario that links together the Jews, Catholicism, the Assassins, the Freemasons, Napoleon, Islamic fundamentalism, the Nazis and the CIA might seem laughable, but the conspiracy theory community is deadly serious. Just as they were slandered in the Middle Ages, so the Nizari Ismailis are still slandered today.

# ASSASSINS' CREED

The Ismaili Heritage Foundation points out that the medieval Nizari were renowned for their libraries and learning; scholars from across the Middle East would visit them to take advantage. The libraries were burned when their strongholds fell. They were also celebrated for their architectural skills, as their castles were famous for their impregnable fortifications and ingenious hydrological engineering, shaping massive water tanks to catch and hold any rainfall in the arid regions they inhabited, which they used to create beautiful gardens.

For conspiracy theorists, however, this all plays into the legend of the Assassins. Their famous gardens and impregnable fortresses, they allege, simply prove several elements of the legend of the Old Man of the Mountains and his wicked tricks. Their libraries and scholars indicate that they guarded ancient wisdom and esoteric secrets. Their skill at architecture suggests links to both the Freemasons and, more directly, the Templars and other knightly orders, who were said

to have learned the arts of fortification from them and used them to such good effect at places like Krak des Chevaliers in Syria.

## GNOSTIC SECRETS OF THE ASSASSINS

A more powerful link between the Assassins and other secret societies is the possibility that their beliefs fit well with the tradition of Gnostic and esoteric belief that connects the ancient mystery cults to the Cathars and Rosicrucians. According to some sources, for instance, Hasan i-Sabah preached reincarnation, or transmigration of the soul, placing him in the same esoteric tradition as Pythagoras (see pages 42–43). His creed 'Nothing is true, everything is permitted', echoes that of Gnostic Christians and Alumbrados (see page 268), who believed that because their divine essences were incorruptible they were incapable of sinning, or that sin did not matter. It also prefigures Aleister Crowley's dictum,

*The battlements of the Crusader castle of Krak des Chevalier viewed from the west.*

POLITICAL AND CRIMINAL SOCIETIES

'Do what thou wilt shall be the whole of the Law' (see page 192).

The Ismailis were called *batiniyya* by their enemies because they believed in *batin*, or the principle of esoteric truth – in other words, that the holy scriptures concealed hidden meanings. These secrets they called *haqa'iq*, and they seem to derive from Pythagoras, Plato and the Gnostics, just as alchemy and Hermeticism did. Supposedly, Hasan taught that ordinary human reason alone could not reveal the *haqa'iq*, but that man must rely on the authority of God and his imam, and therefore they had to give absolute obedience to their imam.

The Ismailis believed in a seven-fold hierarchy of initiation, which the Nizari increased to nine, arranged into three orders in remarkably similar fashion to the arrangement adopted by the Order of the Golden and Rosy Cross (OGRC – see page 114), and after them by the *Societas Rosicruciana in Anglia* (Soc Ros or SRIA – see pages 117–119) and the Hermetic Order of the Golden Dawn (HOGD – see page 186). This is almost certainly not a coincidence. Conspiracy theorists believe that the link is direct, and that the Assassins initiated all

*Illustration of Pythagoras by Masonic artist J. Augustus Knapp. As the godfather of sacred geometry, Pythagoras has a special status for Masons and other mystical brethren.*

subsequent secret societies through their influence on the Knights Templar. According to leading Muslim jurist and historian Syed Ameer Ali:

> From the [Nizari] Ismailis the Crusaders borrowed the conception which led to the formation of all the secret societies, religious and secular, of Europe. The institutions of Templars and Hospitallers; the Society of Jesus, founded by Ignatius Loyola, composed by a body of men whose devotion to their cause can hardly be surpassed in our time; the ferocious Dominicans; the milder Franciscans – may all be traced either to Cairo or to Alamut. The Knights Templar especially, with their system of grand masters, grand priors and religious devotees, and their degrees of initiation, bear the strongest analogy to the Eastern [Nizari] Ismailis.'

In practice, it is more likely that the esoteric scholars who created the first occult Masonic orders in the 18th century had read their history and Orientalist reportage, and drew inspiration at second hand.

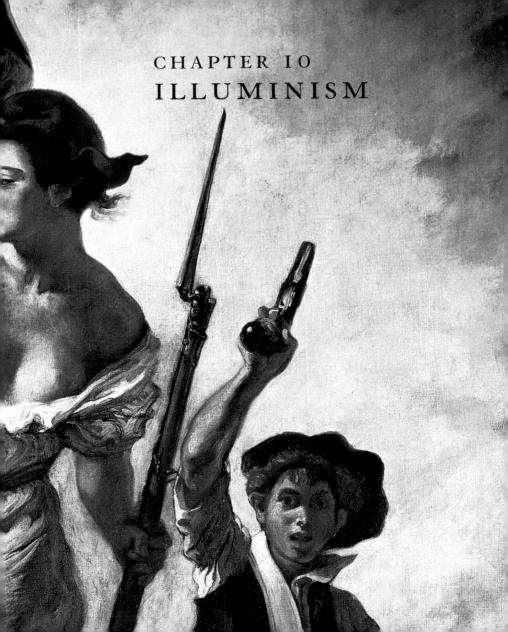

CHAPTER 10
ILLUMINISM

# THE ILLUMINATI

| TYPE | Elite, political, fraternal, esoteric |
|---|---|
| EXISTED | 1776–1787 |
| RELATED TO | Freemasonry, Rosicrucians |
| GOALS AND CONCERNS | Global revolution in religion and society through moral and spiritual enlightenment |

The Illuminati – from the Latin for 'Enlightened Ones' – were a short-lived Masonic secret society in late-18th century Bavaria in modern-day Germany that had grand aims but made little real progress before being uncovered and suppressed. Today, however, they are seen as something much bigger and more sinister, because the Illuminati have become the touchstone for the conspiracy theorists' view of secret societies, an all-purpose bogeyman for anyone and everyone who distrusts or dislikes secret societies and believes they are up to no good. Investigate practically any conspiracy theory and the Illuminati will be mentioned; their exact identity is unclear and changes from one conspiracy theorist to the next. Suggestions range

from the Freemasons and the Jews to the bloodline of Jesus and shape-shifting, baby-eating reptilian aliens. It is necessary to draw a clear distinction between the historical Illuminati and the Illuminati of conspiracy legend.

## HISTORY AND LEGEND

The historical version, the Bavarian Illuminati (also known as the Perfectibilists and the Ancient Illuminated Seers of Bavaria), were created by law professor Adam Weishaupt (1748–1811, or 1830 according to some sources) in 1776. The new secret society, loosely based on the Freemasons, spread slowly at first, but received a boost in 1780 when Weishaupt recruited influential Mason Baron Adolf Franz Friedrich von Knigge

*Freidrich von Knigge, author, diplomat and well-connected Mason, driving force behind the Bavarian Illuminati's brief period of growth and success.*

ILLUMINISM

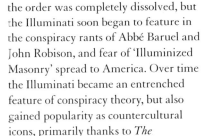

(1752–1796), who helped to recruit other highly placed Masons and spread the order across Europe.

By 1784 there were over 2,000 Illuminati, including famous names and aristocrats, but bickering between the leaders of the order prevented it from making much progress. In the same year their existence was uncovered and they were suppressed in Bavaria and elsewhere. Weishaupt and Knigge fled. Documents were seized and publicized; much was revealed about the order's

organization, aims and methods. In 1787 the order was completely dissolved, but the Illuminati soon began to feature in the conspiracy rants of Abbé Baruel and John Robison, and fear of 'Illuminized Masonry' spread to America. Over time the Illuminati became an entrenched feature of conspiracy theory, but also gained popularity as countercultural icons, primarily thanks to *The Illuminatus! Trilogy* by Robert Anton Wilson (1932–2007) and Robert Shea (1933–1994).

# THE ALUMBRADOS

Long before the Bavarian Illuminati, a different group of people were called by the same name, or by its Spanish equivalent, *Los Alumbrados*. The name 'Alumbrados' described a religious movement that arose in Spain in the early 16th century. It was linked with mystics who believed that it was possible, through contemplation alone, to achieve direct perception of the Light of God – or 'illumination'. By coming into direct contact with this divine essence they achieved perfection of the soul.

The Alumbrados taught that all the other elements of religion – the Church, priests, sacraments, the Bible – were useless and that only contemplation could lead to this experience of the divine. Some also believed that since their souls had attained perfection, they could behave as they liked. At its most extreme, the aim of the Alumbrados was complete absorption in God and the loss of individuality – directly equivalent to the state of nirvana achieved by meditating Buddhists. They also had connections with Gnosticism, which had similar teachings about personal experience of the divine.

To the Catholic Church the Alumbrados were 'false mystics' and their creed, 'Illuminism', was a heresy. The Spanish Inquisition began to attack them in the 1520s. Among those accused was Ignatius Loyola, later the founder of the Jesuits, who was later cleared. Illuminism faded in Spain by the mid-17th century.

The Alumbrados inspired strong reactions and conspiracy theories directed at the Jews. They were linked to the New Christians or *converses*, Jews who had been forced to convert to Christianity when the Christian kings campaigned to drive the Moors out of Spain, and especially after 1492 when Jews were officially expelled from Spain. Anti-Semitic propaganda was widespread and fear of the subversive actions of the *converses* led to the setting up of the Spanish Inquisition in 1478.

*Detail of* The Vision of St. Ignatius of Loyola *by Peter Paul Rubens. Ignatius was a visionary mystic strongly suspected of association with the Alumbrados who survived repeated investigation and trial by the Church authorities before founding the Jesuits (Society of Jesus) in 1540.*

# ADAM WEISHAUPT

The central figure in the story of the Illuminati is the German philosopher Adam Weishaupt. The tale of his life and career is complex and contradictory, reflecting the turbulent history and reputation of the secret society he set up.

According to some, Weishaupt had a Jewish background but he was raised as a Catholic in Ingolstadt in Bavaria, home to one of Europe's most prestigious universities. From a learned family, Weishaupt was academically brilliant and gained a scholarship to a Jesuit school. Although impatient with their restrictive and reactionary teachings, the structure and discipline of the Jesuits impressed him and would become an important influence on the secret society he later set up.

Weishaupt studied at Ingolstadt University and secured an appointment as professor of civil law there when he graduated in 1772. The following year he became the first non-clergyman to occupy the chair of canon law, but he increasingly felt that his career and teaching philosophy was obstructed by the influence of the Jesuits. Although they had officially been disbanded in 1773, they

were suspected of organizing in secret. Partly to counteract their influence, Weishaupt believed he had to play them at their own game. He joined the Freemasons in 1774, but decided they were not up to his grand scheme. Instead he decided to create a new secret society, which he intended to model in part on the Jesuits. According to Baron von Knigge, Weishaupt's 'pet design' was 'to utilize for good purposes the very means which [the Jesuits] employed for evil ends'. Together with four friends he founded the Illuminati on 1 May 1776.

Weishaupt worked hard to promote his secret society, but when it was exposed in 1784 he realized he was in danger. In 1785 he fled Bavaria for the German Duchy of Saxony. Weishaupt weathered the storm that his Illuminati had roused across Europe. He wrote important tracts defending his society, but he seemed to reverse his earlier opposition to Catholicism. According to the records of the Catholic parish in Gotha, he died 'reconciled with the Catholic Church, which, as a youthful professor, he had doomed to death and destruction'.

*Adam Weishaupt, Bavarian jurist, philosopher, professor of civil and canon law and founder of the Bavarian Illuminati.*

# HISTORY OF THE ILLUMINATI

Weishaupt considered naming his new secret society the 'Order of Perfectibilists', but decided on the 'Ancient and Illuminated Seers of Bavaria'. He drew up detailed and ambitious plans for the training and education of initiates, or Minervals (see pages 278–279), which involved considerable direct personal oversight. Weishaupt took the code name 'Spartacus', perhaps indicating his belief that he was leading fellow 'slaves' to freedom from their state of 'servitude' to the establishment and the Catholic doctrines of the day. Despite the apparently egalitarian philosophy he taught, his attitude to the Illuminati was proprietorial and even dictatorial, and perhaps as a result membership increased only slowly, so that by 1779 there were only 54 members.

In 1780 he succeeded in recruiting Baron von Knigge, who took the code name 'Philo'. Von Knigge was a highly

*Prince Ferdinand, Duke of Brunswick (1721–1792), 'princely representative of the illuminism of his age'.*

placed diplomat and leading Mason from the north of Germany, and his involvement opened new doors to the Illuminati, both socially and geographically, helping them spread beyond their restricted Bavarian base. Crucially, von Knigge helped to accelerate a strategy launched by Xavier Zwack, a leading Illuminatus who took the code name 'Cato', and who had managed to take over a Munich Freemasonry lodge. With von Knigge's help, the Illuminati recruited many more leading Freemasons, and succeeded in attracting important people such as Duke Ferdinand of Brunswick, described by the Catholic Church as 'the foremost leader of European Freemasonry and the princely representative of the illuminism of his age', and the writer and polymath Goethe. By 1784 there were colonies, as Illuminati lodges were called, in Germany, Austria, Switzerland, Italy and elsewhere. Their estimated membership was over 2,000, although perhaps only 650 had advanced beyond the most basic grade.

The Illuminati had ambitious plans to perfect human nature and society, overthrow the Catholic Church and introduce a universal system of democratic republicanism, but they were hampered by petty bickering among their leaders. In particular, von Knigge objected to Weishaupt's attempts to micromanage everything, accusing him of 'Jesuitism' and being 'a Jesuit in disguise'. 'Was I,' he lamented, 'to labour under his banner for mankind, to lead men under the yoke of so stiff-necked a fellow? Never!' 'Philo' resigned from the Illuminati in July 1784, but by this time the organization was already doomed.

## FALL OF THE ILLUMINATI

Although the Illuminati were set up to maintain secrecy, rumours of their activities and plans began to leak out. In 1782 they attempted to take over a branch of Freemasonry (Baron von Hund's Rite of Strict Observance – see page 149) at a Masonic conclave at Wilhelmsbad, but were rebuffed by Masons forewarned of their intentions. In 1784 the rumours about secret plots against state and Church had reached a fever pitch in Bavaria, culminating in the issuing of a series of laws against secret societies. In 1785 the Illuminati were banned by name, and a sort of anti-Illuminati Inquisition was launched to root out any Illuminati involvement in the army, clergy, government and education system.

Weishaupt fled to Saxony, leaving orders for the remaining Illuminati to go underground; perhaps he hoped that the panic would blow over and he could pick up the pieces later. The final blow came in 1786, however, when a police raid on the house of Xavier Zwack uncovered a cache of papers and documents. Zwack had already fallen out with Weishaupt and many of his papers may have been fanciful or even delusional. Among them were plans for a female Illuminati order, essays in defence of suicide, recipes for poison and even information on abortion. Whether or not these were genuinely representative of the thinking of Weishaupt's Illuminati, the damage was done and the name of the order was irretrievably blackened. The Illuminati were completely suppressed by 1787, but conspiracy theorists had already started to develop their legend, and when the French Revolution was followed by the Terror, the execution of the King, the de-Christianization of France and attempts to spread revolution across Europe, all the worst fears of the order's reactionary enemies seemed to have come true (see page 266).

There have been some latter-day pseudo-Illuminati. Theodor Reuss, who later founded the *Ordo Templi Orientis* (Order of Oriental Templars, or OTO – see pages 196–197), set up a new Illuminati organization in Berlin in 1895. In California in the 1960s the countercultural appeal of the order led to students in Berkeley setting up a new Bavarian Illuminati in 1968.

*Ruined castle at Hanau-Wilhelmsbad, a fashionable spa town of the late 18th century and location of the Masonic Congress of 1782 at which the Illuminati attempted unsuccessfully to subvert the Rite of Strict Observance. Their downfall came shortly after.*

# AIMS AND ORGANIZATION

Weishaupt was inspired by the intellectual movements of the Enlightenment, which stressed individual liberty and the role of reason, and taught that man could be perfected, hence the alternative name that Weishaupt considered for his order – the Perfectibilists. Like the earlier Rosicrucians, he believed that the inevitable result of a complete philosophical and moral education would be the throwing off of the mental and civic shackles of the established state and Church. Although often accused of atheism, Weishaupt stressed Christianity, but a mystical, esoteric version of it. His vision for the Illuminati, therefore, combined esoteric Christianity with a belief that through pure reason man and society could be transformed. 'Princes and Nations shall disappear from off the face of the earth!' went a quotation attributed to him. 'Yes, a time shall come when man shall acknowledge no other law but the great Book of Nature; this revelation shall be the work of Secret Societies and that is one of our grand mysteries.'

## SECRET SCHOOLS OF WISDOM

The central concept of Illuminism was that of 'enlightenment', in the sense of 'letting in the light of reason', a truth that Weishaupt believed was at the core of what he called 'the secret schools of wisdom' – that is, the Western mystery tradition. Weishaupt declared that these schools:

> ... were always the archives
> of nature and of the rights of
> man; through their agency, man
> will recover from his fall; princes
> and nations, without violence
> to force them, will vanish from
> the earth; the human race will
> become one family, and the
> world the habitation of rational
> beings. Moral science alone
> will effect these reforms
> 'imperceptibly'; every father
> will become, like Abraham and
> the patriarchs, the priest and
> absolute lord of his household,
> and reason will be man's only
> code of law.

*The pyramid shown on the reverse of the Great Seal of the United States signifies strength and durability.*

Weishaupt believed that the true, esoteric doctrine of Jesus was that this original state of 'freedom and equality' could once again be restored through 'illumination', and in setting up the Illuminati his intention was for each colony to form a new 'school of wisdom'.

### PROPER CANDIDATES

Weishaupt claimed that he recruited new members of the Illuminati according to the highest moral standards:

> Whoever does not close his ear to the lamentations of the miserable, nor his heart to gentle

pity; whoever is the friend and brother of the unfortunate; whoever has a heart capable of love and friendship; whoever is steadfast in adversity, unwearied in the carrying out of whatever has been once engaged in, undaunted in the overcoming of difficulties; whoever does not mock and despise the weak; whose soul is susceptible of conceiving great designs, desirous of rising superior to all base motives, and of distinguishing itself by deeds of benevolence; whoever shuns idleness; whoever considers no knowledge as unessential which he may have the opportunity of acquiring, regarding the knowledge of mankind as his chief study; whoever, when truth and virtue are in question, despising the approbation of the multitude, is sufficiently courageous to follow the dictates of his own heart – such a one is a proper candidate.

In practice, more worldly concerns governed Weishaupt's selection, as he mainly recruited rich young men. The radical, liberal ideas he taught appealed to their impressionable young minds, while he hoped that with their wealth, prospects and contacts, he would eventually manage to place Illuminati in influential positions throughout the institutions of society. Later, with the help of von Knigge, more influential people could be recruited directly to the Illuminati.

## NOVICES AND MINERVALS

Weishaupt modelled his new order on both the Masons and the Jesuits. There were three basic grades or degrees to begin with – Novice, Minerval and Illuminated Minerval – although initiates were promised the revelation of greater things to come. The term 'minerval' comes from Minerva, the Roman goddess of wisdom. Possibly to satisfy the appetites of the experienced Masons he recruited, von Knigge later added higher degrees such as Priest, Prince and Magus.

For all his idealistic rhetoric about liberty, fraternity and equality, Weishaupt imposed strict discipline and authoritarian control on recruits. According to von Knigge, Weishaupt regarded the 'despotism of superiors' and the 'blind, unconditional obedience of subordinates' as essential. Novices were expected to prepare a detailed report on their own lives and character, including a list of all their acquaintances, their enemies, the books they owned and so on. They were expected to study for two years and to recruit other Novices, and all the while they were kept in the dark as to the wider nature of the Illuminati. The only other member known to them would be the person who had recruited them. Weishaupt alone would know the full membership list, and only a few close lieutenants knew that he was the founder and general of the order. It has been pointed out that the organization of the Illuminati thus had all the hallmarks of both a cult, in the way that it sought to control the thinking of its recruits, and a terrorist cell, in the way that it compartmentalized its membership. The mind-control aspect had helped to fuel links made by conspiracy theorists between the Illuminati, the Assassins (see pages 238–263) and more recent supposed mind controllers, like the agents of the New World Order (see pages 288–315).

Once a Novice had graduated to the status of Minerval, he could attend meetings of his local 'colony' or lodge. Higher-grade members were organized into 'churches', 'provincials' and 'nationals', who reported to the supreme council of 'Areopagites', named after the ancient Athenian supreme court, but possibly also a nod to a group of

*Minerva, ancient Roman goddess of wisdom. 'Minerval' was the basic rank of Illuminism.*

Elizabethan intellectuals centred on Sir Walter Raleigh and Edmund Spenser who enjoyed esoteric pursuits.

ILLUMINISM

# THE ILLUMINATI CONSPIRACY

If the French Revolution had not taken place so soon after the brief flurry of excitement caused by the Illuminati, they would probably have been forgotten like many other secret societies dating back to around that time. But suddenly Europe was shaken by a violent revolution that brought about many of the seemingly impossible aims of the Illuminati: the monarchy and aristocracy overthrown; the lower and middle classes raised up in their place; liberty, fraternity and equality declared; a new republic instituted; and the power of the Church smashed.

Rather than accept that injustice and the corruption of the old system was the true cause of the revolution, defenders of the establishment started looking for someone to blame. Pinning the blame on a massive international conspiracy of evil secret societies, was easier for many to swallow than grappling with complex problems of justice and inequality – problems that might need solving.

## ROBISON AND BARRUEL

There were a few minor connections between the Illuminati and the French Revolution. Mid-ranking Illuminatus Christoph Bode did travel to France before the Revolution to try to recruit new members, and he succeeded in gaining the interest of Nicholas de Bonneville, who went on to become an important radical journalist during the Revolution. Connections like these were seized upon by the writers John Robison and Abbé Barruel (see page 267) in their pioneering conspiracy theory works, *Proofs of a Conspiracy* and *Memoirs Illustrating the History of Jacobinism*.

Robison claimed that the Revolution had its roots in the success of secret societies, which 'had been used in every country for venting and propagating sentiments in religion and politics, that could not have been circulated in public without exposing the author to great danger'. At their secret meetings, free thinkers and radical liberals had been

*Detail from* Liberty Leading the People *by Eugene Delacroix, 1830. The French Revolution and the Terror shocked reactionaries across Europe; its ripples – in terms of its impact on the world of conspiracy theories – are still being felt today.*

encouraged to 'become more bold, and to teach doctrines subversive of all our notions of morality... of all satisfaction and contentment with our present life, so long as we live in a state of civil subordination'. He went on to claim, in capital letters, that 'AN ASSOCIATION HAS BEEN FORMED for the express purpose of ROOTING OUT ALL THE RELIGIOUS ESTABLISHMENTS, AND OVERTURNING ALL THE EXISTING GOVERNMENTS OF EUROPE'.

More specifically, Robison claimed that Mirabeau and Talleyrand, two influential politicians during the Revolution who also happened to be Masons, had been recruited to the Illuminati cause. Supposedly they had quickly corrupted the rest of French Freemasonry and gone on to found the Jacobin Club, which was to play a pivotal role in unleashing the Terror, when the Revolution descended into violence and anarchy.

Jesuit priest Barruel, meanwhile, drew a similar picture, claiming that the

*John Robison, a distinguished physicist and professor of philosophy, had been an active Mason in his early life. He blamed the Illuminati for leading mainstream Masonry astray and wanted to suspend Masonic lodges in Britain.*

Illuminati had engineered an unholy alliance between the Freemasons and Enlightenment philosophers such as Voltaire and Diderot to produce a 'complete academy of Conspirators', dedicated to destroying 'every religion natural or revealed... every government... all civil society... all property whatsoever'. While Voltaire and Diderot had indeed provided the intellectual inspiration for Weishaupt, Barruel's evidence for direct links was pathetically flimsy, much like Robison's. This did not stop their ideas from becoming enormously popular.

## AMERICAN ANTI-ILLUMINISM

Both Robison and Barruel had dire news for the United States. Robison warned that the Illuminati had already set up cells in America, while Barruel claimed, 'As the plague flies on the wings of the wind, so do their triumphant legions infect America... The immensity of the ocean is but a feeble barrier against the universal conspiracy of the Sect.' Political issues in America meant there was a ready audience for these conspiracy theories. Paranoia led the passing of the Alien and Sedition Acts in 1798, and presidential candidate Thomas Jefferson (1743–1826) was accused of being the chief of the

Illuminati in the States. Politician Theodore Dwight claimed that Jefferson was 'the very child of modern illumination, the foe of man, and the enemy of his country', while his brother the Reverend Timothy Dwight, president of Yale College, warned Americans that it was their 'Duty in the Present Crisis' to destroy the foreign menace with 'the cruelty and rapacity of the Beast', or else their sons would become 'the dragoons of [the Jacobin] Marat' and their 'daughters the concubines of the Illuminati'.

Jefferson fought back against these lurid and hysterical claims, and even defended the reputation of Weishaupt:

> As Weishaupt lived under the tyranny of a despot and priests, he knew that caution was necessary even in spreading information, and the principles of pure morality. This has given an air of mystery to his views, was the foundation of his banishment... If Weishaupt had written here, where no secrecy is necessary in our endeavours to render men wise and virtuous, he would not have thought of any secret machinery for that purpose.

## THE EVOLUTION OF THE ILLUMINATI

Although the anti-Illuminati hysteria of late 18th-century America died down, the Illuminati continued to form the mainstay of conspiracy theorists. Nesta Webster claimed they were part of the Jewish plot that controlled history, and today the term 'Illuminati' is often used as a code for anti-Semitic accusations. From being a Masonic organization, the Illuminati have mutated into many different and strange shapes. They are generally considered to be the ultimate conspirators behind the plot to bring in the New World Order, or perhaps the front for the ultimate conspirators, but wherever there is a conspiracy theory it is almost certain that their name will be invoked. According to David Sutton, editor of the *Fortean Times*, a journal that covers conspiracies and popular delusions, 'Tug on virtually any thread of popular conspiracy theory and it will eventually lead you to the Illuminati. In the Internet age, this network of interconnections is becoming ever more tangled, with many websites having taken paranoia as an art form to a pitch of dizzying baroque splendour.'

*Thomas Jefferson was accused by anti-Masons of Illuminist abomination.*

# THE ILLUMINATUS! TRILOGY

One of the most significant resurrections of the Illuminati was in a science-fiction novel by Robert Anton Wilson and Robert Shea called *The Illuminatus! Trilogy* (1975), which has become a cult classic. Wilson and Shea were editors at *Playboy* magazine before writing their 'fairy tale for paranoids'.

The plot of the novel is deliberately confused and often contradictory. It centres on the apparent discovery of a massive global conspiracy that is masterminded by the Illuminati, who were actually founded 30,000 years ago in Atlantis. The Illuminati are presented as both the agents of control and dictatorship, trying to bring about a New World Order, but also as a front for an even more secret plot to achieve the exact opposite.

In the novels two men, Saul Goodman and George Dorn, each tangle with Illuminati-backed conspiracies and go through a variety of initiatory experiences, including lots of sex and drugs. Goodman joins up with the Justified Ancients of Mummu and is taught to perceive 'fnords' – invisible words implanted in the world's media to generate anxiety so that people will believe they need governments to protect them. Dorn, meanwhile, discovers who assassinated President John F. Kennedy, visits Atlantis, chats with a dolphin and makes love to a divine incarnation of Marilyn Monroe. A variety of apocalypses, including one involving Hitler's lost legion, preserved beneath a lake, are averted, and the novels end with a romance between a giant amoeba and a sentient computer.

## EDUCATING THE READER

Wilson and Shea regarded their novel as part of an education/re-education/de-education programme for the reader, explaining: 'This book, being part of the only serious conspiracy it describes – that is, part of Operation Mindfuck – has programmed the reader in ways that he or she will not understand for a period of months (or perhaps years).' Their intent was that their crazed invention would spread like a cultural virus and help to spark a revolution, and in this sense they might be seen as

'A designated underground classic.' *Booklist*

# THE ILLUMINATUS! TRILOGY

A CULT CLASSIC –
OVER 100,000 COPIES SOLD!
Robert Shea *and* Robert Anton Wilson

*The front cover of Robert Shea and Robert Anton Wilson's 1975 cult classic novel,* The Illuminatus! Trilogy.

ILLUMINISM

the true inheritors of Adam Weishaupt and his revolutionary programme. Weishaupt also features in the book, with the authors claiming that he replaced George Washington during the War of Independence and went on to become the first President of the United States.

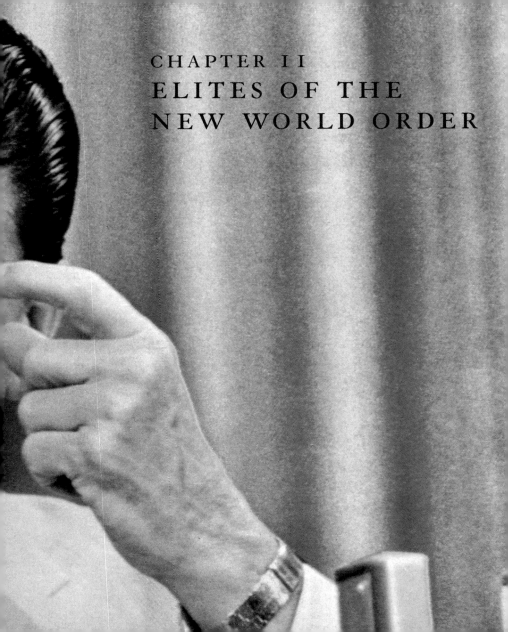

# THEORIES OF THE
# NEW WORLD ORDER

The New World Order is the alleged goal of secret societies that are engaged in a global, history-spanning conspiracy to take control of humanity for their own ends. It is the order that these supposed super-secret societies intend to impose on the planet as part of their evil scheme.

There are many different interpretations of what the New World Order (NWO) will involve, but some elements are common to most: one-world government (a single government ruling the entire planet and superseding national governments); suppression of dissent and suspension of civil liberties; internment of opponents and rebels; covert or overt enslavement of the majority of humanity; money, power and resources concentrated in the hands of a small elite for their exclusive benefit.

The more extreme interpretations of the NWO include programmes for massive culling of the population; global socialism/communism; Satanic worship and mass ritual sacrifices; the coming of the End Times and the Apocalypse; and conspiracies with alien races, including

the harvesting of body parts, breeding of hybrids and preparation for mass alien colonization.

## RIGHT AND LEFT

Such interpretations are mostly characteristic of right-wing conspiracy theorists, but the NWO is also a major feature of left-wing conspiracy theories. In left-wing interpretations, the NWO is usually expected to revolve around globalization, economic control, mass consumerism and corporate control of global power.

For both sides of the political spectrum, the NWO is inextricably linked to many other organizations, institutions and conspiracies, including the Illuminati, the United Nations, the World Trade Organization, the World Health Organization, the Council on Foreign Relations, the Trilateral Commission, the Bilderberg group, Bohemian Grove, the Elders of Zion and the international Zionist-Bolshevik conspiracy, or the Zionist Occupation Government (ZOG). Many NWO theories claim that

international bankers and/or hereditary dynasties form a self-perpetuating oligarchy; typically the Rothschilds, Rockefellers and British royal family are implicated.

*The Rockefeller brothers posing for a photograph at an awards ceremony in New York, 1967. Each brother was the recipient of a gold medal for 'distinguished service to humanity' from the National Institute of Science.*

Most NWO theories are anti-Semitic or have an anti-Semitic element. Some elements are explicitly anti-Semitic, such as accusations about the ZOG or the *Protocols of the Elders of Zion*, a document that is claimed to reveal a secret Jewish conspiracy for world domination, repeatedly proved to be a crude hoax, and though is constantly recycled as genuine to the present day. Others are covertly anti-Semitic – for instance, 'international bankers' is usually, though not always, code for Jews.

### USERS AND ABUSERS

The New World Order first emerged as a focus of conspiracy theorist concern in the 1960s thanks to the John Birch Society, a radical right-wing action group paranoid about a communist conspiracy to undermine the USA. During the 1990s the NWO became the central element of the paranoid fantasies of right-wing militias and fundamentalist Christian millenarians – those who believe that prophecies of Revelation are coming true and that the Apocalypse is due shortly. It briefly entered mainstream politics when President George Bush used the term in a 1991 speech to describe an optimistic view of the future in a post-Cold War world, but its negative, conspiratorial associations made it undesirable. The 1990s also saw the NWO become an object of suspicion for the anti-globalization, anti-capitalist movement.

### NOVUS ORDO SECLORUM

It is a common misconception that the motto on the reverse of the Great Seal of the USA, *Novus Ordo Seclorum*, is Latin for 'New World Order'. Although *seclorum* derives from the same root as the Latin word for 'world', in this case it means 'of the ages', so that the phrase translates as 'New Order of the Ages'. This is a reference to a verse from Virgil's fourth *Eclogue*, interpreted by Christians as a foreshadowing of the coming of Jesus: 'The great order of the ages is born afresh. And now justice returns, honoured rules return; now a new lineage is sent down from high heaven.' The designers of the Great Seal chose the motto to signify the beginning of a new American era with the founding of the new state. It was proposed by classicist Charles Thomson, who was not a Freemason. Although all of this information is widely available online or in most history books, conspiracy theorists seem to persist in misrepresenting the motto as proof that the Illuminati/Masons influenced the Founding Fathers and 'hid' a clue to their covert agenda in plain view for all to see.

*The front of the Great Seal of the United States,
with the motto* E Pluribus Unum *(Out of
Many, One), a statement of unificatory intent.*

# THE JOHN BIRCH SOCIETY

| TYPE | Political |
|------|-----------|
| EXISTED | 1958–present |
| RELATED TO | None |
| GOALS AND CONCERNS | Conservative, anti-Communist agenda |

The John Birch Society (JBS) is an extreme right-wing action group that is dedicated to opposing what it sees as a global communist conspiracy, and to advancing a conservative agenda at the grassroots level through supporting sympathetic political candidates and influencing local politics. It was founded on 8 December 1958 by businessman Robert Welch (1899–1985) as a vehicle for his conspiracy theories and as a result of his disillusionment with the Republican Party, which he considered to be far too moderate. Welch named his society after Captain John Birch, an American serviceman who was killed by Chinese Communists in the closing days of World War II, and was described as 'the first casualty of the Cold War'.

Welch and his supporters were hysterical anti-communists who believed that communists were infiltrating and undermining the US government at every level. They popularized the notion that there was a conspiracy to bring about a New World Order under a one-world government: 'Communism, in its unmistakable present reality, is wholly a conspiracy, a gigantic conspiracy to enslave mankind; an increasingly successful conspiracy controlled by determined, cunning, and utterly ruthless gangsters, willing to use any means to achieve its end.' Birch believed that the Soviets were using the United Nations to usher in the NWO and accused American politicians and judges of complicity, including Supreme Court Justice Earl Warren and even President

*Robert Welch, founder and head of the John Birch Society, photographed in 1966. Welch famously believed that, with the exception of Birchers, there were only four types of American: 'Communists, communist dupes or sympathizers, the uninformed who have yet to be awakened to the communist danger, and the ignorant.'*

Eisenhower, whom he described as a 'tool of the Communists'. Paranoid about its communist enemies, the JBS kept its membership secret. It is believed that by 1962 it had 60,000 members and an annual income of $1.5 million.

At first the JBS successfully influenced mainstream politics, becoming a major force in the Republican Party, culminating in its support for 1964 presidential candidate Barry Goldwater. In the wake of his defeat, Welch became increasingly paranoid, developing a plot theory of history involving Illuminati 'Insiders' who had been conspiring to become 'the all-powerful rulers of a "new order" of civilization' since 1776.

Communism was just the latest manifestation of this 'total conspiracy'. His extremist views – for instance, he believed that as part of the Insider master plan the Soviets had 'goaded the unsuspecting Hitler into attacking Poland' – led to mainstream Republicans disavowing the JBS. Its influence dwindled, but many credit Welch with starting the movement that led to the 'conservative capture' of US politics in the Reagan era, Ronald Reagan having been an early JBS fan. Ironically, the JBS have more recently begun to figure in the lists of suspect organizations accused by conspiracy theorists of being Illuminati fronts and agents of the NWO.

# THE PROTOCOLS OF
# THE ELDERS OF ZION

Probably the most pernicious and vile example of false claims about secret societies and conspiracies is the forged document known as *The Protocols of the Elders of Zion*. It marks the culmination of a millennia-long history of false conspiracy accusations that have been levelled at the Jews.

## BLOOD LIBEL

The Bible records ample evidence of persecution of the Jews going back thousands of years, but they have particularly suffered since the Diaspora, when the Jewish peoples were scattered around the world after the destruction of their state by the Babylonians (8th–6th centuries BCE) and Romans (1st–2nd centuries CE). As a visible, vulnerable ethnic and religious minority widespread across Europe and Asia, the Jews attracted every type of slander and bigotry. A major factor in the growth of anti-Semitism was the development of myths and legends about Jewish conspiracies, most prominently the Blood Libel.

The Blood Libel was the myth that Jews performed human sacrifices,

usually the sacrifice of Christians – especially children – for their dark ritual purposes. This became tied up with accusations of Satanism. It is a common element of modern conspiracy theories about Freemasons, the Illuminati and NWO elites – for instance, the central ritual at Bohemian Grove is said to be the Satanic ritual sacrifice of a child (see page 314). Such conspiratorial Blood Libels often disguise their anti-Semitism.

The Blood Libel was first levelled at the Jews in the pre-Christian era. One of the first recorded instances was the 2nd-century BCE story of a Syrian who claimed to have escaped the clutches of a Jewish coven that had held him captive for a year with the intent of ritually murdering him. It became a common feature of medieval anti-Semitism and there were many instances where wild Blood Libels sparked off riots and pogroms, useful in communities where Christians owed money to Jews and could thus write off their debts.

In 1144, for instance, the Jews of Norwich were accused of murdering a

*Typically grotesque anti-Semitic caricature from the cover of a 1940 version of* The Protocols of the Elders of Zion.

young boy and using his blood to make *matzoh* (unleavened bread). Twelfth-century historian Thomas of Monmouth, 'a man of unlimited credulity' according to the Catholic Church, reported that there was a global conspiracy of Jews plotting annual murders for similar purposes:

> It was laid down by the Jews in ancient times that every year they must sacrifice a Christian in some part of the world... they cast lots for all the countries which the Jews inhabit; and whatever country the lot falls upon, its metropolis has to carry out the same method with the other towns and cities, and the place whose lot is drawn has to fulfil the duty imposed by authority.

The Blood Libel survives to the modern day; in 1983, for instance, Syrian defence minister Mustafa Tlas published *The Matzoh of Zion*, with a cover depicting grotesque Jewish caricatures ritually sacrificing a victim.

*Syrian defence minister, Mustafa Tlas in Damascus, 2001. Tlas has published material repeating the Blood Libel against the Jews.*

## PUBLISHING THE PROTOCOLS

The Blood Libel was by no means the only conspiracy accusation levelled at the Jews. In 15th-century Spain, for instance, there was widespread anxiety among 'Old Christians' against the 'New Christians', or *converses* – Jews who had been forced to convert. A 1466 tract, *Fortalitium Fidei Contra Judeaos* (*Fortress of Faith against the Jews*), spread the notion that the *converses* were infiltrating Church and state in order to take them over.

During the 19th century such conspiracy theories, effectively treating the Jews as a secret society hatching evil plots, became mingled with the anti-Masonry of Robison and Barruel, and the Illuminati became associated with the Jews. Towards the end of the 19th century, anti-Semitic agents in Russia collaborated to forge a document that they claimed to be the secret minutes of a series of meetings of a Jewish secret society called the Elders of Zion. These minutes, or 'protocols', apparently detail their fiendish plans for the takeover of the world and the establishment of their dominance over all the other peoples. For instance, according to Protocol 2, Article 2: 'The administrators... from among the public... will easily become pawns in our game, specially bred from childhood to rule the affairs of the whole world.'

ELITES OF THE NEW WORLD ORDER

These *Protocols of the Elders of Zion* first appeared on the scene in Russia in 1905 and were used to justify state repression of the Jews, even though they were almost immediately identified as forgeries created by Mathieu Golovinski (1865–1920), a virulently anti-Semitic propagandist in league with the Tsar's secret police. In 1921 *The Times* of London ran a series of articles exposing Golovinski and pointing out that the Protocols were merely a crude plagiarism of an 1864 work, *Dialogue In Hell Between Machiavelli and Montesquieu*, written by French satirist Maurice Joly (1829–1878) in 1864. Joly wrote at a time of political tension in France over the ambitions of Emperor Napoleon III, and he penned his tract as a satire/slander of Napoleon's plans for world domination. Golovinski had simply copied the anti-Napoleonic diatribe, replacing 'France' with 'Zion' and 'Napoleon' with 'Jews'. In fact, Joly himself had probably plagiarized his version from an earlier one in which the conspirators were Jesuits.

*The Times* exposé was not the first time that the Protocols were thoroughly debunked, yet they have been repeatedly cited as genuine evidence of a massive conspiracy by Jewish secret societies to bring about the New World Order. In 1920 *The Dearborn Independent*, a newspaper belonging to anti-Semitic US industrialist Henry Ford (1863–1947), published *The Protocols*, and when it was pointed out to him that *The Times* had proven them to be fake, he responded: 'The only statement I care to make about *The Protocols* is that they fit in with what is going on.' A series of articles from *The Dearborn Independent* were collected and published as *The International Jew: The World's Foremost Problem*, which was admired by Adolf Hitler, although Ford disavowed knowledge of its contents. Hitler went on to use *The Protocols* to justify his anti-Semitism, so that they can be said to have played a role in the Holocaust. Today they are still cited as true and touted as evidence by the likes of David Icke, who claims the Elders and their Jewish co-conspirators are really reptilian aliens, and modern neo-Nazis. *The Protocols* are still popular with anti-Semitic propagandists in the Muslim world; in 2004 a copy was displayed as a real work at the Alexandria Library in Egypt. Dr Youssef Ziedan, director of the collection, was reported to have said, 'it has become a holy book for the Jew, their primary law, their way of life'.

*Front cover of the book,* Protocols of the Elders of Zion *by Mathieu Golovinski.*

PROTOKOLY
ZE SHROMÁŽDĚNÍ
SIONSKÝCH MUDRCŮ

# THE DARK SIDE

Some of the wilder versions of the New World Order myth are so extraordinary that they would be laughable if they were not taken seriously enough to incite believers to murder and terrorism.

The far-right in the USA, especially the militia movement, believes that some sort of Illuminati-controlled conspiracy of secret societies is preparing to institute the New World Order with apocalyptic consequences for mankind. Briefly outlined, their beliefs are as follows. The first steps in the plan have already happened, with the setting up of global institutions such as the United Nations, the International Monetary Fund and the World Trade Organization. These have already succeeded in extending their powers and facilitating globalization through instruments such as the North American Free Trade Agreement. The recent financial crisis is seen as part of the plan, leading, for instance, to plans for a new global currency. Even pandemics such as swine flu are viewed with suspicion as elements in the plan, as are efforts to tackle climate change through global treaties and conventions.

Any one of hundreds of websites can be chosen to get an idea of the paranoid fantasies with the NWO as their focus. A useful example comes from the fundamentalist Christian website *Overlords of Chaos* (note the liberal use of capital letters):

> Unfortunately for the people of the world everything is going according to the New World Order Plan. But what is this New World Order Plan? In a nutshell the Plan is this. The Dark Agenda of the secret planners of the New World Order is to reduce the world's population to a 'sustainable' level 'in perpetual balance with nature' by a ruthless Population Control Agenda via Population and Reproduction Control. A Mass Culling of the People via

*A 1943 poster by Leslie Darrell Ragan, declaring 'The United Nations Fight for Freedom'. Not everyone agrees; the UN was founded in 1945 to help prevent conflict, but today it is regarded with suspicion by many conspiracy theorists.*

UNITED

THE UNITED NATIONS FIGHT FOR FREEDOM

Planned Parenthood, toxic adulteration of water and food supplies, release of weaponized man-made viruses, man-made pandemics, mass vaccination campaigns and a planned Third World War. Then, the Dark Agenda will impose upon the drastically reduced world population a global feudal-fascist state with a World Government, World Religion, World Army, World Central Bank, World Currency and a micro-chipped population. In short, to kill 90%

of the world's population and to control all aspects of the human condition and thus rule everyone, everywhere from the cradle to the grave.

## BLACK HELICOPTERS

Common elements of the militia version of the NWO myth include a secret state apparatus that already exists and operates its own military and intelligence agencies. Its signature is the black helicopter: unmarked aircraft equipped with advanced technology that allows them to hover silently, evade radar

detection and even to become invisible. In addition, the NWO uses mind-control techniques to turn people into zombies and unwitting operatives, and to harass and incapacitate opponents. Brainwashing techniques that date back to the Assassins make possible the scenario outlined in Richard Condon's 1959 bestselling novel *The Manchurian Candidate*, first made into a film in 1962 and again in 2004, in which an American is unwittingly turned into the mind-controlled slave of the communists and a political assassin.

Using resources such as these, the NWO conspiracy is covering up its extensive preparations, which include the setting up of concentration camps and massive underground facilities in which opponents will be imprisoned and systematically exterminated. A common belief is that the Federal Emergency Management Agency, which can be given extraordinary powers in times of emergency, will be used to suspend the Constitution and bring about the first steps in the NWO plan. Militia groups take the theory seriously enough to arm themselves against the threat they

*A helicopter flying over the Branch Davidian compound during the Waco siege. The militia movement claims that helicopters like this are characteristic of the secret state apparatus.*

believe is posed by the Federal Government, and incidents like the Waco siege of 1993 are seen as the work of the NWO forces. Paranoia and resentment towards the Federal Government motivated the militia movement sympathizer Timothy McVeigh to bomb the Alfred P. Murrah Federal Building in 1995, killing 168.

## THE DARK SIDE HYPOTHESIS

During the 1980s, conspiracy theories about the NWO merged with theories relating to UFO sightings, alien abductions and cattle mutilation, which is the strange phenomenon whereby cattle are attacked with surgical precision for no apparent reason. Reports from abductees – people who believe they have been abducted by aliens – suggested that the Earth was being visited by 'Greys' – grey-skinned aliens with almond-shaped eyes and few other features. Supposedly, the Greys were abducting people in order to extract biological samples and experiment on them, for some unknown purpose. Ufologists (people who study UFOs) reported sightings of triangular black UFOs associated with cattle mutilations, and also claimed that black helicopters and mysterious men in black (government agents?) harassed anyone who investigated these events.

All these diverse elements seemed to be pieces in a jigsaw, which started to come together through the work of ufologist Paul Bennewitz (1927–2003), who was investigating strange lights near an air base. Bennewitz began to receive classified information from inside the military, which revealed an amazing story that has come to be known as the Dark Side hypothesis. After the crash-landing of an alien spaceship at Roswell, New Mexico, in 1947, President Truman had set up a super-secret council, MJ-12 (where MJ stands for 'Majestic' or 'Majority', depending on the source) to deal with the flying saucers. In 1954 MJ-12 held a meeting with aliens at Holloman Air Force Base where a cooperation pact was agreed. In return for advanced alien technology, MJ-12 gave the aliens secret bases such as Area 51 in Nevada, and used their covert forces to help the Greys gather genetic material through cattle mutilations and abductions, so that they could create an alien–human hybrid.

*The metallic fragments of a weather balloon being examined and identified by Brig. General Roger M. Ramey and Col. Thomas J. Dubose. The material was found in a farmer's field near Roswell, New Mexico. Some believed that an alien spacecraft had crashed to earth and this became known as the Roswell Incident.*

MJ-12 became the secret masters of the world, infiltrating all governments and using mind-control techniques, implants and assassination to cover up their existence and prepare for the launching of the New World Order. They established bases on Mars and on the dark side of the Moon, hence the name of the plot. When they are ready, MJ-12 together with their alien conspirators will launch the NWO, at which point mankind will be enslaved and exterminated, and a new race of alien–human hybrids will rule the planet.

In addition to Bennewitz's inside source, the discovery of leaked MJ-12 documents seemed to back up this story. But they quickly proved to be fakes and eventually it was discovered that Bennewitz was being fed disinformation by the US Air Force, possibly to discredit ufology and protect real-life secret technology and operations that might be compromised by nosy ufologists. The unfortunate Bennewitz had a mental breakdown.

## ILLUMINATI BLOODLINES

Theories about aliens and the NWO are not restricted to the Dark Side hypothesis. Another breed of alien, the Reptoids or Reptilians, are claimed by some to be the true identity of the

POLITICAL AND CRIMINAL SOCIETIES

Illuminati masters who are plotting the NWO. According to theories propounded by David Icke, for instance, the secret dynasties that make up the Illuminati are not human at all but shape-shifting Reptoids who regularly sacrifice children to drink their blood, in rituals led by Queen Elizabeth II.

This in turn is a development of the Illuminati bloodline theory, which claims that the pan-historical plot to bring about the NWO is controlled by a tiny number of families, who represent a secret society of dynasties that has spent most of history trying to subvert Christianity and take over the world. These families are usually said to include the Rockefellers, the Rothschilds, the House of Windsor and the Merovingians. Claims that these families only breed with each other, or are even a different species as the likes of Icke propose, should be seen in the light of 19th-century Theosophical 'root races' doctrine, and the spurious anthropology and occult evolutionary science of Ariosophy, which tried to argue that the Jews were not actually humans but a degenerate subhuman species. The same theories were used to justify the Holocaust, so it is important to stress that they are not simply harmless albeit lunatic fun, but actively dangerous.

## THE END OF DAYS

Yet another variety of NWO theory is the Christian fundamentalist millenarian view. Millenarians are those who believe that the Biblical End of Days will arrive soon, at which time the Second Coming of the Messiah will triumph over the Antichrist at the battle of Armageddon, followed by the Millennium, the thousand-year rule of Christ on Earth (the order of events varies according to the interpretation of scripture).

According to the Book of Revelation, the beginning of the End Times is marked by the arrival of the Antichrist, a beast with ten horns who will rise from the sea to unite 'all kindreds and tongues and nations' and rule the Earth for 'forty and two months'. This period will be the New World Order, a time of apparent peace and prosperity in which most of mankind will be deceived into worshipping the Antichrist and will be marked with the number of the Beast, for 'no man might buy or sell, save he that had the mark'.

Millenarian conspiracy theorists believe that these prophecies are already being fulfilled. Globalization and all the apparatus of the one-world government represent the unification of kindreds, tongues and nations. The Antichrist may actually be an institution, such as the

*The Lizardman of Scape Ore Swamp; a notorious bogeyman said to haunt South Carolina. Some believe it to be a reptile-human hybrid, or 'reptoid'. Similar creatures have been identified as the ultimate architects of global conspiracy and the NWO, although such accusations are often a front for anti-Semitism.*

United Nations, the Bilderberg group, the Illuminati or the Zionist-Bolshevik conspiracy. His ten horns are sometimes interpreted as a reference to the members of the UN Security Council, or the European Union (when it had ten members, before this theory was spoiled by enlargement). The mark of the Beast that everyone will need in order to buy and sell are ubiquitous credit cards or bar codes, or it possibly represents the microchips that will be implanted in every human under cover of vaccination programmes and the like.

## THE COMPLETE PACKAGE

The most impressive conspiracy theories manage to tie together all these disparate elements, following on from the work of Nesta Webster and her all-embracing 'plot theory of history' (see page 172). Examine, for instance, the elaborate theory outlined in David Livingstone's book *Terrorism and the Illuminati: A Three Thousand Year History* (2007), which takes in Illuminati bloodlines, Jews, Assassins, Catholic Church, Islam, Freemasons, occult secret societies, Nazis, CIA and Islamic terrorism in a single overarching scheme.

# THE BILDERBERG GROUP

| TYPE | Elite, political |
|------|------------------|
| EXISTED | 1954–present |
| RELATED TO | New World Order elites |
| GOALS AND CONCERNS | International dialogue |

The Bilderberg group is an informal annual gathering of leading and up-and-coming politicians, businessmen and opinion formers from Western Europe and North America, which meets at an exclusive hotel to network and discuss world issues in private. According to conspiracy theorists it is also a front for the Illuminati, dedicated to bringing in the New World Order, which picks presidents and prime ministers, instigates wars and generally controls world history in absolute secrecy.

The group was started in 1954 by Prince Bernhard of the Netherlands, Polish diplomat and anti-communist Joseph Retinger, former British Foreign Minister Denis Healey and international banker David Rockefeller, whose involvement is like a red rag to a bull for conspiracy theorists. They gathered top policy and opinion makers from either side of the Atlantic for a gathering at the Bilderberg Hotel in the Netherlands, and have since met every year.

The guest list varies, with a steering committee inviting around 100 influential and aspiring individuals for a three- or four-day conference behind closed doors. Journalists who attempt to investigate the meetings or compile lists of attendees may be harassed and intimidated. The Bilderbergers claim that secrecy – or privacy, as they would have it – is essential so that they can discuss issues openly and honestly without having to censor themselves. Although no press is allowed, senior media figures including newspaper editors are sometimes invitees. The guest

POLITICAL AND CRIMINAL SOCIETIES

*Prince Bernhard of the Netherlands, 1956, not long after he helped set up the Bilderberg group to advance trans-Atlantic co-operation and free discussion of global issues.*

list has included many of the most prominent people of the last 50 years.

Even sympathetic critics point out that however well intentioned the Bilderberg group is, it is by its nature anti-democratic, elitist and oligarchic, and it excludes representatives of most of the world's population. Conspiracy theorists go further. Not only does the Bilderberg group decide which country to invade next (Serbians, for instance, claim that the NATO campaign against their country was orchestrated and initiated by Bilderberg), but it may even be a Satanic coven engaged in unspeakable acts of ritual barbarity and devil worship.

# BOHEMIAN GROVE

| | |
|---|---|
| TYPE | Elite, political, recreational |
| EXISTED | 1872–present |
| RELATED TO | New World Order elites |
| GOALS AND CONCERNS | Drinking; camping; open-air urination; Satanic ritual sacrifice |

Bohemian Grove is a forested estate 80 miles (129 km) north of San Francisco that hosts an annual gathering of America's elite for two weeks of camping, entertainment and relaxation, a tradition started in 1872 when bored San Francisco journalists founded the Bohemian Club.

Around 2,500 'Grovers' stay in luxury campsites equipped with hot tubs and bars, and although there is some quasi-Masonic play acting and dramatic ritual, the bulk of the time is taken up with light entertainment, lectures, hiking on forest trails, copious drinking and frequent urination against tree trunks, which appears to be an important Bohemian Grove tradition.

According to the Bohemian Club it is entirely harmless fun, and little more than a summer camp for overgrown kids. The motto of the Club is 'weaving spiders come not here', meaning that there should be no talking shop, doing deals or otherwise detracting from the purpose of the gathering, which is relaxation.

*Photograph c.1967 of Ronald Reagan at a news conference. A journalist had just asked him if he and Richard Nixon would talk about politics at their next meeting at Bohemian Grove in California.*

According to conspiracy theorists, however, Bohemian Grove is the scene of something much darker. To begin with, it is extremely exclusive, admitting only men, almost all of whom are old, rich, white, Christian and conservative Republican. Few Jews and even fewer blacks or Hispanics are admitted. The fee for joining is $25,000 and the waiting list is 15 years or more. Almost all of the movers and shakers of right-wing America have attended at one time or another, including George Bush Sr and Jr, Dick Cheney, Clint Eastwood, Gerald Ford, Dwight D. Eisenhower, Barry Goldwater, Charlton Heston, Henry Kissinger, Ronald Reagan, David and Nelson Rockefeller, Karl Rove, Donald Rumsfeld and Mark Twain.

## THE CREMATION OF CARE

But accusations of elitism are mild compared to the evil things that conspiracy theorists believe are happening at Bohemian Grove. The focus of these claims is the strange and sinister ritual drama that kicks off the annual meeting, known as the Cremation of Care. It is supposed to symbolize the Grovers laying down their wearisome burdens of worldly cares for the duration of the festivities. In front of the Owl Shrine (a gigantic owl statue) on the shores of a small lake, men dressed in

hooded red robes solemnly 'sacrifice' the effigy of a child called 'Dull Care', before placing it in a small boat with a skull on the prow, which is set alight and pushed out across the lake. The Bohemian Grove programme for July 2008 invited Grovers to: 'Come join us as we raise the battle banners in the name of beauty, truth, peace and fellowship. Oh, Beauty's Vassals, let us together seek the counsel of the Great Owl of Bohemia so that we may rediscover the wisdom needed to banish Dull Care once again! "Hail, Fellowship's Eternal Flame!"'

Conspiracy theorists claim that this is a perverted Satanic ritual, that the Owl Shrine is an idol of Moloch, the false god of the Canaanites, and that 'Dull Care' is not an effigy at all but a real child, murdered in a ritual human sacrifice. Worse still, hundreds of other children abducted from across the USA are murdered in the obscene orgiastic rites of the Grovers, who are actually members of the Illuminati bloodline dynasties. A good example of these extreme beliefs comes from the website of conspiracy theorist Henry Makow, who cites as evidence 'a young Las Vegas woman named "Treee", who claims to have contacts inside the secretive club'. According to this unimpeachable source, 'a ritual sacrifice of Mary Magdalene takes place Tuesday July 21; and the

ritual sacrifice of Jesus Christ takes place on Wednesday'.

Makow goes on to relate:

... the Las Vegas woman says the Illuminati are actually an alien reptilian species that occupies human bodies and feeds off our energy... This reptilian species is called 'Sangerians'; they are a 'fourth dimension race' and make up 3% of the world's population... They have three hearts, shift shapes, are cold-blooded, but are developing human feelings from devouring human flesh and blood. 'Ten per cent now get their blood from the Red Cross.' Except for sacrifice, their every ritual involves sex. Queen Elizabeth is a leading reptilian. 'It all sounds sci-fi and unbelievable,' the woman says. 'But everything fits.'

This outlandish account is at odds with the harmless-sounding programme of events circulated to Grovers, which generally includes lots of music, occasional revues featuring drag acts and lectures on topics as diverse as forestry, religion and politics, and nuclear power. Given that the guest list includes such

One of the lavish theatricals staged at Bohemian Grove to entertain the rich and powerful during their break from 'dull care'. Drag acts, spooky quasi-Masonic rituals and urinating on trees are also traditional.

unlikely names as Mickey Hart and Bob Weir, two former band members of the Grateful Dead, it seems hard to believe that Bohemian Grove is entirely evil, but critics point out that extremely exclusive gatherings such as this are inherently anti-democratic, as they maintain unfair levels of access between a tiny, self-selecting, mostly conservative elite.

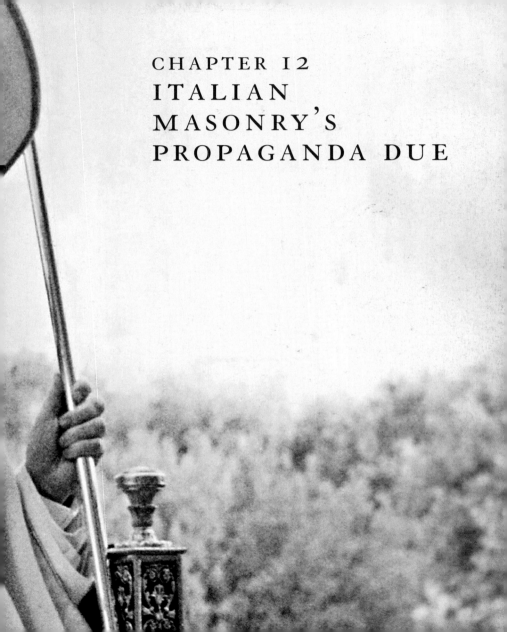

# CHAPTER 12
# ITALIAN
# MASONRY'S
# PROPAGANDA DUE

# P2 — PROPAGANDA DUE

| TYPE | Elite, political, criminal |
|---|---|
| EXISTED | 1877–1981 |
| RELATED TO | Freemasonry, Operation Stay Behind, Operation Gladio |
| GOALS AND CONCERNS | Anti-communism; promoting neo-fascism; embezzlement; personal enrichment |

Propaganda Due, more commonly known as P2, was a private or 'covered' lodge in Italian Freemasonry, which became notorious for its links to political, intelligence and Mafia figures, and its alleged role in a complex web of dirty dealings. These included money laundering and embezzlement on a massive scale, propping up right-wing regimes, 'false flag' terrorist atrocities and a string of murders that may have included a prime minister and a pope.

The original P2 was formed in 1877 by the Grand Master Mason of Italy as a private lodge for members of parliament who wished to flout the Roman Catholic Church's ban on Freemasonry without damaging their reputations. Mussolini's Fascist government made Freemasonry illegal and suppressed P2, but it was revived in 1946 and taken over in the 1960s by Italian fascist Licio Gelli. Under Gelli it became the sort of secret society that conspiracy theorists fantasize about – a super-secret, corrupt body of highly placed right-wing elites, including business and media leaders, politicians, clergy, military and intelligence officers and Mafiosi.

Using high-level contacts with domestic and foreign intelligence agencies and blackmail where necessary, Gelli used P2 to advance his fascist, rabidly anti-communist agenda, support right-wing dictatorships in Latin America, forge unholy alliances between corrupt Vatican officials and the Mafia and become very rich. Gelli and P2 were implicated in Nazi smuggling, covert operations to subvert democratic

*Licio Gelli's Villa Wanda in Arezzo, Italy. It was here that a police raid discovered the membership list of P2, and a later raid found gold bullion hidden in flowerpots.*

governments in Italy and elsewhere, terrorist operations and criminal conspiracies to launder Mafia drug money and embezzle billions from major banks. The secret society was even implicated in the mysterious deaths of Italian Prime Minister Aldo Moro in 1978, Pope John Paul I the same year and Roberto Calvi, nicknamed God's Banker, in 1982 (see pages 328–329). Although its membership list was revealed in a raid on Gelli's villa in 1981 and the lodge supposedly broken up, Gelli himself led the authorities on a merry dance for the next 17 years before finally being brought to justice.

319

# LICIO GELLI AND THE RATLINES

Licio Gelli is the key figure behind the P2 scandal that rocked Italy in the 1980s. Born in Italy in 1919, Gelli was and remains to this day an enthusiastic fascist. During the Spanish Civil War (1936–1939) he volunteered to fight for the Black Shirt Battalion under Franco, and during World War II he served as a liaison officer between Mussolini's Fascists and the Nazis, specifically Herman Goering's SS Division. He was also said to have been a member of the Gestapo. When it was obvious that the war was lost, he saved his skin by becoming an important asset to the American intelligence agencies, helping them to organize 'ratlines'.

## RATLINE NAZIS

Even before the war was over, the Allies had realized that communism would be

*Licio Gelli in 1993. Gelli was one of the most important, divisive and mysterious characters in postwar Italian history. In the 1970s his tentacles of power stretched from the Vatican City to the dictatorships of South America to the heads of Mafia families; he may even have been on good terms with the CIA.*

the next enemy to fight, and that a war with Soviet Russia could possibly be imminent. Combating communism, therefore, took priority over de-Nazification, and working on the principle of 'the enemy of my enemy is my friend', the fascists and the Allies became unusual bedfellows.

To preserve the potentially valuable Nazi assets, US intelligence agencies, who were allegedly in conjunction with the Catholic Church, organized 'ratlines' – underground routes that were used for smuggling Nazis, fascists and Soviet defectors and deserters abroad, mainly to South America, so that they could avoid justice and stay out of jail. Infamous Nazis that are believed to have escaped in this fashion included Klaus Barbie, Adolf Eichmann and Josef Mengele. Licio Gelli was able to use the ratlines as a way to make himself extremely rich, to befriend powerful figures in South American politics, as well as to build up a network of influence within the secret services that would prove highly useful.

# OPERATION STAY BEHIND

In the immediate post-war years, the threat of a Soviet invasion of Western Europe was very real: huge Soviet armies were massed along the Iron Curtain and half the continent was under Soviet rule. Communist political parties were a strong and growing force in many countries. For the West, particularly the USA and especially the military and the secret services, communism was an existential threat on a par with the Nazi menace that had just been defeated. The anti-communist agenda was so important that it over-ruled other considerations such as justice and democracy.

## INSTANT UNDERGROUND

Conspiracy theorists allege that, in preparation for a possible Soviet invasion, the Allies deliberately planted groups of Nazis and fascists in Western Europe in an operation code-named Stay Behind. The idea was that these groups of hardened anti-communist warriors would be activated in the event of a Soviet invasion to create an instant underground or resistance movement, and would also be well placed to help deal with and derail any domestic communist movements. Supposedly, they were even equipped with hidden caches of weapons, and supplied with money and cover.

## OPERATION GLADIO

Among the most worrying countries in Western Europe, from an anti-communist perspective, was Italy, where the domestic Communist Party was making political advances and scoring significant electoral successes during the 1950s. Alarmed, the Americans allegedly activated the Italian arm of Operation Stay Behind to create a secret organization code-named Operation Gladio (sword), recruiting a network of right-wing agents and agitators, ready to resist a communist takeover.

This is where Licio Gelli came in. His extensive contacts in the intelligence and neo-fascist communities made him the ideal man for the job, and he was supposedly a key player in setting up Operation Gladio. Gelli had been initiated into a Masonic lodge in Rome

in 1965, and in 1967 he was appointed secretary of the P2 lodge. This was useful because, while according to Italian law all lodges had to register their membership lists with the government, P2 had been a 'covered' (private) lodge from the start and was thus well suited to his clandestine purposes. He set about transforming it into a political secret society that could serve the anti-communist cause.

*Soviet infantry parading through Red Square in Moscow, 1 December 1954. At the height of the Cold War, scenes like this alarmed the Americans enough to warrant their funding of secret Stay Behind operations involving fascist militia and war criminals. Italy was a hotbed of covert anti-communist activity.*

# THE PUPPET MASTER

Gelli used his extensive contacts to recruit the elite of Italian and South American society, including financiers and businessmen, media people (including Silvio Berlusconi, now Prime Minister of Italy), senior civil servants and politicians, lawyers and judges, generals and admirals, Mafia dons and intelligence agents. When the membership records of the society were seized in 1981, the list included three Italian cabinet ministers, 43 members of the Italian parliament and the heads of the Italian secret service agencies. According to one account, the head of one of the agencies had presented Gelli with files on prominent Italians so that he could blackmail them into joining. Even though the Church threatened to excommunicate anybody who joined the Freemasons, senior clergy signed up, allegedly including Archbishop Paul Marcinkus, the head of the Vatican bank, and other senior members of the Curia, the 'government' of the Vatican City.

Only Gelli knew the complete membership of P2. As well as being

*Il Venerabile*, the Leader, he was also known as *Il Burattinaio*, the Puppet Master. He used his shadowy network of influence to broker deals and help the Mafia launder money. According to some reports he helped sell arms to South American regimes and even helped Juan Peron regain power in Argentina, and there is a tale that Peron knelt at Gelli's feet to thank him for his help. Through his Vatican contacts he was allegedly involved in a deal in which the Vatican bank sold massive shareholdings to the Mafia in return for hundreds of millions of dollars of drug money.

## MURDERS IN HIGH PLACES

As part of Operation Gladio, P2 was alleged to have been behind a number of 'false flag' operations as part of a 'strategy of tension' – attacks that would

*Italian Prime Minister Silvio Berlusconi. Once a member of P2, Berlusconi is believed by some to have put into action Gelli's 'plan for democratic rebirth'.*

appear to have been carried out by Communist terrorists so as to mobilize public opinion against them and blacken the name of legitimate Communist politicians. To act as its *agents provocateurs*, P2 allegedly colluded with the CIA and the Italian secret services to set up the Red Brigades, a radical leftist terrorist group, which in 1978 kidnapped the Italian Prime Minister Aldo Moro when he was on the verge of a historic accommodation with the Italian Communist Party. After he had been held in captivity for 55 days, during which time the Italian police and secret services notably failed to rescue him, he was murdered. Supposedly, Moro had been warned by senior Americans that his life would be in danger if he made deals with the Italian Communists.

An even more incredible murder plot surfaced when popular Cardinal Albino Luciani was elected Pope John Paul I, but died just 33 days later. Conspiracy theorists allege that he had vowed to clean up the rotten state of the Curia and Vatican finances by getting rid of P2 members and affiliates in the Vatican, and that Marcinkus and his P2

*Pope John Paul I (Albino Luciani 1912–1978) is seen being carried aloft in the Papal Chair. He died just 33 days after taking office.*

allies had him killed. Suspicions were fanned by the fact that he was not given an autopsy and there were allegations of missing evidence and stolen papers.

In 1980 came the worst outrage yet, the Bologna Massacre. On 2 August 1980 a massive bomb at Bologna train station killed 85 people. The true story behind this atrocity remains murky and contentious, with the trials of alleged perpetrators dragging on for decades. It is generally thought that a neo-fascist terrorist group, the *Nuclei Armati Rivoluzionari*, were responsible, but one of the top men in Italian military intelligence was accused of fabricating evidence to help divert attention from Licio Gelli, and P2 are widely assumed to have been involved at some level.

## THE MASTER PLAN

All of these actions were part of P2's anti-communist agenda. In parallel with these was a political and propaganda programme set out in documents later found secreted in the false bottom of a suitcase. These included Gelli's *piano di rinascita democratica* – 'plan for democratic rebirth' – in which he advocated taking over the mainstream media and generally shifting Italian politics towards the right, while working to undermine the Italian Communist Party.

# THE END OF P2

P2 became entangled in a complex web of financial crime that eventually brought about its downfall. Two important members of P2 were the financiers Michele Sindona (1920–1986), a Sicilian believed to have been one of the Mafia's top money men, and Roberto Calvi (1920–1982), the head of Banco Ambrosiano, Italy's largest private bank. With help from Licio Gelli, these men and the institutions with which they were involved were implicated in a variety of massive financial irregularities, including the 'disappearance' of hundreds of millions of dollars of funds stolen from, among others, the Vatican.

Banking scandals in the late 1970s led the Italian authorities to investigate both Sindona and Calvi. Although the investigations were impeded by the arrest, imprisonment and even murder of key investigators and journalists, both men were eventually brought to trial. Sindona was jailed for 25 years, but died in prison, claiming that he had been poisoned. Calvi was sentenced to four years in jail in 1981, but was freed pending an appeal.

## THE MURDER OF GOD'S BANKER

The investigations led the authorities to raid Gelli's villa in Arezzo, where they found a membership list for P2 that shocked the country. There were over 900 names on the list and indications that more than a thousand other names were missing, although many of the names that were listed have since been proven to have nothing to do with P2. Nonetheless, the roll-call of top officials, especially politicians, dirty bankers and Mafiosi, led to an outcry and brought down the government. The Italian parliament passed a law banning secret associations, and P2 was officially defunct. Gelli had already been expelled from mainstream Italian Masonry after a series of altercations with the Grand Orient Lodge that ran the Craft in Italy, and which had declared P2 illegal around the same time.

The story was far from over, however. In 1982 Banco Ambrosiano was found to have a $1.287 billion 'black hole' in its accounts and soon collapsed. Roberto Calvi, widely believed to have cheated the Mafia as well as engaging in

*Michele Sindona after extradition from the US in 1984. He was suspected of having Mafia links and he died in prison in 1986; many people believe he was murdered.*

massive financial fraud, fled to London, but was found on 18 June hanging underneath Blackfriars Bridge with bricks in his pockets. The same morning his long-time secretary 'jumped' from her office window in an apparent suicide. Incredibly, Calvi's death was initially ruled to be a suicide as well. His wife succeeded in having the case reopened and it is now believed he was murdered, probably by the Mafia, but in a deliberately mock-Masonic style, possibly indicating P2 involvement. Gelli has been accused of complicity in Calvi's murder.

## GREAT ESCAPES

Wanted in connection with these scandals and crimes, Gelli fled to Switzerland, where he was arrested in Geneva attempting to withdraw millions of dollars from a secret bank account. He escaped from prison in Switzerland and fled to South America, but gave himself up to the authorities in 1987. He was extradited back to Italy to face charges relating to the Bologna Massacre, impeding investigations into P2, his role in the Banco Ambrosiano collapse and other crimes. A series of trials and appeals lasting until 1998 saw him receive various jail sentences, culminating in a 12-year sentence relating to the Ambrosiano affair, but while under house arrest at his villa he again managed to escape.

Six months later he was tracked down on the French Riviera where he had been holed up in an apartment in Cannes. Taken to hospital after suffering a minor stroke, he was said to have attempted suicide. Meanwhile, police found documents that led them to search six large flowerpots that were standing on the terrace of his Tuscan villa, which held 165 unmarked gold ingots. In October 1998 he was deported back to

Italy to begin serving his sentence, although it is not clear whether he is still in prison.

Gelli is said to have sold the film rights to the story of his life, and a film entitled *Conspirator: The Licio Gelli Story* is reportedly in production, with George Clooney linked to the title role. In 2008 Gelli sparked outrage by starring in an Italian TV documentary series in which he defended his life and work, declaring at a press conference, 'I will die a fascist'. He also heaped praise on Silvio Berlusconi, current Prime Minister of Italy. Disturbingly, Berlusconi, who was a fully paid-up member of P2, is believed by many critics to have successfully implemented Gelli's *piano di rinascita democratica* or 'plan for democratic rebirth'. As called for under the P2 plan, Berlusconi has succeeded in amalgamating most of the Italian media under his direct or indirect control. Meanwhile, his government has passed many laws that appear to benefit and/or protect himself and his partners, launched neo-fascist controls on immigrants, put soldiers and paramilitaries on the street, overseen attacks on left-wing protestors and advanced the cause of anti-communism while shifting Italian politics far to the right by bringing neo-fascist parties and politicians into government.

*Roberto Calvi, 'God's Banker', was murdered in 1982. Shortly before his death, Calvi threatened to spill shocking facts about the Vatican finances.*

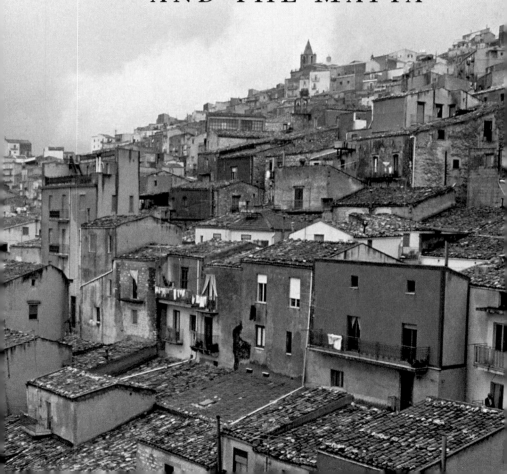

# CHAPTER 13
# THE DARK
# BROTHERHOODS
# AND THE MAFIA

# THE MAFIA

| | |
|---|---|
| TYPE | Criminal, fraternal, political, paramilitary |
| EXISTED | 1860s–present |
| RELATED TO | Dark Brotherhoods, Black Hand Gangs |
| GOALS AND CONCERNS | Racketeering; extortion; drug trafficking; prostitution; stealing; financial fraud; gambling; corruption; community policing |

'Mafia' has become the generic name for any organized crime outfit, and particularly for Italian organized crime groups. It originally referred solely to the Sicilian organized crime society that calls itself the Cosa Nostra (Our Affair), although now there are four recognized mafias in Italy – Cosa Nostra in Sicily, 'Ndrangheta in Calabria, Camorra in Campania and Sacra Corona Unita in Puglia – with a fifth, the Basilischi, emerging in the region of Basilicata (also called Lucania). The Mafia have become famous thanks to their exploits in America, but in reality organized crime syndicates in the States are harder to categorize as secret societies than their Italian forebears; despite public perception, they are not such distinct or culturally specific entities.

Mafia organizations have many of the characteristics of secret societies: secret membership, aims and proceedings; initiation ceremonies; code words and secret symbols; internal hierarchies; and legends of origin. The Mafia date back to Sicily in the late 19th century when social and political changes, especially the unification of Italy, led to the criminalization of pre-existing groups and social structures with roots in the Middle Ages. Clans defined by class, locale and tradition evolved into societies known as the Dark Brotherhoods, later calling

*This photograph taken in 1928 shows members of the Mafia organization, handcuffed and guarded by police, awaiting trial after their capture in Sicily, Italy.*

themselves the *Cosa Nostra* or *La Società Onorata*, the Honoured Society. In America the Mafia coalesced out of the Black Hand phenomenon; the extent to which it actually reflects genuine and direct transfer of Italian Mafia structures is a matter of debate. Many feel that the authorities and the media are largely responsible for this impression (see pages 352–353).

## ORIGIN OF THE NAME

Many different origins have been suggested for the word 'mafia'. The most common is that it derives from the Arabic word *mafiyya*, 'place of refuge', a reference to the mountain villages where generations of Sicily's downtrodden inhabitants endured the depredations of a succession of invaders and exploiters (see pages 338–339), and where the Mafia had its roots.

Alternatively, *mafie* was the name for the small private armies hired by absentee landlords to protect their estates. A charming if improbable legend recounted by former 'wiseguy' (one of

the names for a Mafia mobster) Sonny Girard traces the origin of the name back to the Night of the Sicilian Vespers, in 1283:

> The story is that one day, while a soon-to-be bride waited for her groom to fetch the priest from a village church, she was approached by a Bourbon Army Lieutenant, Pierre Drouet. The lieutenant, who was drunk at the time, tried to have his way with the girl, who resisted his advances. During the struggle, the bride-to-be fell, hit her head on a stone and died. When word of the girl's murder spread, enraged Sicilians began planning to finally reclaim their independence and rose up at the ringing of the Easter Vesper bells to drive the French from their land. The acronym of their shouts, Morte Alla Francia, Italia Anella – 'Death to the French is Italy's cry' – supposedly became the name of their sub-rosa government: MAFIA.

As Girard himself points out, however, Sicilians of the time would never have described themselves as Italians.

*Tommaso Buscetta, Sicilian mafioso who turned* pentito *(informant), exhausted by internecine warfare and repeated arrests. He was the first to break the code of* omertà *and his testimony led to many convictions in Italy and the US.*

# ORIGINS OF THE MAFIA

Sicily is a large island in the Mediterranean situated at the strategic crossing of trade and transport routes, and its long history has been one of almost continuous rule by foreign powers. The island was successively invaded and exploited by Arabs, Normans, French, Spanish and mainland Italians. Mistreated Sicilians developed a long tradition of self-reliance, distrust of the authorities and violent self-defence. The rugged interior with its fortified villages became the refuge for gangs of bandits and native militia, who both protected the indigenous Sicilians and offered the only style of justice and order available to them. Out of sight of the authorities, concealed behind a cultural wall of silence, a caste of outlaws became entrenched in Sicilian society, respected and feared for its strong code of honour. This was the probable origin of the Mafia, which developed 'families' that

were actually more like clans, extended social networks based on geography and centred on villages like Corleone, Prizzi and Bagheria.

## THE DARK BROTHERHOODS

By the 1870s these clans or proto-mafias were known as the *Tenebrosi Sodalizi*, the Dark Brotherhoods, among other names. They included Fratuzzi di Bagheria, Scattialora di Sciacca, Scaglione di Castrogiovani, Fontana Nuova di Misilmeri, Fratellanza di Favara and Zubbio di Villabate, but the most powerful was the Stoppaglieri di Monreale. Each was an independent organization based around a village, but they shared common features such as similar initiation rituals (see pages 341–345), code words for mutual recognition and respect for each other's hierarchies. The Stoppaglieri of the village of Monreale, in the hills above Palermo, was formed as an example of a counter-mafia; they were founded by Giuseppe Palmeri of Nicosia to protect the locals from the threat posed by the Palermo brotherhood, the Giardinieri. The two organizations engaged in one of the first documented mob wars in the 1870s.

*Prizzi, a mountain village in Sicily, deep in the heartland of the original mafia clans.*

## TAKING OVER

Sicily had traditionally been divided into large estates, the landlords of which rarely lived on them. These absentee landlords used local gangs to run the estates and maintain order; the gangs became rich in the process. As the foreign feudal landowners lost power in the 19th century, the local gangs became more powerful. After the unification of Italy these Mafia gangs controlled most of Sicily's economy, and they formed a close alliance with politicians of the new state; they delivered votes on demand in return for immunity from harassment and government collaboration. By the end of the century the Mafia, calling themselves the Cosa Nostra, had become completely entrenched in Sicilian society, controlling most aspects of life with the collusion of the official authorities. Although this arrangement was briefly disturbed during Mussolini's Fascist government, when he instituted a crackdown and locked up hundreds of suspected Mafiosi in 1922, it reasserted itself by the end of World War II. The invading Americans, keen to make use of Mafia help in defeating their enemies, freed many Mafiosi from prison. In post-war Italy the Mafia forged close links with the Christian Democratic Party that were to last for more than 50 years.

# CODE OF HONOUR

Mike La Sorte, Emeritus Professor at the State University of New York, describes the defining characteristics of 'a mafia-like association' as: 'centralized organization, top capo [boss], initiation ceremony, sense of brotherhood and swearing to codes of honour and fidelity to one's dying breath'. Mafias in both Italy and the USA generally share a similar organization, with a defined area controlled by a single, clan-like 'family'. The family is ruled by a *capofamiglia*, who has a lieutenant and a counsellor or *consigliere* to help him run things. Below them are captains, each of whom controls a number of soldiers. Each soldier might have a specific area of responsibility, such as control of a venue. Soldiers are expected to show complete obedience to their superiors, and the capo's word is law. In theory, the capo never deals with the soldiers or any of

*Sicilian-born American gangster Charles 'Lucky' Luciano (1897–1962) walking with friends in Lercera, Sicily. There is disagreement over the extent to which the Mafia in Sicily and the Mafia in America are really comparable.*

the illegal activities directly, so that he never gets his hands dirty. Tithes on earnings are passed upwards in pyramid-scheme fashion. A group of families in one region might recognize a *capo dei capo*, or chief of chiefs.

## OMERTÀ

Initiation was central to the success of the Mafia – members had to surrender their former lives and become completely transformed into *Mafiosi*, so that they would not break the all-important code of *omertà*. Although this refers to a code of silence, the word derives from *omu*, Sicilian for man. 'Manliness', or machismo, is the central concept of Mafia life; only fully initiated Mafiosi are considered to be real men – everyone else is a lesser breed. True men follow a strict code of honour, the code of omertà, and everyone living under the Mafia system is expected to abide by it as well. Mafiosi never speak to or seek justice from the authorities, they never go outside the family to resolve disputes and they never, ever rat out a family member or squeal to the police. Ideally, the real man does not speak much at all, following the Sicilian proverb, *'L'omu chi parra assai cu la so stissa vucca si disterra'* ('The man who talks too much will ruin himself through his own mouth').

To symbolize the transference to a new life, a new state of being, new Mafia members went through an initiation that has changed little in more than a century. Compare these three accounts of initiation:

> Marsala tied my index finger of my right hand tightly with a string. He pricked the finger with a pin. The blood dripped on the image of a female saint. He burned the image, divided it into two portions and gave me one. We ground up our portions in our hands and then threw the result into the air. As part of the ceremony I swore that I would remain a member of the *Società* [*Onorata* – the Honoured Society] that has as its capo Don Vito Vita, and its aim is to commit crimes against persons and property. I was told that the *Società* has affiliates in other towns, each town with its own capo, and if an affiliate does not carry out his assigned duties he would be judged by the *Società* and condemned to death. Then they taught me the mode of recognizing other affiliates.

Testimony of Leo Pellegrino from Sicily, talking in 1876.

> One evening I was driven to a village on the slope of Mount Etna. We stopped in the courtyard of a small house. The owner was a member of the mafioso family, obviously. At a certain point Uncle Peppino Indelicato entered and said to us, 'You boys stand over there,' indicating a corner of the room. 'Dear young men,' he began, 'we are here this evening to present to you a nice gift. You know the mafia? But look, the true mafia is not the same mafia of which others speak. This is Cosa Nostra. It is called Cosa Nostra. Now for the rules. First thing, if you ever encounter a man of honour who is on the lam [on the run], you have the obligation to hide him, even in your own house, if necessary. Woe to the person who approaches his

*A cage holding 34 accused men during the Camorra trial in Viterbo, March 1911.*

daughter, or wife of another man of honour. He who does must be killed. Third: it is prohibited to steal. ...At this point Uncle Peppino took a needle, a big one, and asked me, 'Which is your shooting hand?' 'With this,' I responded. He pricked a finger, causing my blood to drip onto a small picture of a sacred image. I looked at it. It was the Madonna dell'Annunziata [Our Lady of the Annunciation], the patron saint of Cosa Nostra, whose holy day falls on 25 March. Uncle Peppino lit a match and set aflame a corner of the sacred image, asking me to hold the burning paper in my hand until it turned to ash. According to the rule, if an affiliate betrays the commandments of Cosa Nostra, he must burn like Saint Annunziata. Once the oath of allegiance was completed, all those in attendance came forward to kiss me. I had become *un uomo d'onore*.

Testimony of Antonino Calderone from Sicily, in 1992.

There was a wooden table in the centre of the room. On it was a knife and a loaded blue-black pistol, each there to symbolize the most important tools in this trade – deadly force. Gaspipe stood at the table with the gun and knife and a picture of St Peter. Vinny Beans intoned the oath as Casso repeated: 'I, Anthony Casso, want to enter this organization to protect my family and to protect my friends.' He was then ordered to never betray the family or break his vow of silence. Casso's trigger finger was pricked and blood dripped onto an image of St Peter. The image was set aflame with Casso holding the burning paper until it turned to ash.

Testimony of Anthony 'Gaspipe' Casso from Brooklyn, in 1994.

Common to all three accounts is the marking with blood of a picture of the patron saint of the Mafia clan's home town, after which the picture is burned to ashes, symbolizing the irreversibility of the initiate's commitment. Calderone's account also includes some of the Mafia 'commandments'. A raid on a Mafia meeting in Palermo in November 2007 uncovered a document with ten such commandments. Supposedly top

'Godfather' Salvatore Lo Piccolo carried the document with him everywhere:

1  No one can present himself directly to another of our friends. There must be a third person to do it.
2  Never look at the wives of friends.
3  Never be seen with cops.
4  Don't go to pubs and clubs.
5  Always be available for Cosa Nostra, even if your wife's about to give birth.
6  Appointments must be respected.
7  Wives must be treated with respect.
8  When asked for any information, the answer must be the truth.
9  Money cannot be appropriated if it belongs to others or to other families.
10 People who can't be part of Cosa Nostra are anyone with a close relative in the police, with a two-timing relative in the family, anyone who behaves badly and doesn't hold to moral values.

## CAMORRA INITIATION

The Mafia around Naples on the Italian mainland are known as the Camorra. An account of 1885 describes the lengthy and arduous system of training and initiation that a Camorra recruit had to undergo, which included 'the scientific use of the knife, and such rough fencing as the weapon permits, various exercises that tend to develop strength and agility, and teach how to endure long fasts and a prolonged want of sleep' and instruction in 'the use of disguises, and in the means by which he may avoid attention or elude pursuit'. The initiation ceremony took the form of a brutal knife fight, an ultimate test of machismo:

> When a capo believes that his pupil is sufficiently instructed to advance a stage, he communicates with other officers of a similar kind in different parts of the town. At an appointed place and hour they appear with their respective charges and pit them against each other. A series of fights with knives then takes place, and whoever shows sufficient skill in the use of his weapon and stoicism in bearing his wounds is promoted to the rank of a *Picciotto di Sgarro*. The greatest proof of hardiness is to seize the opponent's knife by the blade and to wrench it from his hands, a feat which is frequently attempted, but rarely succeeds. When the police find that the interior of one of their prisoner's right hand is marked by deep scars, they at once conclude that he belongs to the Camorra.

# THE BLACK HAND

The popular account of how the Mafia came to America is that they simply transferred their operations across the Atlantic along with the Sicilians who emigrated there during the 19th and 20th centuries – up to a million of them. The first inkling of a Mafia presence in the USA came around the turn of the century with the appearance of *la Mano Nera*, the Black Hand. 'There is talk of this terrible society of delinquents called "la Mano Nera" here in America, and in New York above all, one hears and one reads every day of terrible crimes,' reported Adolfo Valeri in the New York newspaper *Stamperia del Bollettino della Sera* in 1905.

The Black Hand Gang or the Blackhanders were so called for their habit of sending threatening letters or messages, extorting money with threats of violence, marked with the imprint of a hand in black. Supposedly, it developed from a Sicilian custom of the 1880s, when a hand blackened with coal dust would be used to make an imprint on a wall. From around 1900 members of the immigrant communities, mainly shopkeepers and small businessmen, began receiving such letters. If they failed to pay they might be attacked or have their premises bombed.

There was a widespread fear that the Black Hand Gang was an organized conspiracy, but in fact the notes were written in a variety of dialects and took different forms, revealing their true origin. They were simply the work of individuals or small gangs of criminals who had no association with each other and came from widely different parts of the Old World. Many were not Italian, and Black Hand threats were issued to Jewish and other Eastern European immigrants by thugs from their own communities. In his 1977 book *The Black Hand*, Thomas Pitken described them as 'more a rabble than an organized crime enterprise... unorganized thieving groups and individuals with no central leadership or hierarchical structure'.

The Black Hand phenomenon faded in the 1920s. This may have partly been due to better law enforcement and detection, but it has also been attributed to the coming of Prohibition.

*Denizens of* Bandits' Roost, *a notoriously lawless area of Manhattan's Little Italy in the early 20th century. Areas like this were believed to be the haunt of the Black Hand Gang, but in fact Blackhanders were just as likely to come from Eastern European immigrant communities.*

# THE MAFIA IN AMERICA

In 1919 the Volstead or National Prohibition Act was passed, making it illegal to produce, transport or sell intoxicating liquor in the USA. Bootlegging became big business and there were vast profits to be made by criminal gangs. The era of organized crime in America had begun.

## CAPONE AND LUCIANO

According to the conventional account of the American Mafia, the criminal gangs involved in bootlegging were dominated by Mafia clans transferred direct from the old country. Although at first they squabbled and fought, they were brought together as a nationwide cooperative of criminal syndicates by Alphonse 'Al' Capone (1899–1947), who had established control in Chicago with the help of the St Valentine's Day Massacre of 1929, in which seven of his opponents were brutally gunned down.

Meanwhile, in New York Charles Luciano (1897–1962), who had acquired the nickname 'Lucky' after surviving being tortured and left for dead by a rival gang, had risen to prominence.

Luciano and Capone represented a new breed of Mafiosi, keen to move beyond the traditional parochial restrictions of the older generation, who would refuse to deal with gangsters from different Sicilian villages, let alone non-Sicilians. Supposedly, Capone and Luciano arranged a meeting of national bosses in Atlantic City in 1931 to announce a new order and the creation of a national network of gangs – the true beginnings of the American Mafia. On 10 and 11 September 1931, over 60 'Moustache Petes', or members of the old guard of Sicilian émigrés who might stand in the way of this grand plan, were murdered in what became known as the Second Night of the Sicilian Vespers. Capone was put away by special law enforcement agent Eliot Ness (1903–1957) of Untouchables fame, but Luciano

*Al Capone in relaxed mood, photographed in May 1932, on the train taking him to a federal penitentiary in Atlanta where he was due to begin serving an 11-year sentence after indictment for tax evasion. Revisionist historians claim he was only ever a minor player in organised crime.*

continued to modernize the Mafia, setting up the Commission that regulated crime families in New York. He became de facto *capo di tutti i capi* – the head of the Mafia in America.

With the end of Prohibition the Mafia concentrated on labour racketeering and infiltrating the trade unions, and began to move into drug distribution. During World War II they colluded with the secret services, first of all agreeing not to disrupt the war effort and later helping to set up the resistance movement in Sicily. After the war they began to focus on gambling and the development of Las Vegas, massively enlarged the international heroin trade and poured millions into developing Cuba as a gangster's paradise. All the while they were largely immune from serious prosecution thanks to their success at keeping capos separate from the day-to-day business of crime, and their alleged possession of incriminating photos of the head of the Federal Bureau of Investigation (FBI), J. Edgar Hoover (1895–1972), a closet homosexual. Right up until 1963, Hoover maintained that there was no such thing as the Mafia.

## MODERN MAFIA

A series of government investigations and new leadership at the FBI after Hoover's death led to increasing public awareness of the Mafia and pressure to crack down on them. The Racketeering Influenced Criminal Organization (RICO) law of 1970 made it an offence to be a member of the same organization as someone who has committed crimes. Mafia bosses were no longer safe because they kept clear of routine criminal activities, and a series of top Mafia bosses went to jail. At the same time, the omertà-based wall of silence began to come down as Mafiosi were increasingly willing to testify against their colleagues.

Nonetheless, the Mafia continued to modernize, gaining massive profits from the increasing international drug trade, but also moving into white-collar crime: financial fraud and legitimate business enterprises. In Italy, Mafia influence grew, and the vast profits from illegal arms trading and control of the transatlantic heroin trade saw the black economy bring in billions of dollars a year. Eventually, the entire Italian economy came to depend on the Mafia, and in the late 1980s it was estimated that almost a third of Italian government bonds – the financial instruments that prop up the state – were bought with money from the drug trade. In 1991 the Ministry of the Interior estimated that 450 gangs were operating in Italy with 15,000 members, and that a million people were involved

*Director of the FBI, John Edgar Hoover seated at his desk, c.1940.*

in drug smuggling and extortion. As in the USA, Italy has seen a series of high-profile crackdowns and super-trials in which dozens of top bosses were locked up at once. The traditional alliance between the Mafia and Italian politics has also been weakened with the breaking up of old political parties and the emergence of new ones. Meanwhile, organized criminal gangs from other nations, including South America, China, Russia, Turkey and Central Asia, have increasingly taken over control of the international drugs trade.

# THE INVENTION
# OF THE MAFIA

POLITICAL AND CRIMINAL SOCIETIES

Critics of this conventional history argue that, in the USA in particular, the Mafia are a myth, invented by the authorities and reinforced by a constant cycle of media reporting and fictional versions such as *The Godfather* and *The Sopranos*. Although some Italian-Americans have been engaged in organized crime, the notion that they have ever controlled or monopolized it is a fiction. For instance, a minority of the Prohibition-era bootleggers were Italian, while Al Capone was a relatively minor figure in Chicago crime.

The myth of the Mafia really began to take hold in 1951, with the widely publicized investigations of Senator Estes Kefauver into organized crime in interstate commerce. The Kefauver Crime Committee uncovered genuine crimes, but it also claimed that the Mafia was a shadow government controlling virtually every aspect of politics and commerce in the USA. The legend of the Mafia was born, and grew from there. Mark Haller, writing in *The Oxford Companion to United States History*, explains that post-war investigators:

... constructed a history based upon the assumption that the generally independent businessmen in the families were instead controlled by and worked for the profit of the 'mafia'... non-Italian entrepreneurs were subservient to the Italians. In this history, the 'mafia' rose to a central place in coordinating crime nationally through the power of Italian-American bootleggers... As the fight against the 'mafia' menace became a central focus of law enforcement... the focus of federal, state and local prosecutions almost solely on Italian-Americans, combined with the media attention, necessarily publicized the exaggerated notions of the power of 'the mafia' while obscuring the complexity and diverse roots of criminal activities and generally ignoring similar activities by persons not of Italian-American background.

The way that the authorities and the media colluded to create a mythical narrative of an overarching international conspiracy of organized crime, in order to mobilize and direct public opinion, is reminiscent of the creation of Jewish conspiracy myths for similar purposes (see page 296–301).

*Democratic Senator from Tennessee, Estes Kefauver, at his desk in 1951, the year of his Congressional investigation into organized crime that did so much to create the myth of the American Mafia.*

CHAPTER 14
THE TRIADS
AND THE TONG

# THE TRIADS

| | |
|---|---|
| TYPE | Criminal, fraternal, political, paramilitary, mystical |
| EXISTED | 1761/2–present |
| RELATED TO | White Lotus Society, the Tong |
| GOALS AND CONCERNS | Fraternal support and protection; restoring Ming dynasty; criminal enterprises |

'Triads' is a collective description for a number of Chinese criminal secret societies, or *hui*. *Hui* has no precise English translation, but 'society' and 'association' are the nearest approximations. The word 'triad' means a group or arrangement of three, and in this context is a reference to man, heaven and earth.

Modern triad societies can trace their origins back to the Heaven and Earth Society (Tiandihui), or to related *hui*, including the Three Dots Society (Sandianhui), the Three Unites Society (Sanhehui) and the Hong League (Hung Mun). These may all have been different names for the same things, but the early history of the *hui* is murky. Today there are an estimated 80,000 members in 60 societies around the world.

## ORIGINS OF THE TRIADS

According to internal Triad legends, especially the Xi Lu Legend, the Triads were founded to overthrow the Manchu Ch'ing or Qing dynasty (1644–1911) and restore the native Chinese Ming dynasty. The Manchu – a warrior people from Manchuria to the north of China – invaded China in 1644 and quickly established control over the whole country. Many of their Han Chinese subjects resented rule by foreigners, and in the late 17th century grassroots movements mixing mystical and millenarian religious beliefs with martial arts evolved into *hui* in the southern Chinese province of Fujian, taking 'defeat the Ching, restore the Ming' as their motto. They also adopted the dynastic colour of the Ming, which was red, and the family name of the Ming emperors, 'Hung', hence the alternative Triad name of 'Hung Mun'. Supposedly, like the early Mafia in Sicily, the Triads were the protectors of their people against the repressive and cruel regime of the Manchu overlords.

In reality, this is a romantic myth with little more credibility than Masonic Legends of Perpetuation (see page 149). The Heaven and Earth society was actually founded at the Guanyinting (Goddess of Mercy pavilion) in Gaoxi township, in Fujian province in the south-east of China, in 1761 or 1762. According to Dian H. Murray and Baoqi Qin, authors of *The Origins of the Tiandihui: The Chinese Triads in Legend and History*:

> The Tiandihui emerged as a mutual aid fraternity in response to the demographic and economic crises of the late 18th century, and that it was but one of several societies, or *hui*, to appear at this time... During the Qing dynasty, *hui* were organizations characterized by a ceremonial ritual, often in the form of a blood oath, that brought people together for a common goal.

*A Ch'ing nobleman and his wife, 18th century. The Ch'ing were Manchu from northern China, and were resented by dispossessed ethnic Chinese who mythologized the previous Han dynasty.*

# ORGANIZATION AND INITIATION

Some of what we know about the organization of Triad societies is coloured by the fact that the original Victorian descriptions were based on Western ideas about secret societies. It is telling that the *hui* were described as having lodges and chapters. In practice, the lack of a centralized organization was an important feature of the triads. Although several *hui* in an area might form a loose association, generally they are independent and self-sufficient.

## BLOOD BROTHERS

The key principle of the Triads is *guanxi*, swearing brotherhood. In traditional Chinese society not all brothers are equal – seniority is all-important, and younger 'brothers' are expected to defer to their elders. Traditionally, within each *hui* there were three senior officers: a leader or chief and his two main lieutenants, who occupied the ceremonial roles of Incense Master and Vanguard. The Incense Master was the high priest of a *hui*, guardian of its core religious principles and mystical elements. The Vanguard was in charge of administrative

functions, including recruiting members, expanding into new areas and looking after its weapons. Even today Triad members favour the traditional weapons – machetes and modified meat cleavers.

Below these three senior officers were five others, making a total of eight, a number of great significance in Chinese culture. Numerology – the mystical, esoteric and symbolic meanings of numbers – is a vital concern in Triad lore. For instance, high-ranking Triad members use code numbers 489 and 438, while common members use the number 47. Each of the five junior officers controlled an area of responsibilities. One of the most important was the Welfare section, which was responsible for arranging funerals. This became particularly important in the Tongs – the Chinese gangs overseas – because traditional Chinese were desperate to be buried in their homeland and needed Tong help to ensure this.

## HANGING THE LANTERN

The initiation ceremony for Triad recruits is of vital importance in

*Suspects of one of Hong Kong's crime rings are arrested in 1993. Their heads are covered in hoods to protect their identity.*

moulding a new, criminal identity, outside the rules of normal society. Triad initiations are elaborate, lengthy and mystical. Typically, initiation is seen as a ceremonial journey, both literal and symbolic, through city and countryside, across water and over bridges, under and above ground, representing the journey to a new identity. An example of a typical initiation ceremony is 'hanging the lantern', in which initiates are bound together to reinforce fraternal bonding. Incense is burnt while members make numerous oaths recited in Chinese. In the 'hanging the lantern' ceremony, 36 oaths are taken. The oaths include an oath of silence and a promise to protect fellow members.

# A BRIEF HISTORY OF THE TRIADS

As in 19th-century Sicily, close-knit societies of armed men from impoverished backgrounds with few prospects inevitably became involved in criminality. The Triads were particularly associated with gambling before moving into drug trafficking as well. During the 1970s and '80s the 'Golden Triangle' region of South East Asia supplied most of the world's heroin, and the Triads controlled the majority of the international distribution, sometimes employing especially ingenious methods to smuggle the drug abroad. One clever ruse was to dissolve heroin in water, which was then frozen to produce ice for shipping shrimp from Thailand. Once delivered, the ice could be melted and the heroin recovered by evaporating the water. Additionally, modern Triads control the smuggling of endangered species and related products.

## FIGHT THE POWER

As well as their criminal activities, the Triads and related societies became involved in Chinese politics and the long history of rebellions against Ch'ing dynasty rule. One of the greatest of these was the White Lotus rebellion of the mid-1790s, led by a mystical Buddhist *hui* known as the White Lotus Society. The Triads were also heavily involved in the 'Cudgels' uprising of 1847–1850, the Taiping rebellion of 1850–1864 and the Boxer Rebellion of 1896–1900. The revolutionary Sun Yat Sen (1866–1925) led a sustained campaign to end imperial rule of China and institute a republic, finally succeeding in 1911; the Triads played an important role in a decade of insurrections leading up to this.

In the post-imperial era the Triads were broadly anti-Communist and pro-Nationalist, although they were accused of collaborating with the Japanese after Japan invaded China in the 1930s. After World War II the Nationalists relied heavily on Triad support in their struggle with the Chinese Communists, and the location of Nationalist headquarters at 14 Po Wah Road in Canton is thought to be the origin of the name of the 14K Triad, which in 1947 was estimated to have 300,000 members in Hong Kong alone. After the

*Two members of the Boxer society kneel before the Chinese High Court, 1919. Boxers were a mystical hui with millenarian tendencies. Their 1896–1900 rebellion was aided by the Triads.*

Communists came to power they ruthlessly suppressed the Triads, effectively breaking their power in mainland China. However, they continued to flourish in Hong Kong and Taiwan, and throughout Chinese colonies overseas, especially in Vietnam, Malaysia, Singapore, USA, Canada, Australia and Britain. Overseas Triads became known as the Tong.

GLOSSARY

**Adept** Someone highly trained and skilled in **occult** practices.

**Alchemy** An early form of chemical research that was concerned with the discovery of the **Philosopher's Stone**, which was thought capable of transmuting base metals into gold and might also hold the key to eternal life. Alchemists were particularly focused on spiritual transformation and the recovery of ancient wisdom.

**Alumbrados (Illuminati)** Adherents of a mystical Christian movement in 15th- and 16th-century Spain, including many Jewish and Moorish convert members, who were much persecuted by the Spanish Inquisition.

**Ancient Mystical Order Rosae Crucis (AMORC)** A neo-Rosicrucian (see **Rosicrucianism**) order established in North America in the 1920s by occultist H. Spencer Lewis, which subsequently spread to Britain and Europe.

**Ariosophy** An **occult** anti-Semitic belief based on Germanic mysticism and spurious anthropology, which argues that Jews are a sub-human race.

**Ark of the Covenant** Originally a chest containing the tablets of the Ten Commandments of the ancient Israelites, placed in the Temple by Solomon and lost at the time of the Babylonian destruction in 586 BCE. It subsequently took on iconic importance for many sects.

**Assassins (Hashashin)** An Ismaili Muslim sect at the time of the Crusades, allegedly responsible for the killing of a number of political and religious opponents. They also supposedly had links with the Christian **Knights Templar**.

**Astral Plane** In **Theosophy** and other related beliefs, the place of ethereal existence and life after death.

**Atlantis** A legendary land of great beauty and prosperity lost under the Atlantic Ocean and an important mystical location for many sects.

**Baphomet** A legendary pagan deity whom the Templars were accused of worshipping. Interest in Baphomet was revived in the 19th century as a satanic deity, half-goat, half-man. Possibly derived from medieval corruption of 'Mahomet'.

BCE Before the Common Era (CE); a religiously more neutral form of BC.

**Bilderberg group** An informal meeting of leading Western politicians, business leaders and opinion formers founded in 1954 to discuss world issues. Some conspiracy theorists see it as part of the **Illuminati** plot to introduce the **New World Order**.

**Black Hand, the (***a Mano Nera***)** Criminal gangs in late 19th- and early 20th-century America. They supposedly developed through immigration from Sicilian origins and coalesced into the American **Mafia**, though they were by no means all Italian/Sicilian.

**Bloodline** A number of pseudo-historical **occult** theories claim that there is a royal bloodline of inheritance running from Jesus and Mary Magdalene to the Merovingian kings and various modern dynasties, including the Stuarts. Greatly popularized in Dan Brown's 2003 novel *The Da Vinci Code*.

**Boedromion** The third month of the ancient Athenian calendar (late summer) when the first act of the Eleusinian Greater Mysteries (see **Eleusinian Mysteries**) took place.

**Bogomils** A Gnostic sect that emerged in Bulgaria in the mid-10th century and

spread through the Byzantine Empire, the Balkans and parts of Western Europe.

**Bohemian Grove** A men's club founded in the late 19th century in California, which has developed into an annual social meeting for the (mostly conservative) elite of America. It is seen by some conspiracy theorists as part of the plot to bring about the **New World Order**.

**Cathars** A Gnostic (see **Gnosticism**) Christian sect that emerged in 11th-century Italy, Germany and especially southern France. Despite stubborn resistance, the Cathars were ruthlessly suppressed by the time of the 14th century.

**CE** The Common Era; a religiously more neutral form of AD.

**Chthonic** Literally Greek for 'underground', hence of the Classical Underworld. Also refers to pre-Olympian gods of prehistoric Greece.

**Craft, the** Another term for **Freemasonry**.

**Dark Brotherhoods** Clan gangs in Sicily and elsewhere in Italy that developed into the mafia.

**Degree (Masonic and other orders)**
**Freemasonry** and other similar
organizations are frequently structured
with a hierarchy of degrees: from
novices, through adepts or more
spiritually or intellectually developed
members, to fully initiated masters.

**Demeter** The ancient Greek goddess
of the crops and agriculture in whose
honour the Eleusinian Mysteries
were held.

**Dionysus** The Greek god of fertility and,
later, wine, also known as Bacchus, whose
worship often involved ecstatic rites.

**Dualism** The religious and philosophical
concept that the universe is divided into
opposing realms of spirit and matter.

**Eleusinian Mysteries** Rites held in
ancient Greece at Eleusis in honour of
**Demeter** and her daughter **Persephone**.

**Esoteric** Secret, intelligible only to the
initiated or those with special knowledge.

**Exoteric** Public reality; knowledge that
is available to anyone.

**Fraternitas Rosae Crucis (Fellowship
of the Rosy Cross, FRC)** A neo-
Rosicrucian (see **Rosicrucianism**) order

founded in the late 19th century in
America that still exists today.

**Freemasons/Freemasonry** Also known
as the Masons. An international
fraternity for fellowship and spiritual
self-improvement, with elaborate rites
and secret signs. It supposedly
developed from associations of 14th-
century stonemasons into brotherhoods
of like-minded people in 18th-century
London, and became a worldwide
network with links to Rosicrucianism
and other closed organizations. While
essentially theist, Freemasonry has been
persecuted by Roman Catholic,
communist and fascist regimes, and
has been suspected by many of unfair
dealings between its members.

**Gematria** One of the mystical tools of
the **Kabbalah**, involving assigning
numerical values to letters, names and
words to reveal hidden meaning.

**Gnosticism** A heretical branch of
Christianity that flourished in the early
centuries CE. Gnosticism was itself
influenced by Greek philosophy and
earlier pagan beliefs, and there were
also Gnostic strands in Judaism and
Islam. Gnostics contrast the spiritual
realm of light and good with the evil
material world, from which

individuals may escape by direct experience of the divine rather than the mediation of organized religion. Manicheans (see **Manichaeism**), **Bogomils** and **Cathars** all developed from the Gnostic tradition.

**Gormogons** The Ancient Noble Order of the Gormogons was a short-lived Scottish secret society supporting the Jacobite cause and was opposed to mainstream Freemasonry.

**Haschischin, the Club des** This club flourished briefly in mid-19th-century Paris as a meeting place for poets, artists and other intellectuals to engage in Orientalism and the taking of recreational drugs, especially hashish. It claimed spiritual links with the **Assassins** of the Middle Ages, who were allegedly associated with the taking of mind-altering drugs.

**Hashashin** See **Assassins**.

**Hermes Trismegistus** In the ancient world, the 'thrice great' Hermes was a combination of the Greek god Hermes and the Egyptian god **Thoth**, deities of magic in their different traditions. He was credited with the production of a great body of pre-Christan sacred writing of special interest to astrologers and alchemists. Interest in him revived in the Renaissance and in modern New Age movements.

**Hermetic** Relating to **alchemy** and other **occult** sciences.

**Hermetic Order of the Golden Dawn (HOGD)** A secret society founded in late 19th-century London with an invented history and rites and structure based on the Rosicrucian tradition (see **Rosicrucianism**). It attracted a number of famous adherents, but fell apart as a result of vicious in-fighting. It spawned various daughter orders, some of which still exist.

**Heterodoxy** The converse of orthodoxy, contrary to authorized or generally accepted theories and beliefs.

**Holy Grail** Supposedly the vessel from which Christ drank at the Last Supper. An object of quest in medieval and subsequent legends, it was said to have mystical powers.

**Homeric Hymns** A series of 33 anonymous hymns to celebrate the ancient Greek gods, written from the 7th century BCE. They were attributed to Homer because they use the same metre as the *Iliad* and *Odyssey*.

**Houri** A beautiful young woman in legends of Muslim paradise.

**Illuminati** The name given to a number of secret societies, historical and modern, real and fictitious. In 18th-century Germany the Illuminati were an organization of progressive thinkers and activists drawing on some aspects of **Freemasonry**. In modern times they are the group alleged by conspiracy theorists to be behind the plot for the **New World Order**.

**Invisible College** The followers of Christian Rosenkreutz, supposedly the founders of **Rosicrucianism**, formed an Invisible College of **occult** savants. The historical Invisible College was a group of 17th-century English natural philosophers, or scientists, who were given a Royal Charter by Charles II to found the **Royal Society**.

**John Birch Society** An extreme anti-communist right-wing American pressure group opposed to US involvement in the United Nations and concerned about the perceived threat of the **New World Order**.

**Kabbalah (also Cabala and Qabala)** The ancient Jewish tradition of mystic interpretation of holy works using

**esoteric** practices. Present also in Christian (Cabala) and Islamic traditions. Associated with mystic ciphers and **occult** lore.

**Knights Hospitaller** A military religious order, the Knights of the Hospital of St John in Jerusalem, founded in the early 11th century originally to protect pilgrims and care for the sick. They became a powerful military force, eventually based in Malta after the Christians were driven from the Holy Lands.

**Knights Templar** A military religious order, the poor Knights of Christ and of the Temple of Solomon, founded in 1118 to protect pilgrims. They amassed great wealth as well as military power and became the object of enmity and envy among rulers and other Christian organizations. Accused of heresy and forbidden practices by King Philip IV of France in 1307, they were eventually suppressed in 1312. They remain a source of **occult** myths.

**Legends of Perpetuation** Various pseudo-historical claims, some backed by forged/spurious documents, that the Templars survived in secret and re-emerged in Masonic and related organizations.

**Lemuria** A hypothetical lost land under the oceans. It was posited by some 19th-century scientists, but subsequently lost credibility. It remains part of the mythology of some occultists.

**Mafia/Mafiosi** Criminal secret societies and their members, originating in Sicily in the 19th century, with equivalents on the Italian mainland, which later spread through emigration to the USA.

**Magus/magi** Originally a member(s) of the priestly caste in ancient Persia; later a term for magicians, sorcerers or possessors of advanced secret knowledge.

**Manichaeism** A dualistic (see **Dualism**) religious system with Christian, Gnostic (see **Gnosticism**) and pagan elements, first developed in Persia in the 3rd century and widespread in the Roman Empire. It was based on the concept of the conflict between the evil material world and the divine spirit potentially present in all individuals. It was heavily persecuted by orthodox Christian authorities.

**Masons** See **Freemasons**.

**Merovingians** A Frankish dynasty that ruled Gaul and parts of Germany from the early 6th century until 750 CE.

Identified by some bloodline theorists as the descendants of Christ and Mary Magdalene.

**Millenarianism** Various beliefs associated with the timing of the second coming of Christ and the 1,000 years he was predicted to rule on Earth thereafter.

**Mithras/Mithraism** A god of light and truth of Persian origin. His worship, known as Mithraism, was popular with soldiers of the Roman Empire and was a significant rival to Christianity in the first three centuries CE.

**Mysteries** Secret forms of worship only accessible to the initiated in various **occult** religions. The most famous were probably the **Eleusinian Mysteries** in honour of **Demeter** and **Persephone**.

**Neo-Platonism** A religious and philosophical system based on the teachings of Plato and other Greek philosophers and also Eastern mysticism. Popular in the medieval and Renaissance world, it proposed a pathway of enlightenment by which the individual could rise above the material world.

**Neo-Pythagoreanism** Mystical and **occult** beliefs based on the teachings of the ancient Greek philosopher, mathematician and mystic, Pythagoras.

**New Aeon** A new, post-Christian age envisaged by the late 19th- early 20th-century occultist Aleister Crowley.

**New World Order (NWO)** In modern conspiracy theory, a collectivist world government that is being planned and implemented by secretive elites, variously comprising communists, Jews, Masons (see **Freemasonry**) and even extraterrestrials. Frequently, international bodies such as the United Nations, the World Bank and the World Trade Organization are cited as agencies of the NWO. Such theories are advanced especially in the USA by extreme right-wing and Christian fundamentalist organizations.

**Occult** Literally, 'hidden'; refers to mystical, magical or secret knowledge.

**Old Charges** Evidence that claims to trace modern **Freemasonry** back to ancient and biblical times. The basis of the constitution of the modern Masons drawn up in 18th-century London.

**Old Man of the Mountain** The legendary leader of the **Assassins** in medieval times in the Middle East.

**Opus Dei** A secretive Roman Catholic organization of lay people, founded in Spain in 1928, but now with worldwide membership, dedicated to advancing conservative Christian ideals in secular society.

**Order (religious, Masonic)** A fraternity, sometimes secretive and frequently with a complex hierarchy, rites of initiation and progression, regalia and symbols.

**Order of the Golden and Rosy Cross (OGRC)** A neo-Rosicrucian (see **Rosicrucianism**) **esoteric** order founded in Germany in the 1750s. It attracted a number of powerful figures including King Frederick William of Prussia, but withered after his death in 1797. However, its model was very influential in the foundation of other neo-Rosicrucian orders in the 19th century.

**Order of the Solar Temple** *(Ordre du Temple Solaire,* OTS) An extreme secret society, claiming lineage from the Templars, founded in 1984 in Switzerland, with members also in France and Canada. It was accused of money laundering and gunrunning, and came to an end with a macabre series of mass suicides and apparent murders between 1994 and 1997. Its two founders were among the dead.

**Ordo Novi Templi (Order of the New Temple, ONT)** A quasi-monastic **occult** order founded in Germany in 1907 with the aim of recapturing for the Aryan races their ancient psychic powers and racial dominance. The order claimed lineage from the Templars (see **Knights Templar**) and Rosicrucians (see **Rosicrucianism**), and was a forerunner of the Nazi Party.

**Ordo Rosea Rubeae et Aureae Crucis (Order of the Rose of Ruby and the Cross of Gold, RR et AC)** The second or inner order of the Hermetic Order of the Golden Dawn.

**Ordo Supremus Militaris Templi Hierosolymitani (Sovereign military order of the Temple of Jerusalem, OSMTH)** A modern international ecumenical Christian organization that claims links with the best of the **Knights Templar** tradition, but not direct lineage.

**Ordo Templi Orientis (Order of the Oriental Templars, OTO)** A secret society with Masonic (see **Freemasonry**) origins founded at the end of the 19th century in Germany or Austria. Under the leadership of the British occultist Aleister Crowley, it focused increasingly on Gnostic (see **Gnosticism**) and Thelemic doctrines (see **Thelema/Thelemic**). It was accused of, but strongly denied, practising Satanism. It almost died out during World War II, but has subsequently revived, especially in the USA.

**Orpheus/Orphism** A mythical ancient Greek poet and musician, the son of the god Apollo. Orphism was a related mystery cult with secret rites and incantations.

**P2 (Propaganda Due)** Masonic lodge founded after World War II when **Freemasonry** was once again legal in Italy, later developed by Licio Gelli as a secret lodge for powerful figures throughout Italian politics and society. It has been accused of many forms of corruption, including banking scandals and links with the Mafia.

**Palladian Order** A supposed Masonic order engaged in Satanism and deviant sexual practices, revealed as a hoax perpetrated by anti-Catholic Leo Taxil in 1894 in mockery both of the gullibility of devoted Catholics and of the practices of **Freemasonry**.

**Perfecti Cathar** adherents who adopted a life of extreme austerity, including the renunciation of sexual activity.

**Perfectibilists** The name adopted by adherents of the **Illuminati** movement.

**Persephone** In Greek mythology the daughter of Zeus and Demeter, celebrated in the **Eleusinian Mysteries**. The symbol of spring and nature's return to life.

**Philosopher's Stone** The iconic object of **alchemy**, supposedly able to transform base metal into gold.

**Plato** A Greek philosopher from the 5th and 4th centuries BCE whose teachings had a profound influence on Christian theology and metaphysics. See also **Neo-Platonism**.

**Priory of Sion** An alleged **esoteric** Christian chivalric order of great antiquity revealed in France in 1956 and concerned with the propagation of bloodline theories. It was soon shown to be a hoax, but continues to be regarded as a real and threatening agent of the New World Order by some conspiracy theorists.

**Propaganda Due** See **P2**.

**Protocols of the Elders of Zion** A forged document supposedly revealing plans for Jewish world dominance, published in Russia in 1905. Despite being thoroughly discredited, it has subsequently been used by the Nazis and others to fuel anti-Semitic campaigns.

**Pythagoras** A Greek philosopher, astronomer and mathematician of the 6th–5th centuries BCE. He propounded a theory that the physical world can be explained by numerical ratios. He also founded a secret religious and political sect in southern Italy. See also **Neo-Pythagoreanism**.

**Renewed Order of the Temple (ORT)** A modern neo-Templar/Rosicrucian order led by Luc Jouret before he went on to co-found the notorious **Order of the Solar Temple**.

**Rite of Strict Observance** Influential Masonic rite of the 18th century, founded by Baron Karl Gotthelf von Hund, combining spurious claims of Templar descent with occult and esoteric teachings.

**Root races** The theory of 'root races' was developed by Madame Blavatsky as part of her cult of **Theosophy**. It was concerned with the ancient emergence of the original races of mankind, notably on the lost continents such as **Atlantis**

and **Lemuria**, and with the emergence of superior, Aryan races.

**Rosicrucianism** A legendary 17th- and 18th-century metaphysical and mystical **occult** society with a programme of spiritual, cultural and social revolution. Many modern **occult** orders claim an inheritance from the Rosicrucians, although they are mainly offshoots of **Freemasonry**.

**Rosicrucian Manifestos** Anonymous documents published in the early 17th century supposedly based on ancient wisdom and associated with the legendary figure of Christian Rosenkreutz, the founder of the mystical Rosicrucian (see **Rosicrucianism**) movement. They have subsequently been dismissed by some as hoaxes.

**Royal Society** A society that developed from the informal group of natural philosophers in 17th-century England called the **Invisible College**, gaining the seal of royal approval from Charles II in 1660. It became the crucible of the Scientific Revolution.

**Scientology** A religious cult founded by science-fiction author L. Ron Hubbard in California in 1954. Based on his theory of dianetics, it claims to raise spiritual awareness through self-knowledge. It has attracted some famous adherents, but has been accused of manipulative and coercive practices.

**Shaman** A person, especially in tribal societies, with **occult** powers, including the ability to access the spirit world.

**Sharia** The sacred law of Islam based on the teachings of the Koran and the traditional sayings of Mohammed.

**Shi'ite** One of the two main branches of Islam. See also **Sunni**.

**Shriners** Members of the Ancient Arabic Noble Order of the Mystic Shrine, a fraternal and charitable offshoot of **Freemasonry** founded in the 1870s and with widespread membership in the USA today.

**Societas Rosicruciana in Anglia (Soc Ros, SRIA)** An independent Christian fraternal society open only to Master **Masons**, though separate from the formal structure of **Freemasonry**. Soc Ros was founded in 1867. There are parallel societies in Scotland and North America, and Soc Ros lodges in Australia and elsewhere.

**Stella Matutina** A magical society established in the early 20th century to propagate the teachings of the **Hermetic Order of the Golden Dawn (HOGD)** in Britain and later the Antipodes. Like the HOGD it has suffered from a number of schisms, but still exists today in various forms.

**Sunni** The larger of the two main branches of Islam. Sunnis differ from **Shi'ites** mainly in the acceptance of the Sunna (customs and practices based on Mohammed's words and acts), and over the question of the legitimate succession of the caliphs (chief civil and religious leaders) after Mohammed's death.

**Tarot (the)** Playing cards with origins thought to date back to the early 15th century in Italy, featuring mystical images linked to astrology and the Kabbalah. Renewed interest in the **occult** has led to a modern revival in the use of the Tarot for divination.

**Templars** See **Knights Templar**.

**Temple Mount** The site of the two great temples, Solomon's and Herod's, destroyed respectively by the Babylonians and the Romans. In the Jewish tradition, the place where God created Adam, and for Muslims, the point from which Mohammed ascended to heaven. A site of complex archaeological remains and supposedly **occult** secrets, such as the resting place of the Ark of the Covenant.

**Teutonic Knights** A military and religious order founded in the early 12th century as the Knights of St Mary of Jerusalem. After the expulsion of Christian forces from the Holy Land in 1225, they conquered large areas of non-Christian territory south and east of the Baltic. Their beliefs included the theory of Teutonic superiority over their Slavic neighbours.

**Thelema/Thelemic** A religious philosophy developed in the early 20th century by Aleister Crowley based on the dictum 'do what thou wilt'. Although this was often taken as a licence for hedonism and sexual indulgence, Crowley argued that it was concerned with self-knowledge. He was associated with a number of Masonic (see **Freemasonry**) and neo-Rosicrucian (see **Rosicrucianism**) orders.

**Theosophy** A variety of philosophies examining fundamental truths common to all religions and professing that knowledge of God can be achieved through spiritual ecstasy and intuition.

The Theosophical Society was founded in America in 1875 by Helena Blavatsky, to promote her mishmash of metaphysics, world religions, pseudoscience and occultism.

**Thoth** The ancient Egyptian god of wisdom, associated by the ancient Greeks with their own god Hermes.

**Thule** Legendary land of the far north, adopted by Arianism as a mythical homeland of the Aryan peoples.

**Thule Society** An anti-Semitic, mystical Aryan society set up in 1917; played an important role in the founding and ideology of the Nazi Party.

**Tong, the** Chinese secret societies, especially among overseas Chinese in North America and elsewhere.

**Triads** Chinese secret societies originally formed in the 18th century to oust the alien Manchu dynasty. They subsequently developed into fraternal and criminal gangs with some political influence in the war between the Chinese Nationalists and Communists, and are now mainly concerned with organized crime.

**Zoroaster (Zarathustra)** A 6th-century BCE Persian prophet and founder of a monotheistic (belief in a single God) but dualistic (see **Dualism**) religion. The subject of many legends, he is believed to have been a magician, astrologer and mathematician.

# BIBLIOGRAPHY

## ONLINE SOURCES

*American Mafia*, www.americanmafia.com

'Beyond *The Da Vinci Code*: History and Myth of the Priory of Sion', Massimo Introvigne, www.cesnur.org/2005/pa_introvigne.htm

*Catholic Encyclopedia*, www.newadvent.org/cathen

*Grand Lodge of British Columbia and Yukon*, www.freemasonry.bcy.ca

'The History of the Golden Dawn', *The HOGD in Britain*, Chic Cicero and S. Tabatha Cicero, www.hogd.co.uk/gd_history_ciceros.htm

*Internet Medieval Source Book*, Paul Halsall, Fordham University Center for Medieval Studies, www. fordham.edu/halsall/source/1173williamnorwich.html

'Operation Gladio', David Guyatt, www.deepblacklies.co.uk/operation_gladio.htm

*Oxford Dictionary of National Biography*, www.oxforddnb.com

*Paschal Beverly Randolph and The Anseiratic Mysteries*, Catherine Yronwode, www.luckymojo.com/tkpbrandolph.html

'The Real History of the Rosicrucians', 1887, Arthur Edward Waite, www.sacred-texts.com/sro/rhr/rhr20.htm

*Societas Rosicruciana in Civitatibus Foederatis*, Washington College, www.sricf-wa.org/about.html

## PRINT SOURCES

*Alchemy & Mysticism*, Alexander Roob, Taschen, 2009

*The Assassin Legends: Myths of the Isma'ilis*, Daftary Farhad, I. B. Tauris, 1994

*The Atlantis Encyclopedia*, Frank Joseph, Career Press, 2005

*Atlantis: Lost Lands, Ancient Wisdom*, Geoffrey Ashe, Thames & Hudson, 1992

*The Atlas of Atlantis*, Joel Levy, Hamlyn, 2007

*The Atlas of Lost Treasures*, Joel Levy, Hamlyn, 2008

*The Black Hand: A Chapter in Ethnic Crime*, Thomas Pitken, Littlefield Adams, 1977

*Blowback: America's Recruitment of Nazis and Its Effects on the Cold War*, Christopher Simpson, Weidenfeld & Nicolson, 1988

'Bohemian Tragedy', Alex Shoumatoff, *Vanity Fair*, May 2009

*Borderlands: The Ultimate Exploration of the Unknown*, Mike Dash, Arrow, 1998

*The Boxer Rebellion*, Diana Preston, Robinson, 2002

*Brewer's Dictionary of Phrase and Fable* (17th ed.), Chambers Harrap, 2005

*The Cambridge Dictionary of Philosophy*, Robert Audi (ed.), Cambridge University Press, 1999

*Chambers Dictionary of the Unexplained*, Una McGovern (ed.), Chambers Harrap, 2007

*The Classical World: An Epic History from Homer to Hadrian*, Robin Lane Fox, Allen Lane, 2005

'Cognoscenti of Cannabis: Jacques-Joseph Moreau', Ethan Russo, *Journal of Cannabis Therapeutics*, Vol. 1(1), 2001

*The Concise Oxford Companion to Classical Literature*, M. C. Howatson and Ian Chilvers (eds), Oxford University Press, 1996

*Conspiracies and Conspiracy Theory in Early Modern Europe: From the Waldensians to the French Revolution*, Barry Coward and Julian Swann (eds), Ashgate, 2004

*Conspiracies: Plots, Lies and Cover-Ups*, Richard M. Bennett, Virgin, 2003

*Conspiracy Theories in American History: An Encyclopedia*, Peter Knight (ed.), ABC-CLIO, 2003

*The Count of Monte Cristo*, Alexandre Dumas, Penguin, 1996

*The Druids*, Peter Beresford Ellis, Robinson, 2002

*The 80 Greatest Conspiracies of All Time*, Jonathan Vankin and John Whalen, Citadel Press, 2004

*The Element Encyclopedia of Secret Societies*, John Michael Greer, Element, 2006

*Emperors of Dreams: Drugs in the Nineteenth Century*, Mike Jay, Dedalus, 2000

*Encyclopedia of Freemasonry*, Albert Gallatin Mackey and H. L. Haywood, Kessinger Publishing, 2003

*Encyclopedia of Violence, Peace and Conflict*, Lester Kurtz (ed.), Elsevier, 2nd ed., 2008

'The Enlightened Ones', David Hambling, *Fortean Times*, 239, August 2008

*The French Revolution*, Christopher Hibbert, Penguin, 1980

*Iberia and the Americas: Culture, Politics, and History*, J. Michael Francis, ABC-CLIO, 2006

*In God's Name: An Investigation into the Murder of Pope John I*, David Yallop, Jonathan Cape, 1984

'The Jewes shall be blamed', Bob Rickard, *Fortean Times*, 136, July 2000

*The Little Book of Conspiracies*, Joel Levy, Allen & Unwin, 2005

*Lost Civilizations of the Stone Age*, Richard Rudgley, Arrow, 1998

*Lost Histories*, Joel Levy, Vision, 2006

*The Lost Land of Lemuria: Fabulous Geographies, Catastrophic Histories*, Sumathi Ramaswamy, University of California Press, 2004

*The Lost Lemuria*, William Scott-Elliot, The Theosophical Publishing House, 1904

*The Magicians of the Golden Dawn: A Documentary History of a Magical Order, 1887–1923*, Ellic Howard, Taylor & Francis, 1972

*The Masks of God: Creative Mythology*, Joseph Campbell, Souvenir Press, 2001

*Masonic Manual and Code of the Grand Lodge of Georgia, Free and Accepted Masons*, 8th ed., 1963

'Mischief Myths', Roy Bainton, *Fortean Times*, 136, July 2000

*The Mystic Symbols*, Brenda Mallon, Godsfield, 2007

'New England and the Bavarian Illuminati', Vernon Stauffer, *Studies in History, Economics and Political Law*, Volume LXXXII:1, 1918

*Newton's Notebook*, Joel Levy, Quid Publishing, 2009

*Occult Roots of Nazism: Secret Aryan Cults and Their Influence on Nazi Ideology*, Nicholas Goodrick-Clarke, New York University Press, 1993

*The Origins of the Tiandihui: The Chinese Triads in Legend and History*, Dian H. Murray and Baoqi Qin, Stanford University Press, 1994

*The Oxford Companion to Classical Civilization*, Simon Hornblower and Antony Spawforth (eds), Oxford University Press, 1998

*The Oxford Companion to Military History*, Richard Holmes (ed.), Oxford University Press, 2001

*The Oxford Companion to United States History*, Paul S. Boyer (ed.), Oxford University Press, 2001

'Plotting the Mason-Taxil Line', David Barrett, *Fortean Times*, 179, January 2004

'Police Discover Mafia's "Ten Commandments" After Arresting Godfather', *Daily Mail*, 8 November, 2007

*The Problem of Lemuria: The Sunken Continent of the Pacific*, Lewis Spence, Rider & Co., 1932

*The Quest for the Phoenix: Spiritual Alchemy and Rosicrucianism in the Work of Count Michael Maier (1569–1622)*, Hereward Tilton, Walter de Gruyter, 2003

*Ritual and Mythology of the Chinese Triads: Creating an Identity*, B. J. Ter Haar, Brill, 1998

*Satan's Circus: Murder, Vice, Police Corruption and New York's Trial of the Century*, Mike Dash, Granta, 2007

*Secret Agenda: The U.S. Government, Nazi Scientists and Project Paperclip, 1945–1990*, Linda Hunt, St Martin's Press, 1992

*The Secret Doctrine: An Abridgement*, Helena Blavatsky, Quest Books, 1967

*Secret History: Hidden Forces that Shaped the Past*, Joel Levy, Vision, 2004

*Secret Societies*, David Barrett, Blandford, 1997

*Sex and Rockets: The Occult World of Jack Parsons*, John Carter with an introduction by Robert Anton Wilson, Feral House, 2000

*The Signs and Symbols Bible*, Madonna Gauding, Godsfield, 2009

'Solar Temple Pilots: Reading the End Times with Luc Jouret', Erik Davis, *The Village Voice*, 25 October, 1994

*Strange Angel: The Otherworldly Life of Rocket Scientist John Whiteside Parsons*, George Pendle, Weidenfeld & Nicolson, 2005

*A Suggestive Inquiry into the Hermetic Mystery*, Mary Anne Atwood, T. Saunders, 1850

'10 Illuminati Conspiracies', David Sutton, *Fortean Times*, 239, August 2008

*Their Kingdom Come: Inside the Secret World of Opus Dei*, Robert Hutchison, Corgi, 2005

*Them: Adventures with Extremists*, Jon Ronson, Picador, 2001

*A Thief in the Night: Life and Death in the Vatican*, John Cornwell, Simon and Schuster, 1989

*Three Early Modern Utopias: Utopia, New Atlantis and The Isle of Pines*, Susan Bryce (ed.), Oxford University Press, 1999

*The Travels of Marco Polo, Marco Polo and Rustichello of Pisa, the complete Yule-Cordier edition* (1920), Dover, 1993

*Who's Who in the Classical World*, Simon Hornblower and Antony Spawforth (eds), Oxford University Press, 2000

# INDEX

Figures in italics indicate captions.

## A

14K Triad 360
Abbey of Thelema, Sicily 194
Abiff, Hiram 140, 143, 158, 163
Achamoth 83
Adam 374
adept 364
*adytum* (inner sanctum) 29, *159*, 189
Aga Khan 259
Agape Lodge OTO 197, 202, 203
Agrae, near Athens 34
Ahura Mazda 46
Akhenaten 123
Alamut castle, Persia 238, 241, *243*, 252, *252*, 254
Albertus Magnus (Saint Albert the Great) *82*
Albigensians 56
alchemy 19, 43, *58*, 59, 60, *60*, 63, 99, 110, 112, *112*, 115, 149, 176, 178, 194, 364, 367, 372
Alexander the Great 59
Alexandria, Egypt 46, 53, 59, 88
Alfred P. Murrah Federal Building, Oklahoma 305
Ali, Syed Ameer 263
alien abductions 305
Alostrael (Leah Hirsig) *192*
Alpha et Omega group 188, 189

Alpha Galates 230
Alumbrados (Illuminati) 260, 268, *268*, 364, 365
America, discovery of 76, 84, 89
American Revolution 164, 166–7
Anaktoron 34, 39, 40
Ancient Arabic Noble Order of the Mystic Shrine 151, *151*, 373
Ancient Illuminated Seers of Bavaria 266
Ancient Mystical Order Rosae Crucis (AMORC) 122, 123, 197, 207, 230, 364
Ancient Noble Order of Gormogons 145–6
Anderson, James 138
Andreae, Johann Valentin 103, *103*, 105, 106, 225
Angra Mainyu 46, 49
Anti-Masonic Party 170
anti-Semitism 199, 200, 206, 230, 268, 284, 292, 296–301, >*309*, 364, 372, 375
Antichrist 169, 208, 308–9
Apocalypse 290, 292
Apollo 28, 371
Apollonius of Tyana 179
'Areopagites' 279
*Argenteum Astrum* (Silver Star, AA) 191, 192
Arianism 375
Ariosophy 199–200, 206, 230, 308, 364
Ark of the Covenant 70, 72, *72*, 89, 228, 364, 374

Armageddon 308
Armanen 200
Aryan races *198*, 199, 200, 373, 375
ascended masters 181, 208
Ashmole, Elias *110*, 111, 135
Assassins (Hashashin) 15, 18, 21, 71, 74,
    75, 89, 235, 236–63, 279, 305, 309, 364,
    367, 370
    Assassins' creed 260–63
    behind the legend 252–7
    Club des Haschischin 248–51
    end of the Assassins 258–9
    the Garden of Paradise 240–43
    legends of the hashish eaters 244–7
astral plane 187, 364
astrology 96, 176, 374
atheism 129, 247
Athelstan, King 140
Athenian calendar 365
Atlanteans 74, 89
Atlantis 182, 183, 199, 286, 364, 372
Augustine, St 53
Augustus, Emperor 40
Aumont, Pierre d' 88–9
Australian Aborigines 26

**B**
Babylonians 296, 374
Bacchus (Dionysus) 36, 38, 366
Bacon, Sir Francis 109, *109*, 110
Baigent, Michael 222
Baldwin, King of Jerusalem 66
Balzac, Honoré de 251
Banco Ambrosiano 219, 331
Baphomet 69, 80, *80*, 83, 89, *172*, 247, 364
Barbie, Klaus 321
Barruel, Abbé Augustin 167, 169, 267,
    280, 283, 299

Baudelaire, Charles 251
Bavarian Illuminati 266, *267*, *271*, 275
Beans, Vinny 344
Benjamin of Tudela 241, *241*
Bennewitz, Paul 307
Berlusconi, Silvio 324, *324*, 331
Bernard de Clairvaux 67
Bernhard, Prince of the Netherlands 310,
    *311*
Bible, the 176, 268, 296
Biblical End of Days 308
Bilderberg group 290, 309, 310–11, *311*,
    365
Birch, Captain John 294
Black Hand, the (*a Mano Nera*) 337, 346,
    *347*, 365
black helicopters 304–5, *305*
Black Shirt Battalion 321
Blavatsky, Madame 42, 123, 180–83, *180*,
    *183*, 187, 191, 199, 208, 372, 374–5
Blood Libel 296, 299, *299*
bloodline 72, 83, 225, 226, 228, 266, 308,
    309, 365, 372
Bode, Christoph 280
Boedromion 365
Boehme, Jakob 100
Bogomils 50, *53*, 55, *55*, 56, 71, 252, 365,
    367
Bohemian Grove 290, 296, 312–15, 365
Bologna Massacre (1980) 327
Bolsheviks 172
Bonneville, Nicholas de 280
bonshommes 55–6
Boston Tea Party (1773) 166, *166*
Bourbon dynasty 225
Boxer Rebellion (1896–1900) 360, *361*
Boyle, Robert 111
Brotherhood of Eulis 122

Brown, Dan 230
*The Da Vinci Code* 52, 72, 216, *217*, 222, 226–7, 233, 365
Brunswick, Prince Ferdinand, Duke of 273, *273*
Buddha 50, 52
Buddhism 49, 181
Builders of the Adytum (BOTA) 189
Bulwer-Lytton, Edward 116, 117, *117*, 179
*Zanoni* 116–17
Burchard of Strassbourg 241
Buscetta, Tommaso *337*
Bush, President George 292

C
Cadet de Gassicour, Charles-Louis 89
Cagliostro, Alessandro di 115
Calderone, Antonino 344
Caliphate OTO 197
Calvi, Roberto 154, 219, 319, 328–9, *331*
Cameron, Marjorie 'Candy' 205
Camorra Mafia 345
Camorra trial (Viterbo, 1911) *342*
Campbell, Joseph 58
Capone, Alphone 'Al' 352, 358, *358*
Carbonari (Charcoal Burners) 15
Carolingians 222, 225
Case, Paul Foster 189
Casso, Anthony 344
categorization of secret societies 18–21
Cathars 40, 46, 50, 52–3, *53*, 55–6, *56*, 89, 226, 260, 365, 367
Catholic Church 49, 56, 72, 99, 171, 172, 213, 219, 226, 268, 270, 273, 274, 280, 299, 309, 318, 321
Catholicism 259, 270
cattle mutilation 305
cave paintings 24

Central Intelligence Agency (CIA) 259, 309
*Centro Romano di Incontri Sacerdotali* 219
Charles II, King 111, 112, *112*, 368, 373
Charles Edward Stuart (Bonnie Prince Charlie; 'Young Pretender') 144, 148
Charter of Larmenius 88
Chávez, Hugo 219
Chinese Nationalists 375
Christian Democratic Party (Italy) 339
Christian fundamentalist millenarians 292, 308–9
Christian fundamentalist organizations 370
Christianity
    development of 31, 38–9, 52
    founding myth of 83
    Gnostic 50, 52
    heterodox beliefs *51*
    orthodox 53, 55
    rivalled by Mithraism 45
chthonic 26–7, 31, 365
*Chymical Wedding of Christian Rosenkreutz, The* 94, 96, 103
Cicero 40
Cipher Manuscript 185
Cistercian order 80, 83
Classical Underworld 365
Clement V, Pope 69, 72
Clement XII, Pope 169, *169*
Clement of Alexandria 39
Clooney, George 331
Club Archédia 207
Club des Haschischin 248–51
Clymer, R. Swinburne 122, 123
Cocteau, Jean 225
Columbus, Christopher 84
Communism, Communists 294, 295, 322, 327, 370, 375

Condon, Richard 305
*Confessio Fraternitas* (*Confession of the Fraternity*) 94, 102, 105
Conrad of Montferrat, King of Jerusalem 257
Constant, Alphonse Louis *see* Lévi, Eliphas
Constantiens, Theophilus Schweighardt 99
*Constitution of Freemasons, The* (Anderson's Constitution) 138, 145
Cooper, Bill: Behold a Pale Horse 12
Corbu, Noël 229, 233
*Corpus Hermeticum* 59, 99
Cosa Nostra *see* Mafia
Council on Foreign Relations 290
Cousos, John *13*
Craft, the *see* Freemasonry
Creation 50
Cremation of Care 313–14
criminal acts 15
criminal societies 21
Crowley, Aleister (Edward Alexander) 42, 89, 176, 187, 188, 190–95, 196, 197, 202, 203, 205, 260, 263, 370, 371, 374
Crusades, Crusaders 55, 66, 69, *69*, 74, 83, 87, 146, 160, 232, 239, 241, 257, 263, 364
'Cudgels' uprising (1847–50) 360
Curia 324, 327

**D**
Dante Alighieri 241
Dark Brotherhoods 334, 339, 365
Dark Side hypothesis 307
Darwinism 63
David, King *72*
Debussy, Claude 225
Dee, Dr John 100, *100*, 110, 144, 192, 194

degrees (masonic and other orders) 10, 127, 132, 143, 148–9, 163, 196, 278–9, 366
Deism 129
Delacroix, Eugene *280*
Delaforge, Gaetan 71
Delphi oracle 28–9
Demeter 31, 33, *33*, 34, 36, *36*, *39*, 366, 369, 372
Descartes, René 106
*Deutsche Arbeiterpartei* 200
Di Mambro, Joseph 207–8, *208*
dianetics 373
Dickens, Charles 116
Diderot, Denis 283
Dion Fortune (Violet Mary Firth) 189
Dionysian rites 28
Dionysus (Bacchus) 28, 38, 366
divination 60, 374
Doctrine of Correspondences 60
*Dossier Secrets d'Henri Lobineau* (*Secret Files of Henri Lobineau*) 225, 226, 233
Drouet, Pierre 337
Druze 245
dualism 46, 52, 366, 369, 375
Dubose, Col. Thomas J. *307*
Dumas, Alexandre 251
Dunkarton, Robert *105*
Dunn, Theron 158
Dutoit, Nicki 208
Dwight, Theodore 284

**E**
Ebbo of Rheims, Archbishop *135*
ecstatic dances 27
Egyptian religion 49
Eichmann, Adolf 321–2
Eisenhower, President Dwight 294–5

Elders of Zion 290, 299, 300
Eleusinian Mysteries 28, 30–41, 365, 366,
    369, 372
    Demeter and Persephone 31
    the Eleusinion 33–4
    legacy of the mysteries 40–41
    the Lesser and Greater Mysteries 34, 36
    procession to Eleusis 36, 38–9
    revealing the mysteries 33
    revelation 39–40
Eleusis, near Athens 31, 33, 34, *34*, 36, 39,
    *39*, 129
Elizabeth II, Queen 308
Elysian Fields 33
End Times 290, 308
Enlightenment 176, 276
Eschenbach, Wolfram von 72
Escrivá de Balaguer, Saint Josemaria
    212–16, *213*, 219
esoteric 16, 366, 370, 372
esoteric societies 18–19, *19*
esoteric tradition 63
Essenes 115
Euclid 140
European Union 309
evolutionary theory 63
exoteric 16, 366
extreme right-wing 370

**F**
Fabré-Palaprat, Bernard Raymond 88,
    206
*Fama Fraternitas Rosae Crucis* (*Discovery
    or Report of the Brotherhood of the Rose
    Cross*) 93–4, *94*, 102, 103, 105
fascism 21, 206, 216, 230, 318, 321, 322, 339
Federal Bureau of Investigation (FBI)
    350, *351*

Federal Emergency Management Agency
    305
Fellowship of the Rosy Cross 188
fertility cults 89
Fibonacci Sequence *137*
Fichtuld, Herman 114
Firth, Violet Mary *see* Dion Fortune
Flamel, Nicolas 225
Fludd, Robert *93*, *96*, 102, 106–7, *107*, 110,
    225
Ford, Henry 300
*Fortean Times* 284
Franco, General 216, 217, 321
Franklin, Benjamin 164
fraternal societies 15, 18, *19*
*Fraternitas Rosae Crucis* (Fellowship of the
    Rosy Cross, FRC; Beverly Hall
    Corporation) 122, 366
fraternity 15, 130, *160*
Fraternity of the Inner Light 189
Frederick V of the Rhine Palatine 105,
    *105*
Frederick William II, King of Prussia
    114, *115*, 370
Freemasonry/Freemasons (Masons) (main
    references) 124–73, 366
    anti-Masonry 127, 128, *145*, 151, 163,
    168–73, 299
    beliefs and goals 128–31
    degrees and rites 132, *132*
    emblems *132*
    in history 164–7
    operative and speculative 126–7, 154–5,
    157, *157*, 158
    origins 134–43
    rise and fall of 144–51
    ritual and symbolism 152–63
Freemasons' Hall, London 117, *118*

French League *15*
French Revolution 89, 167, 170, 172, 230, 274, 280, *280*, 283
Freudian psychoanalysis 194

**G**

Gautier, Theophile 251
Gelli, Licio 219, 318, 319, *319*, 321–4, *321*, *324*, 327, 328, 329, 331, 371
gematria 19, 60, 100, 176, 366
geomancy 226
George I, King 144
George Washington Masonic National Memorial, Alexandra, Virginia *127*
*Germanenorder* (Order of Germans) 200
Girard, Sonny 337
Gnostics/Gnosticism 13, 46, 49–50, *49*, *51*, 52, 53, *53*, 55, 58, 59, 72, 74, 83, 89, 100, 130, 226, 260, 263, 268, 365, 366–7, 369, 371
goddess worship 227
Godefroy de Bouillon, King 222, *222*, 225
Godhead 49, 55
Goering, Herman 321
Goethe, Johann Wolfgang von 273
Golden Dawn 185, 187
golden ratio (golden section) 137–8, *137*
'Golden Triangle' 360
Golden Way Foundation 207
Goldwater, Barry 295
Golitsyn, Prince Aleksandr 181
Golovinski, Mathieu 300, *300*
Gormogons 367
Grant, Kenneth 197
Grateful Dead 315
Great Seal of the United States 166–7, *277*, 292, *293*
Greater Mysteries 34, 40

Greek Dark Ages 34
Greer, John Michael 15
Greys 305, 307
Guido von List Society 200
guilds, medieval 18, 135, 137

**H**

Hades (god) 31, 36
Hadrian, Emperor 34
Hall, Prince 151
Haller, Mark 352
Hammer-Purgstall, Joseph von 83, 89, 247, *247*
Hanau-Wilhemsbad castle *275*
'hanging the lantern' ceremony 359
Harding, Warren Gamaliel *151*
Hart, Mickey 315
Hasan-i-Sabah 75, 245, *252*, 254, *254*, 257, 260
Haschischin, Club des 367
Haselmayer, Adam 103
Hashashin *see* Assassins
hashish 247, 248, *248*, 251, 252, 257
Healey, Denis 310
Henry, Count of Champagne 242
Henry III, King 69
heretics 13
Hermes 59, 367, 375
Hermes Trismegistus *58*, 59, 140, 367
hermetic 367
Hermetic Brotherhood of Light 196
Hermetic lore 19
Hermetic Order of the Golden Dawn (HOGD) 36, 41, 79, 114, 118, 149, 178, 184–9, *189*, 191, 192, 263, 367, 371, 374
Hermeticism 43, 59, 63, 115, 130, 138, 178, 194, 263
Herod's Temple 374

Hess, Dr Tobias 105
heterodoxy 13, 15, 16, 18, *51*, 367
Hitler, Adolf 198, 200, *200*, 216, 295, 300
Hoene-Wronski, Józef 178
*Höhere Armanen-Orden* (Higher Armanen
    Order) 200
Holocaust 300, 308
Holy Grail 66, 72, 89, 93, *225*, 226, 228,
    233, 367
Holy Land 66, 67, 69, *69*, 72, 74, 79, 115
Homer 367
*Homeric Hymn to Demeter* 40
Homeric Hymns 367
Hooke, Robert 111
Hoover, John Edgar 350, 351
Hotel Pimodan, Paris 251, *251*
Houri 368
House of Stuart 87, 112
House of Windsor 308
Howe, Ellic 118
Hubbard, L. Ron 205, *205*, 373
Hugo, Victor 225
Hugues de Payens 66, 67
*hui* 356, 357, 358, *360*
Hulagu Khan 258, *258*
Hund, Baron Karl Gotthelf von 89, *148*,
    149, 181, 187, 274, 372

**I**

Icke, David 300, 308
Illuminati 89, 167, 169–70, 235, 239,
    266–7, 290, 295, 299, 308, 309, 368, 372
Illuminism 264–87
    Adam Weishaupt 270, *271*
    aims and organization 276–9
    the Alumbrados 268, *268*
    history of the Illuminati 272–5
    the Illuminati 266–7

the Illuminati conspiracy 280–85
*The Illuminatus! Trilogy* 286–7, *287*
Illuminized Masonry 169–70, 172, 267
incantations 10
Independent and Rectified Rite of the
    Golden Dawn 188
initiates 10, 16, 17, *41*
initiation 10, 16–17, *17*, *19*, 26, *75*, 80, 154,
    161, 342, 344–5
Innocent II, Pope *56*
Innocent III, Pope 56
Inquisition 56
International Monetary Fund 302
Inuit peoples 26
Invisible College 108–11, 368, 373
invisible jungle *11*
Isis 185
Isis-Urania Temple of the HOGD 185
Islam 55, 74, 75, 83, 252, 259, 309, 366, 373
Islamic fundamentalism 259
Islamic groups 18
Islamic terrorism 309
Ismaili Heritage Foundation 252, 260
Ismaili Muslims 245, 247, 252, 254, 256,
    259, 263
Israelites 364
Ivanow, Wladimir 252

**J**

Jack the Ripper 154
Jacobin Club 283
Jacobite cause 112, 144–5, 148, 367
Jacobite Rising (1645–6) 149
Jacobites 87, 144, 148, 149
James I, King 106, 112
James II, King 87, 144
James Stuart ('Old Pretender') 144
Jefferson, Thomas 283–4, *284*

Jerusalem, fall of 69, *69*
Jesuits *see* Society of Jesus
Jesus Christ 50, 52, 72, 83, 222, 226, *227*,
    233, 266, 292, 314, 365, 367, 369
Jews *15*, 199, 216, 259, 266, 268, 292,
    296–301, 308, 309, 313, 353, 364, 370,
    372
John, apostle *227*, *227*
John Birch Society 292, 294–5, *295*, 368
John Paul I, Pope (Albino Luciani) 327,
    *327*
John Paul II, Pope 219, *219*
John the Baptist 83
Joly, Maurice 300
Jouret, Luc 207–8, 372
Judaism 59, 366

**K**

Kabbalah (also Cabala and Qabala) 19,
    59–60, 63, 95, 99, 100, 110, 123, 149, 176,
    178, 194, 366, 368, 374
Kabbalism 50
Kefauver, Senator Estes 352, *353*
Kelley, Edward 192
Kellner, Carl 196
Knigge, Baron Adolf Franz Friedrich
    von 266–7, *267*, 270, 273, 274, 278
Knight, Stephen 163
Knights Hospitaller of St John 83, 263,
    368
Knights of St John of Jerusalem 146
Knights of St Mary of Jerusalem 374
Knights Templar (Templars) 10, 21, *21*,
    29, 46, 52, 56, 66–9, 214, 226, 239, 263,
    364, 368, 370, 371, 372
    Assassins and Templars 74–5, *75*
    neo-Templars 18, 21, 66, 84–9, 206–8,
    372

Scottish survivors? 76–7, *77*
a secret society? 78–83
treasure of the Templars 70–73
Koran 176, 252, 254, 373
Krak des Chevaliers castle, Syria 260, *260*
Ku Klux Klan *11*
!Kung of the Kalahari 26

**L**

La Sorte, Mike 341
Lamech 140
Lanzinger, Hubert *200*
Larmenius, Johannes Marcus 88
Last Supper 367
Law of Thelema 192
Legends of Perpetuation 87, 88, 114–15,
    149, 232, 357, 368
Leigh, Richard 222
Leighton, Frederic *33*
Lemozy, Daniel *56*
Lemuria 123, 182, 199, 369, 373
Lennhoff, Eugen *13*
Leonardo da Vinci *130*, 225, *225*, 227, *227*
Less, Eliot 348
Lesser Mysteries 34, 40
Lévi, Eliphas (Alphonse Louis Constant)
    118, 178–9, *179*, 180, 194
Lewis, Bernard 254
Lewis, H. Spencer 122–3, 197, 364
Libavius, Andreas 106
Liebenfels, Jörg Lanz von 199–200
Lilly, William 111
Lincoln, Henry 222, 226
Little, Robert Wentworth 117, 118, *118*
Livingstone, David 309
Lo Piccolo, Salvatore 345
lodges 10, 126, *129*, 138, *138*, 143, 151, 158,
    196, *283*

Loyola, St Ignatius of 263, *268*
Luciano, Charles 'Lucky' *341*, 348, 350
Lucifer *49*, 50
Luther, Martin 105

**M**
McClure, Kevin 71
Mackenzie, Kenneth 117, 185
McMurty, Grady Louis 197, 205
McVeigh, Timothy 305
Mafia 15, 219, 235, 318, 319, *321*, 324, 328, 329, *329*, 334–53, 365, 369, 371
   in America 348–51
   Black Hand 346, *347*
   code of honour 340–45
   the invention of 352–3, *353*
   origin of the name 337
   origins 338–9
magic 21, *58*, 59, 60, 89, 95, 96, 100, 176, 178, 179, 187
   black 177, 205
   folk 176
   natural 21, 96
   religious 176
   sex 89, 120–21, 123, 192, 194, 205
   white 177
magical societies 21
magus/magi 96, 369
Maier, Michael 106, 110
Makow, Henry 314
Mamelukes 258–9
Manchu 356, *357*, 375
Mani 52, *53*
Manicheanism, Manicheans 52–3, *53*, 55, 367, 369
Marat, Jean–Paul 284
Marcinkus, Archbishop Paul 324, 327
Marcus Aurelius, Emperor 34

Marshal, Master William 69
Mary, Virgin 92
Mary Magdalene 72, 222, 226, 227, *227*, 314, 365, 369
*Masonic Manual and Code* 155, 157–8
Masons *see* Freemasons/Freemasonry
Masyaf fortress, Syria 256, 257
Mathers, Moina 189, *189*
Mathers, Samuel Liddell MacGregor 185–9, *187*, 191, 194
Mengele, Josef 321
Merovingians 72, 222, 225, 226, 228, 232, 308, 369
metaphysics 18, 60
Middle Ages 56, 63
Millenarianism 369
Millennium 308
Minerva 278, *279*
Minervals 273, 278, *279*, *279*
Ming dynasty 356–7
Mirabeau, Honoré Gabriel Riqueti, comte de 283
Miro, Aldo 319
Mithraeum 45
Mithras/Mithraism 44–5, *45*, 52, 58, 369
MJ-12 307
Mohammed 50, 252, 373, 374
Molay, Jacques de 69, 79, *79*, 88, 167
Mongols 239, *239*, 258, *258*
monotheism 375
Montagu, Duke of 143, *143*
Montségur castle, France 56, *56*
Moreau, Gustave *29*
Moreau de Tours, Jacques-Joseph 248, *248*, 251
Morgan, William 170, *171*
Moro, Aldo 327
Mount Olympus 26

Mount Zion, near Jerusalem 232–3
Mozart, Wolfgang Amadeus *129*
Murray, Dian H. 357
Muslim Brotherhood 259
Mussolini, Benito 318, 321, 339
Mustalian Ismailis 254
Mycenaean civilization 34
mystery religions 28–9, *29*, 89
mystical societies 18, *19*
mysticism 25, 58, 59
    Christian 178, 188
    Jewish 49
    Pythagorean 43

### N

Nag Hammadi Gnostic gospels 50, *51*, 72
Napoleon Bonaparte 206, 245, 259
Napoleon III, Emperor 300
NATO 311
natural philosophy 110
nature 21, 60, 96
Naxos, Greece: Temple of Demeter *31*
Nazis, Nazi Party 21, 89, 172, 189, 198,
    *198*, 200, 259, 309, 318, 321, 322, 371,
    372, 375
Neo-Platonism 369
Neo-Pythagoreanism 369–70
neo-Rosicrucian 370, 374
neo-Templars 18, 21, 66, 84–9, 372
Neoplatonists *58*
Nerval, Gerard de 251
New Aeon 370
New Aeon of Thelema 202
New Age 89, 183, 207, *207*, 208, 233, 367
New Testament 50
New World Order (NWO) 172, 235, 239,
    259, 279, 284, 286, 288–315, 365, 368,
    370, 372

Bilderberg group 310–11, *311*
Bohemian Grove 312–15
the Dark Side 302–9
John Birch Society 294–5, *295*
*Protocols of the Elders of Zion* 296–301
theories of 290–93
Newton, Sir Isaac 111, 225
Night of the Sicilian Vespers (1283) 337
Nixon, Richard *313*
Nizari Ismailis 252, 254, 257, 258, 259,
    263
Noah's Ark *99*
Nostradamus 225
Novices 278–9
*Novus Ordo Seclorum* 292
*Nuclei Armati Rivoluzionari* 327
numerology 358

### O

Oak Island Money Pit, Nova Scotia 76
Occult Revival 259
occult societies 21, 176–7
occultism, occultists 60, 182
Oddfellows sect *17*, 18
Olcott, Henry Steel 181, *183*
Old Charges 139–40, 370
Old Man of the Mountains 238, 241, 242,
    *243*, 245, 247, 251, *256*, 257, 260, 370
Olympic gods 31
omertà 341–2, 344–5
Operation Gladio 322, 324
Operation Stay Behind 322–3, *323*
Opus Dei 210–19, 227, 370
    divine revelation 212–13
    a secret society? 216–19
    structure 214–15, *215*
Order of Christ 84, *84*
Order of Montesa 84

Order of the Golden and Rosy Cross (OGRC) 88, 112–15, 117, 118, 149, 185, 263, 370

Order of the Solar Temple (*Orde du Temple Solaire*, OTS) 71, 88, *88*, 206–9, 370, 372

orders 10, 186, 263, 370–71

*Ordo Novi Templi* (Order of the New Temple, ONT) 21, 89, 200, 206, 371

*Ordo Rosea Rubeae et Aureae Crucis* (Order of the Rose of Ruby and the Cross of Gold, RR et AC) 187, 371

*Ordo Stella Matutina* (OSM) 177

*Ordo Supremus Militaris Templi Hierosolymitani* (Sovereign military order of the Temple of Jerusalem, OSMTH) 87, 371

*Ordo Templi Orientis* (Order of the Oriental Templars, OTO) 89, 122, 191, 192, 194, 196–7, 202, 205, 275, 371

Orientalism 248, 367

Origas, Julien 207

Ormus 115

Orpheus 28, *29*, 36, 371

Orphic mysteries 28

Orphism 371

Osiris 163

OTO *see Ordo Templi Orientis*

*Overlords of Chaos* website 302, 304

**P**

P2 (Propaganda Due) 15, 219, 316–31, 371
  the end of P2 328–31
  Licio Gelli and the ratlines 321, *321*
  Operation Stay Behind 322–3, *323*
  the Puppet Master 324–7

Palladian Order 171, 172, 371

Palmeri, Giuseppe 339

papacy 99

paramilitary societies 21, *21*

paranormal powers 21

Parsons, Jack 197, 202–3, *203*, 205

Parthenon, Athens 137, *137*

Paulicians 55

*Perfecti* 40, 55–6

Perfecti Cathar 371

Perfectibilists 266, 276, 372

Pericles 34

Peron, Juan 324

Persephone 31, *33*, 34, 36, 38, 366, 369, 372

Peter the Great 242

Phelps, General John Wolcott 170

Philip IV 'the Fair', King of France 69, 72, 75, 76, 84, 368

Philosopher's Stone 60, 99, 149, 364, 372

Phrygian cap 45, *45*

Picart, Bernard *153*

Pike, Albert 171–2

Pindar 28

Pitken, Thomas 346

Plantard, Pierre 222, 225, 226, 229, 230, 232–3, *232*

Plato 19, 36, 40, 41, 43, 106, 263, 369, 372

Platonic philosophy 59

Platonism 49, 59

Plutarch 33

political societies 21

Polk, James K. 167

Polo, Marco 241, 242

Poor Fellow Soldiers of Christ and of the Temple of Solomon *see* Knights Templar

Poussin, Nicolas 225

Prince Hall Masonry 151

Priory of Sion 222–7, 228, 372
  true origins of 230–33

Prohibition 346, 348, 350, 352
Pronaos 189
Propaganda Due *see* P2
Protestantism 105, 148
*Protocols of the Elders of Zion* 292, 296–301
pseudoscience 63, 182
psychedelics 27
psychic powers 21, 63
psychophysical practices 176–7
pyramid builders, Egypt 74
Pythagoras 19, 42, 43, *43*, 106, 137, 138, 260, 370, 372
Pythagorean Brotherhood 42–3
Pythagoreanism 49, 59
Pythia 28

**Q**
Qafzeh, Israel 24–5, *25*
Qin, Baoqi 357

**R**
Ragan, Leslie Darrell *302*
Ramey, Brig. General Roger M. *307*
Ramsay, Chevalier Andrew Michael 87, *87*, 146, 148, 158, 160–61
Randolph, Paschal Beverly 120–22, *121*, 196
ratlines 321
Reagan, Ronald 295, 313, *313*
Red Brigades 327
Red Square, Moscow *323*
Reformation 148
regalia 10, 17, 154–5, *155*, 157, 177, *187*, 208
Regardie, Israel 189
Regius Manuscript (Halliwell Manuscript) 140
reincarnation 183, 260

religious societies 18, *21*
Renaissance 63, 74, 99
Renewed Order of the Temple (ORT) 207, 372
Rennes-le-Château, France 225, 228–9, *229*
Reptoids, Reptilians 300, 307–8, *309*
Republican Party (US) 294, 295
Retinger, Joseph 310
Reuss, Theodor 192, 194, 196–7, *197*, 275
Revelation, prophecies of 292, 308
Richard I, King, the Lionheart 257
Richter, Sigmund (Sincerus Renatus) 111, 114
Riley, John *110*
Rite of Memphis and Misraim 196
Rite of Strict Observance 89, 149, 274, *275*, 372
rites 28, 132
ritual 10, 17, 41, *41*, 80, 130, 177, 187, 189, *207*
ritual and symbolism of Freemasonry 152–63
Robert the Bruce 76, 149
Robison, John 167, 169, 247, 267, 280, 283, *283*, 299
Rockefeller, David 310
Rockefeller family 291, *291*, 308
Roman Empire 58
Romans 296, 374
root races 182, 199, 308, 372–3
Rosenkreutz, Christian 94–6, 100, 368, 373
Rosicrucian Knights 112
Rosicrucians, Rosicrucianism 10, 13, 15, 29, 43, 56, 60, 88, 89, 90–123, 129, 178, 194, 260, 366, 367, 368, 371, 372, 373
American Rosicrucians 120–23

Christian Rosenkreutz 95–6
the Invisible College 108–11, 368, 373
Manifestos 93–5, *94*, 100, 102–3, *103*,
    105, 106, 109, 123, 138, 187, 373
motifs *185*
the Order of the Golden and Rosy
    Cross 112–15
the real Rosicrucians 102–5
the rose and the cross 92–3, *93*
the Rosicrucian agenda 96, 99
Rosicrucian defenders 106–7, *107*
Societas Rosicruciana 116–19
sources 99–100
Rosslyn Chapel, Lothian, Scotland 76, 77,
    89
Roswell Incident 307, *307*
Rothschild family 291, 308
royal family, British 291
Royal Order of Scotland 112
Royal Society 110–11, 112, 368, 373
Rubens, Peter Paul *268*
Russian Revolution (1917) 172

**S**
sacred architecture 130
sacred geometry 130
Sacy, Silvestre de 245, *245*, 247
al-Sadiq, Jafar 252
St Germain, Comte de 115
St Valentine's Day Massacre (1929) 348
Saladin 69, *69*, 238–9, 256
Salafi reform movement 259
Salomon's House 109
salvation 49, 52
San bushmen *27*
Sanjar, Sultan 254
Saracens 80, 161, 233
Satan 55, 172

Satanism 16, 21, 83, 144, 163, 171, 172,
    176, 194, 296, 371
Saunière, Bérenger 225, 226, 228–9, *229*,
    *230*, 233
Sayer, Anthony 138
science 63, 179, 183
Scientific Revolution 176, 373
Scientology 205, *205*, 373
Scottish Rite 151, 157, 259
Second Coming of the Messiah 308
Second Night of the Sicilian Vespers
    (1931) 348
secrecy 12–15, 16
Sède, Gérard de 225, 233
shaman practices 26, 27, *27*, 28, 373
Shapur I, Emperor 52
sharia law 12, 252, 373
Shea, Robert 267, 286–7, *287*
Shi'ite Muslims 245, 252, 254, 373, 374
Shriners 373
Sinan ibn-Salman *256*, 257
Sinclair, Henry 76
Sinclair, William 76
Sinclair family 76, *77*, 87
Sindona, Michele 328, *329*
Smith, Pamela Coleman *177*
*Societas Rosicruciana in America* (SRIA)
    119
*Societas Rosicruciana in Anglia* (Soc Ros,
    SRIA) 114, 117–19, 185, 186, 263, 373
*Societas Rosicruciana in Civitatibus
    Foederatis* (Rosicrucian Society of the
    United States) 119
*Societas Rosicruciana in Scotia* 119
Society for Psychical Research 183
Society of Jesus (Jesuits) 263, *268*, 270
Solidarity 219
Solomon, King 140, 364

Somer, Paul van *109*
Spanish Civil War (1936–39) 213
Spanish Inquisition 268, 364
Spenser, Edmund 100
spirit world 25, 60
spiritualism 21, 63, 183
spirituality in the ancient world 24–5, *25*
'Sprengel, Fraülein' 185, 188
Squaring the Lodge 158
SS Division 321
Stella Matutina Society 188, 189, 373–4
Stolac, Herzegovina 55
Stone Age cults 26–7, *27*
Sufism 50
Sun Yat Sen 360
Sunni Muslims 245, 252, 254, 374
Sutton, David 284
symbolic architecture 19, 29
symbolic mathematics 19
symbolism 10, *19*, 130
    Mithraic 45
    ritual and symbolism of Freemasonry
        152–63
Synod of Hippo (393 CE) 50

**T**
Taiping rebellion (1850–64) 360
Talleyrand-Périgord, Charles Maurice de
    283
Tanier the Younger, David *60*
Tarot, the 19, 39, 59, 63, 176, *177*, 178, 194,
    374
Taxil, Leo (Gabriel Jogand–Pagès) 105,
    171, 172, *172*, 371
Taxil-Schwindel 105, 170–72
Telesterion 34, *34*, 39
Templars *see* Knights Templar
Temple in Jerusalem 77

Temple Mount, Jerusalem 6, 71, *71*, 72,
    374
Temple of Solomon 66, 74, 140, 143, *155*,
    161, 374
Ten Commandments 364
Terror, the 274, 283
Teutonic Knights 84, 199, 374
Thelema/Thelemic 371, 374
Thelemic doctrine 192, 194, 196
Theodosius I, Emperor 31, *34*
theosophical mysticism 115
Theosophical Society 123, 180, 181, 183,
    196, 199, 374–5
theosophy 183, 187, *198*, 200, 208, 364, 372,
    374–5
Third Temple of the Rosie Cross, San
    Francisco 120
Thirty Years War 105
Thomas of Monmouth 299
Thomson, Charles 292
Thoth (Egyptian god of wisdom) 59, 367,
    375
Thule 375
Thule Society 200, 375
Tigers Eye Society *11*
Tlas, Mustafa 299, *299*
Tommaso da Modena *80*
Tongs 358, 361, 375
Tower of Babel 140, *140*
trance 27, 28–9
transformation 15, 99
transmutation of base metals into gold 60
Tree of Life 60, 178
Triads 15, 21, 356–61, 375
    brief history 360–61
    organization and initiation 358–9
    origins 356–7
Trilateral Commission 290

Triptolemus *36*
Truman, Harry S. 307
Tübingen circle 105, 106, 107
Turin Shroud *225*
Typhonian OTO 197

**U**

UFO sightings 305
ufologists 305, 307
UN Security Council 309
United Grand Lodge of England (UGLE) 143
United Nations (UN) 87, 290, 302, *302*, 309, 368, 370
Unknown Superiors 149, 181, 187
Urania 185

**V**

Vaughan, Diana 172
Villa Wanda, Arezzo, Italy *319*, 328
Virgil 292
Visigoths 228
Volkische Movement 199, 200
Voltaire 283

**W**

Waco siege (1993) 305, *305*
Waite, A.E. 188
Warren, Supreme Court Justice Earl 294
Washington, George 164, *164*, 167, 170
Webster, Nesta 172, 284, 309
Weir, Bob 315
Weishaupt, Adam 266, 267, 270, *271*, 273, 274, 276–9, 283, 284, 287
Welch, Robert 294, 295, *295*
Westcott, Dr William Wynn 118–19, 178, 185–8
Western esoteric tradition 58–9

Wharton, Philip Duke of 145–6, *146*
White Lotus rebellion (mid-1790s) 360
White Lotus Society 360
William of Rubruck 241
William of Tyre 241
Wilson, Robert Anton and Shea, Robert: *The Illuminatus! Trilogy* 267, 286–7, *287*
Wirt, William 170
witchcraft 21, 144, 176
Woodford, Reverend A. 185
Woodman, Dr William Robert 185, 187
World Bank 370
World Health Organization 290
World Trade Organization 290, 302, 370

**Y**

Yahweh 49–50, 163
Yeats, W.B. 187, 191
York Rite 151

**Z**

Zeus 26, 31, 372
Ziedan, Dr Youssef 300
Zionist Occupation Government (ZOG) 290, 292
Zionist-Bolshevik conspiracy, international 290, 309
zodiac 45
Zoroaster (Zarathustra), Zoroastrianism 46, *46*, 49, 52, 375
Zwack, Xavier 273, 274

# ACKNOWLEDGEMENTS

**akg-images** 1, 53, 78, 103, 115, 198; Bildarchiv Steffens 256; Erich Lessing 234; Sotheby's 272 **Alamy** Bertrand Rieger/Hemis 220, 229; Classic Image 6, 22, 30, 147; Historical Art Collection 165; Interfoto 38, 54, 267; Judith Tewson 77; Lebrecht Music and Arts Photo Library 117, 224; Mary Evans Picture Library 58, 80, 171, 223, 240, 271; Photos 12 173; Royal Geographical Society 315; The Art Archive/Gianni Dagli Orti 57, 152; The Art Gallery Collection 184; The Print Collector 141; World History Archive 107; **Bridgeman Art Library** © Leeds Museums and Galleries (City Art Gallery) 32; Archives Charmet 20, Archives Charmet/Bibliothèque Nationale, Paris 182, Archives Charmet/Private Collection 297; Ashmolean Museum, University of Oxford 110; Bibliothèque Nationale, Paris 64, 75, 239; Edinburgh University Library/With kind permission of the University of Edinburgh 282; Ken Welsh 13, Ken Walsh/Private Collection 156; Lauros/Giraudon 44; Museu de Marinha, Lisbon/Giraudon 85; Museum of London 139; National Army Museum, London 142; Peter Newark Military Pictures/Private Collection 201; Private Collection 108, 186, 189; **California Institute of Technology** Courtesy of the archives 203; **Corbis** 361; Bernd Weissbrod/epa 325; Bettmann 11, 218, 285, 288, 306, 311, 312, 323, 335, 336, 347, 349, 353; Christophe Boisvieux 354; Free Agents Limited 136; Gianni Dagli Orti 43, 134; Hulton-Deutsch Collection 17, 351; KJ Historical 303; Macduff Everton 332, 338; Orjan F Ellingvag 210, 217; Royal Ontario Museum 357; Stefano Bianchetti 277; Sygma/Gianni Giansanti 329, Sygma/Jacques Langevin 359; The Art Archive 264, 281; The Gallery Collection 29, 124, 131, 227, 269, 293; **Fraternitas Rosae Crucis Archives**, Quakerstown, Pennsylvania 121; **Getty Images** 8, 19, 101, 113, 151, 166, 190, 204, 213, 291, 316, 326; AFP/Louai Beshara 298, AFP Tim Roberts 304;

De Agostini/A Garozzo 35; Bridgeman Art Library/French School 155; Cosmo Condina 62, 70; Franco Origlia 215; Ignaz Unterberger 128; LaWanda Wilson 122; Scott Barbour 119; Slim Aarons 340; **Hessische Hausstiftung, Museum Schloss Fasanerie**, Eichenzell 275; **Institute for Antiquity and Christianity**, Claremont California 51; Courtesy of **Joe Roberts** 287; **Lebrecht Collection** Leemage 244, Leemage/Fototeca 255, 301, Leemage/Gusman 231; **Mary Evans Picture Library** 179, 232; Courtesy of **P R Koenig** 197 **Photolibrary** John Warburton-Lee Photography/Mark Hannaford 236, 261, John Warburton-Lee Photography/Nigel Pavitt 27 **Photos12.com** ARJ 258; **Picture Desk/The Art Archive** 47; Alfredo Dagli Orti 90, 97; Archaeological Museum, Ferrara/Alfredo Dagli Orti 37; Archives Nationales, Paris/Kharbine-Tapabor/Collection Jean Vigne 67; Biblioteca Nazionale Marciana Venice/Alfredo Dagli Orti 48; Bibliothèque des Arts Décoratifs, Paris/Gianni Dagli Orti 41; **Press Association Images** AP 295, AP/Fabrice Coffrini 209, AP/Studio Imago 320 **Rex Features** John Pickering 88, 174, 207; Olycom spa 319; **Photo Scala**, Florence 82, 168; Heritage Images 68, Heritage Images/Ann Ronan 104, 279; White Images 73; **Science Photo Library** Mission Archeologique de Qafzeh/Look at Sciences 24; Sheila Terry 61; **SuperStock** Newberry Library 262; **TopFoto** 162; Art Media/HIP 145; Charles Walker 159, 177, 195; Fortean 309; Imagno/Austrian Archives 246; Roger-Viollet 14, 98, 250; The Granger Collection 2, 93, 94, 133, 160, 253; The Image Works 127; Topham Picturepoint 193, 330, 343; World History Archive 180, 243